D0914984

Water Resources Management

Declining water and alkalai at the Stillwater National Wildlife Refuge, terminus point for water from the Truckee River near Fallon, Nevada. Millions of waterfowl and fish died due to disease and selenium poisoning during 1986–1988. Photograph by Peter Goin, 1989. Original in color.

Water Resources

≋ **In Search of an Environmental Ethic**

Management

David Lewis Feldman

The Johns Hopkins University Press   Baltimore and London

The Johns Hopkins University Press
701 West 40th Street, Baltimore, Maryland 21211
The Johns Hopkins Press Ltd., London

∞

The paper used in this book meets the minimum requirements of
American National Standard for Information Sciences—Permanence
of Paper for Printed Library Materials, ANSI Z39.48-1984.

Library of Congress Cataloging-in-Publication Data

Feldman, David Lewis, 1951–
    Water resources management : in search of an environmental ethic /
    David Lewis Feldman.
          p.   cm.
    Includes bibliographical references and index.
    ISBN 0-8018-4075-9
    1. Water supply—Government policy—United States. 2. Water
resources development—Environmental aspects—United States.
I. Title.
HD1694.A5F46   1991
333.91'00973—dc20   90–43987

Contents

Preface and Acknowledgments

This is a book about environmental policy whose argument reflects both of my careers: college teacher and government policy analyst. While focusing upon how people and nature can live together in an orderly and just political community, I also consider why achievement of this ideal remains elusive. As might be expected of someone trained in political theory, I also examine what makes public policy equitable, why and how a good public policy should encompass impacts upon nature as well as people, and how it can reflect certain standards of liberty, freedom, equality, and democracy. I pondered these issues over nine years of teaching seminars in political thought and environmental policy.

The book is also a personal statement about the consequences for public policy of wrong, faulty, ill-thought-out, or merely inconsistent values. I learned these lessons while working in a state natural resources agency and continue to relearn some of them as a staff member of the Energy Division of the Oak Ridge National Laboratory. Chapters 4, 6, and parts of chapter 8 were previously published. Chapter 4 was published under the title "The Great Plains Garrison Diversion Unit and the Search for an Environmental Ethic," *Policy Sciences* 22 (1989). An earlier version of chapter 6 appeared as "The Defeat of the Blue Ridge

Pump Storage Project as Microcosm of Environmental Policy Change,"
Policy Sciences 20 (1987). Parts of chapter 8 appeared under the title
"Comparative Models of Civil-Military Relations and the U.S. Army
Corps of Engineers," *Journal of Politics and Military Sociology* 15 (1987).

How has someone trained in political theory come to work in water
policy? More to the point, how might a political theorist's training help
us understand natural resources problems and how we might better
manage them? The discussion of my own experience answers the first
question. The book itself is an answer to the latter question. Retracing
the path that linked theory and policy in my own career may serve to
show the reader why the connection between the two disciplines is
essential for good public policy.

My exposure to water policy came about quite accidentally while I
was completing my doctoral dissertation at the University of Missouri.
My name had been sent by way of the Presidential Management Intern-
ship Program to the director of the water resources planning program
of the Missouri Department of Natural Resources. The director was
dedicated to sound environmental management and the protection of
his state against inappropriate encroachments by federal agencies.

For me, the offer was particularly fortuitous. Although I had opportunities to apply for federal agency positions, this state position offered
me the chance to continue to teach part time at a small liberal arts
college while "getting my feet wet" in government. Moreover, the director of the program enthusiastically supported his staff, its responsibilities, and my possible contribution. Finally, I was interested in environmental issues and the director was willing to overlook my relative
lack of information about them.

I began my work in 1980, the last year of Jimmy Carter's presidency.
At that time, environmental policy was at the vortex of national controversy. Water issues prompted considerable discussion and study and
at least some movement toward what was then too optimistically termed
a national water policy. Almost all of my agency's efforts reflected this
controversy. Squabbles over supplemental appropriations bills for the
Water Resources Council, changes in principles and standards governing
water resources projects, and almost daily discussion about the goals of
water planning interfered with our work. To understate matters, it was
an exciting time to be learning about, and working in, water policy.

I was hired to help write a state plan to manage its water resources
for recreation, agriculture, industry, utilities, municipalities, and navigation. The document, partially funded by Water Resources Council state
planning grants (which, like the council itself, no longer exist), would
elucidate strategies for achieving water conservation and control of nonpoint agricultural runoff. Most of all, it would tell citizens of Missouri

how their state saw its most pressing water problems and what it expected to do about them with the help of upstream states and the federal government.

In the several months I interned in this program, I also reviewed federal agency plans and environmental impact statements and helped to assess the policy implications of various river basin commission reports. Most challenging of all, I composed drafts of letters for the director of the council, which, in final iteration, represented state policy on such matters as proposed Corps of Engineers' mitigation measures to prevent further fish kills at Harry S. Truman Dam on the Osage River. Once, I even prepared the state's formal request for Corps of Engineers' help for a resort owner on Table Rock Lake who wanted to move his fishing dock, which was caught high and dry (like his fishing business) when drought prompted a greater than normal reservoir drawdown for power and instream flow quality on the White River.

I learned a great deal about the substance of water policy, its stakeholders and their concerns, the inner workings of state bureaucracy, and how governments use knowledge and information for making policy. It was frustrating to me that my detailed (and, I thought, well-conceived) reports were eventually reduced to the briefest of memoranda, stating recommendations without rationale.

Most of all, I learned three lessons, which are reflected in this book. First, most people who work in government are conscientious and dedicated. They may not always be able to define good public policy, but they have some intuitive sense of what it should be. For my colleagues at the Missouri Department of Natural Resources, such a policy would attempt to honestly, openly, and equitably accommodate the interests of a number of divergent stakeholders, and it would establish rules for water management that assured abundant, clean water for present and future Missourians. Civil servants may not often reflect on intergenerational justice, but they know that good policy entails a long-term commitment to sound, scientific management supported by scrutable ethical justification. This commitment represents a promise by government that the implications of its decisions have been carefully studied. Our planning efforts were not only designed to meet a legislative mandate or deadline; they were elegant statements of the priorities valued by water resources professionals, articulating goals important to a just society.

Second, natural resources issues spark contentious debate precisely because they strike at the core values of fairness, equity, and even aesthetics. Honest, fair-minded people can have honest, well-founded disagreements over priorities and programs. For example, when does government have the authority to order a family from its land? How does government assess a new dam that would attract significant tourism at the same time that it would inundate farms? Do the beauty and recreational quality of a white-water stream outweigh the benefits of improved navigation and additional electric power? To a greater degree than I then realized, my colleagues were fighting battles in the trenches of American federal-state relations over economic development and environmental preservation. Policy makers' ethical justifications for their decisions are their weapons.

Third and finally, I learned that political scientists trained in political theory have many important things to say about the two concerns expressed above. Some of the most cogent observations on the failings of natural resources management come from those who, like Lynton Caldwell, Theodore Lowi, Grant McConnell, point to the shortcomings of the liberal state and its tenuous foundations for moral authority. These tenuous foundations explain, among other things, why established environmental policies pit region against region; resist centralized, rational management; are powerfully linked to conventional notions of private property; too often disregard the consequences of cavalier abuse of resources; and require a formal deontology of decision making—such as a procedure for assessing environmental impacts of proposed agency actions—in order to assure the accountability of government to its citizens.

These observations and their basis in political theory extend far beyond water policy to a number of pressing environmental issues, including global climate change, transboundary air and water pollution, and deforestation and desertification. That is precisely the point of this book; although our scientific understanding of the causes and consequences of environmental problems has steadily increased, the ways in which governments—local as well as national—react to these problems lag far behind our knowledge. I contend that the major reason for this lag is that this understanding challenges the positions of stakeholders, whose perceptions, interests, and goals hinge upon contending views of property, of our responsibility to protect and use nature, and even of our obligation to future generations.

This book is aimed at an audience of social scientists, environmentalists, and environmental professionals eager for a vision of how to better manage the ethical issues prompted by these environmental dilemmas. I would like to bridge the void between the policy makers concerned with managing these issues and the political theorists who are aware of the value dilemmas posed by natural resources issues. More than anything, these environmental issues pose a herculean challenge to the goals of balancing sustainable development, feeding the world's hungry, and assuring our survival as a species.

If this book prompts a dialogue between practitioners and theorists,

I will have attained my goal. Natural resources policies are not simply the result of cumulative preferences or a reflection of the prevailing distribution of power in society. They are commitments—sometimes explicit, more often tacit—made to citizens by government. To be effective, these decisions need to be seen as legitimate and trustworthy.

In any project of this magnitude, for which ideas were nurtured and refined over a long period of time, an author owes a debt of gratitude to a great many people. I wish to especially thank Bob Dunkeson of the Missouri Department of Natural Resources for giving me the chance to learn about water policy and for exemplifying the type of civil servant I describe above. I also thank the Department of Political Science at the University of Missouri–Columbia, especially Art Kalleberg, Paul Wallace, Robin Remington, and Dean Yarwood, for understanding the need for a link between theory and policy and for sustaining my own curiosity about that link.

I am also grateful to George F. Thompson at the Johns Hopkins University Press for inquiring about my interest in such a project, guiding it along, and helping me sustain my enthusiasm for it. At Oak Ridge National Laboratory, a number of colleagues, including Sam Carnes, George Rogers, and John Sorensen, suggested changes in parts of the manuscript, referred me to additional sources of material, or discussed ideas with me. I would also like to thank Bill Cabage for his editorial assistance and his help compiling the index. Wilma Minor and Cindy Coomer typed parts of the draft patiently and diligently. Martin Marietta Energy Systems, Inc., the managing contractor for the National Laboratory, allowed me time to complete the project in spite of deadlines for other work. Of course, all errors of fact and interpretation are mine alone.

Finally, to my wife, Debbie, I owe the greatest debt of all—she shared each step of the career odyssey that saw many of the ideas expressed in this book develop. Without her encouragement, patience, friendship, confidence, and love, the book never would have been possible.

Water Resources Management

1 Values, Political Theory, and Environmental Policies

Values in Natural Resources Policy: The Case of Water

This is a book about American water policy. Its central concern is the need for reform in the way water policy is made and implemented. It argues that serious crises confront our society's use and abuse of water. While these crises (flooding, drought, pollution, energy production, groundwater depletion, agricultural irrigation, and recreational demand) require technological solutions, they also require political reform. Thus, the book is not an engineering treatise or a refinement of river basin planning. Rather, it is a call for political change.

Although this book contends that government programs to generate hydroelectric power, to prevent floods by damming rivers, and to supply cheap water for farms and homesteads have often been wasteful of tax-payers' money, capricious in their assessment of benefits and costs, ignorant of injurious environmental impacts to entire regions, and inequitable toward some groups, it does not advance the facile claim that more rigorous benefit-cost analyses will solve our water problems.

Finally, the book asserts that water policy is flawed because of the overrepresentation of a few dominant interest groups in the policy-making process and the fragmentation of policy-making institutions. However, it does not plead for the reorganization of natural resources agencies, as the Office of Management and Budget often does, nor does it call, as various presidential commissions occasionally do, for the curtailment of congressional committee influence upon water policy. It does not suggest the abolition of the U.S. Army Corps of Engineers or the Bureau of Reclamation. Nor does it call for the nationalization of water policy, which environmental groups sometimes urge.

Instead, the purpose of this book is to show how our most severe water resources problems are caused by a reliance upon narrow and often inappropriate acquisitive values that are harmful to nature and to the satisfaction of a wide range of human needs, including biological exigency and living in harmony with nature and in community with other people. While various approaches have guided water resources management in the United States, decision makers have traditionally chosen development-oriented policies on the basis of the improved economic efficiency they offer. These policies are normatively indefensible because they do not adequately consider the environmental and social costs of water projects or sufficiently encompass democratic representation and participation (Dickson, 1981; Ingram, 1978; Ostrom and Ostrom, 1971; Young, 1982).

In employing these narrow, acquisitive values as guiding principles in water resources management, decision makers overlook policies that are more likely to encourage equity as well as efficient distribution of benefits. They also overlook the potentially positive impact of wide public participation in the formulation of these policies. Public participation would mean consideration of noneconomic values, of local concerns and traditions, of promises made to regions and of the impact of policy upon present and future generations. The concept of efficiency, employed in justification of water policy by federal agencies and others, often reflects poorly conceived preferences held by a relatively small elite of engineers, planners, and water project beneficiaries. The narrow, technocratic approaches to efficiency promoted by this elite have severely and irreversibly affected nature. They have also produced short-term gains for some regions at the expense of long-term benefits for the rest of society.

The thesis of this book is that public policies should be defended on ethical grounds, by reference to principles that elucidate the desired consequences of government action or inaction (C. Anderson, 1979). In addition to economic efficiency, these principles include the equitable distribution of natural resources; the protection of flora and fauna; political feasibility; and finally, the fulfillment of human needs, ranging from mere survival to an enlightened existence in a just community.

These ethical principles I call a political theory of the environment. Such a theory would promote values toward nature that are coherent, that are consistently logical, and that share an epistemology.

In natural resources policy, governments, interest groups, party platforms, and elected officials publicly acknowledge the need to justify political practice with such ethical principles in order to establish the legitimacy and rationality of decisions. Unfortunately, no appropriate political philosophy for water policy encompasses these diverse concerns. Thus, policy makers often make decisions without reference to fairness or the enhancement of the natural environment. Likewise, they are unable to encompass intergenerational justice, the reduction of risk, political feasibility, or citizen participation.

As a result, the narrow, acquisitive approaches to policy discussed here conform to a pluralistic concept of democracy characterized by a sometimes pathological interest in group competition. This competition does not allow groups to transcend self-interest, because each group enters the policy-making process intending to negotiate and trade off preferences. Participants do not become enlightened through the process or concerned with the broader interests of nonstakeholders. Moreover, in the long run the process is detrimental to an enlightened notion of democratic government, which presumes that good policy emerges not from the mere aggregation of preferences but from deliberation and discussion in an open public forum that serves to educate citizens.

The implications of this argument extend to the management of other natural resources, including forests, minerals, energy resources, flora, fauna, and national parklands. They also apply to the general use and exploitation of the biosphere as a natural commons. In analyzing the absence of a political theory of the environment for water resources management, I will draw attention to similar problems encountered in the management of other natural resources. In addition, I will note how the absence of an environmental ethic in these areas has produced public policies inconsistent with principles of justice and rationality.

The basic thesis of this book is neither new nor startling. Failures in water policy have been chronicled by political scientists for decades. In historical perspective, many Corps of Engineers and Bureau of Reclamation projects in regions as diverse as the Colorado, Columbia, and Missouri river basins are only explainable in the politically narrow struggle for bureaucratic survival and interest group aggrandizement characteristic of American subsystem politics. Such constituency-based decision making has facilitated the building of dams and other public works projects to fuel regional economic growth (Ferejohn, 1974; Hart, 1957; Mazmanian and Nienaber, 1979; McConnell, 1966; Murphy, 1974; Seidman, 1970; Freeman, 1965).

Yet, despite numerous reforms in the process by which water policy is made—beginning with the establishment of river basin planning during the 1930s and extending through the ambitious, if largely thwarted, efforts of the Carter administration to bolster the so-called principles and standards of the Water Resources Council—these agencies continue to propose solutions to water problems that may inflict massive social and environmental upheavals. In short, they continue to resist serious challenges to the way they formulate water policy. They still rely upon structural solutions such as dams, dikes, and water diversion schemes to resolve problems of flooding, drought, irrigation, energy production, and water-based recreation (Miller, 1985; Derthick, 1970; Holmes, 1979; U.S. Senate, 1978a, 1985).

One reason reform has been resisted is that the fragmentation of American politics—traceable to the character of the liberal state—divests government of adequate authority to make policy without interference or reprisal from powerful, strategically placed interest groups. At the national level, this is reflected by the dominant role in policy formulation of congressional public works committees, which encourage river and harbor improvements to benefit local constituents. These projects often serve no compelling needs beyond the immediate vicinity of a project (Lowi, 1979; Mann, 1985). This is unfortunate, because water by its very character is a common property whose misuse affects people outside an immediate locale. In order to mitigate environmental impacts upon resources that affect others as well as oneself (a precondition, as shall be seen, for justice), we need to assess these impacts in our immediate vicinity daily. This is the true meaning, I argue, of the phrase "think globally, act locally."

At the state level, fragmentation of authority is partly caused by competing systems of water law, which discourage efficient use of water or its conservation, promote litigation, and discourage public participation in water resources management (Busby, 1955; Viessman, 1978; V. Ostrom, 1971). Instead of finding fault with this fragmentation, many Americans applaud the fact that considerable authority for the management of natural resources is placed in the private sector. They assume that the determination of need for water projects, the appropriateness of resource exploitation, and the costs of environmental impacts are all borne by a free market, which sorts out the best political decisions. The presumed existence of an almost unlimited supply of virgin resources—a popular myth throughout the nineteenth and early twentieth centuries—coupled with the unabated demands of a vigorous frontier society, have become wedded to the utilitarian criterion that the best public policy is that which produces the greatest net material benefits for the largest number of citizens. Policy so defined fails to provide a satisfactory basis for justice, because it is calculated to satisfy only the pre-existing preferences of citizens and not their unexpressed need for an enlightened existence.

Within this traditional approach to natural resources policy, it has been viewed as appropriate to ignore impacts upon the environment as well as the uneven distribution of benefits among ethnic groups, regions, or social classes. It has been argued that the forces of the marketplace can resolve these problems if the pricing system for natural resources promotes prudent use and discourages disuse and overuse (Young, 1982: 10, 15, 119–30; Sproule-Jones, 1982), even though such a market-oriented solution has been found wanting.

This fragmentation and its popular acceptance have led to rejection of a political philosophy for natural resources development, with three consequences. First, when water policies do not encompass utilitarian ends, there is periodic demand for structural reform of the process by which this policy is made. This has entailed calls for reorganization of water resources agencies to make them less subservient to bureaucratic, self-interest, and regional pressures and more accountable to presidential attempts to coordinate the goals of river basin planning on behalf of a wider, yet still elusive, public interest (DRP, 1971; MacNeil and Metz, 1956). The problem with this strategy, as shall be seen, is that, in the absence of an overriding concern on the objectives of policy, administrative centralization only heightens and intensifies conflict between different agencies and their clientele. One result of such conflict is that agreement over the goals of water policy becomes more, not less, difficult to attain. Case studies of the Garrison diversion project and the development of the Colorado River basin, discussed in chapters 4 and 5, exemplify this problem.

Second, many critics of water policy assume that merely changing the priorities of water resources agencies from river basin development to conservation of water and other natural resources will make natural resources decisions responsive to broad public concerns and inflict fewer irreversible impacts on the environment. One shortcoming of this approach is that the meaning of conservation encompasses a number of different strategies for natural resources management, which are neither synonymous nor compatible.

Conservation can mean the exploitation of resources by maximizing their efficient utilization on behalf of present and future generations. This definition suggests that development, if it is guided by science and done prudently, can be good for society and the environment by measurably improving both. On the other hand, conservation can also be construed (and has been construed by some environmentalists) to mean sharply reducing our demand for scarce, nonreplenishable natural re-

sources by curtailing exploitation and preserving natural resources in
a pristine state (Hays, 1961; Pinkett, 1978). This latter view places a
premium upon minimizing environmental impact and values nature as
an intrinsic, rather than extrinsic, commodity. While these two views
are not mutually exclusive, they emphasize sharply differing goals and
objectives. The former view, sometimes also referred to as the sustainable development position, assumes that economic growth, development, and environmental protection are largely compatible, while the
latter view, sometimes termed preservationism, fears that grave catastrophe may result if nature's fragile limits are exceeded (Cotgrove,
1982).

Finally, since the 1930s, a variety of political actors in the field of
water policy—ranging from the Congress, the Office of Management
and Budget, the former Water Resources Council, and various construction agencies—have placed considerable reliance upon easily quantifi-
able benefit-cost analyses of river basin projects. This has been done to
justify these projects' economic viability and, thus, these agencies' right
to act as stewards of natural resources. Benefit-cost analysis has been
inappropriately applied to water resources problems. Its basic goal, the
assessment of efficiency, requires comparing one strategy for solving a
resource problem with an alternative designed to solve the same problem. Government agencies rarely make such a comparison. Moreover,
even when they do, they rarely defend the results they obtain by the
larger goal of structural efficiency, an important constituent of justice
that conforms to our intuitive sense of what is fair (Rawls, 1971). Structural efficiency is the allocation of goods in such a way that, if it is
changed in order to make one person better off, another is not made
worse off.

In the justification of water projects, benefit-cost analysis has often
been used to justify a preformed agency decision that is politically palatable to Congress (White, 1969; Eckstein, 1958). It thus inadequately
accounts for environmental impact and fails to elucidate the objectives
of public policy. It also ignores the range of concerns that people have
about the uses of natural resources. For this reason, it cannot be normatively defended by reference to some compelling social good that is
reached through careful deliberation.

The proper comparison of policy alternatives through benefit-cost
analysis requires that efficiency and equity be directly tied to one another. Contemporary political philosophers such as John Rawls (1971)
point to one mechanism for accomplishing this connection—Pareto optimality. Under Pareto optimality, the concept of efficiency is considered
to apply to the basic structure of decision making in society, not just
to the allocation of goods or services. Thus, it is not ethically sufficient

to justify a water project by reference to a net increase in goods or services to one group, region, or segment of society unless it can be demonstrated that this increase would not make others worse off, or that the inequality would ultimately make everyone better off by, for example, assuring a more productive, useful, or practical exploitation of those goods beneficial to society.

The essential point of Rawls's theory for the argument of this book is that a fair distribution of natural resources requires agreement over decision-making rules for the allocation and use of natural resources that takes into account the broad range of human needs noted previously (and which will be expanded upon momentarily), as well as our intuitive desire, as rational, reasonable beings, for justice. This desire for justice, as well as conformance with rules for allocating and distributing resources, should take precedence over consideration of the practical means of achieving these policy goals.

Why There Is No Political Theory for Water Resources Management

The federal government has been actively involved in water resources management from its inception. Historically, the first priority addressed was inland navigation, followed by flood control, irrigation, hydroelectricity, and, only lately, comprehensive planning for river basins. Projects and policies had little overall coordination or guidance but were undertaken as simple responses to the particular needs and interests of one region at a specific time. In this limited sense, it could be said that the ranking of these priorities was determined by the most pressing needs of established communities and westward settlers.

Below the national level, and for almost as long, states have engaged in efforts to articulate and clarify water rights, manage in-stream flow, regulate floodplains, and provide water-based recreation. The scope of these programs has been traditionally narrow enough to permit their management by one or two state agencies working closely with a particular federal program. This has been the prevailing pattern in fish and wildlife enhancement, erosion control, and instream flow management programs, for example (Davis and Cunningham, 1977).

Cooperative efforts by states and the national government, involving the sharing of technical expertise and the division of costs, did not promote, nor were they intended to promote, long-range environmental planning. They also failed to provide any comprehensive umbrella for a broad-based, multipurpose natural resources policy. These efforts were merely intended to solve highly visible problems on an ad hoc basis. They were not consciously guided by an intention to address long-term issues of natural resources management. Instead, these efforts were constrained by disjointed utilitarianism. They were designed to serve the needs of the greatest number of potential beneficiaries, but they responded only to those parties vocal enough or well situated enough to make themselves heard. Such ad hoc resolution of water problems did not advance the causes of environmental protection or balanced exploitation of natural resources.

This lack of comprehensiveness is precisely why the federal government attempted comprehensive water resources planning in the 1960s. In the wake of serious droughts in the East and growing demands for more irrigation projects in the West, it gradually came to be understood that the failure to assess a broad range of interests made it difficult to anticipate water problems. It was nearly impossible to undertake long-range planning in response to social changes brought about by in-migration, new or different water uses, or short-term, dramatic changes in weather patterns. These problems were insurmountable under the guidelines of traditional water resources policy making, because water projects were constructed without regard for who should pay for water resources improvements, for the reciprocal benefits that could be rightfully expected by those who paid for them, and for these projects' impacts upon natural systems, for which adaptability to human engineering was little understood. In assessing the results of these comprehensive planning efforts, we must place them in a broader philosophical context. Comprehensive planning in water resources policy attempts to coordinate public participation in policy formulation with the efforts of agencies at all levels of government (Fox, 1966: 282; White, 1969: 34). As such, it may be viewed as an attempt to go beyond ad hoc policy. How successful have these efforts been?

Federal water resources policy has aimed at regional and national economic development. Early federal involvement in water policy stemmed from navigational concerns prompted by westward settlement and by pressing needs for an improved inland transportation system after the War of 1812. From the beginning, the federal government was involved in water policy in order to placate powerful regional interests that wanted their activities subsidized to minimize the risks and hardships of the frontier. Decisions over who would pay for these projects were deferred, sometimes far into the future. Moreover, environmental and social impacts were not carefully weighed.

The distinguished efforts of a small military and topographical engineering unit during the War of 1812 prompted Congress to form the Corps of Engineers in order to widen the channel of the Ohio River. After the Board of Engineers for Internal Improvements was formed in 1824, President Monroe assigned army engineers to what was initially a three-member civilian body, because the military was the only government organization with the expertise necessary to construct roads, canals, and harbors (Goetzmann, 1959: 4–6, 13–14; Clarke and Mc-Cool, 1985: 13–14). Afterward, and well into the early twentieth century, army engineers remained closely identified with the development of water resources.

The corps's Civil Works Directorate, successor to the Internal Improvements Board, became adept at identifying and lobbying on behalf of river and harbor improvements, flood control, and later on, hydropower. These efforts were viewed as vital to economic prosperity, regional growth, and national security, because they made efficient inland communication viable—a good initial reason for their pursuit. The reason such efforts continued was a fortuitous combination of circumstances only indirectly related to natural resources policy.

In essence, water resources development by army engineers was linked to the desire to avoid creating an aloof and highly educated military establishment that might become contemptuous of democratic values. The use of West Point as a civil engineering training center, and of the Corps of Engineers as the principal agency for water resources development, prevented the emergence of a highly professionalized officer corps, segregated from civilian society. It also placated groups in favor of using government to stimulate development of the nation's interior. Reliance upon the armed forces for water resources development in the United States was animated by some of the same concerns currently confronting many developing nations that rely upon their armed forces for interior development and other so-called civic action (Gribble, 1974: 9; Weigley, 1973; Rourke, 1984: 94; Feldman, 1987a).

Initially, this strategy constituted a practical use of military skills during a critical stage in American political development, when civilian bureaucratic expertise necessary for natural resources management was insufficiently developed. However, dependence upon a technically proficient body of narrowly trained specialists retarded a fuller appreciation of the social, economic, and environmental impacts of water resources development. It also minimized public participation, excluded consideration of nonengineering solutions to water problems, and ignored the relation between water and other natural resources.

As a result of this reliance on Corps of Engineers' expertise, the federal government was slow to address multipurpose water resources concerns in a coherent manner. It was more than seventy-five years after the Rivers and Harbors Act of 1824 that Congress formally addressed concerns for flood control, irrigation, hydroelectricity, and river basin planning in a unified, programmatic fashion. Following passage of the 1909 Rivers and Harbors Act, requiring the Corps of Engineers to "consider the potential for power in all preliminary surveys for navigation projects," Congress established the National Waterways Commission to examine water resources development issues. The final report of this commission, released in 1912, cautioned that, from a constitutional point of view, the federal government has authority only to promote navigational improvements. Nevertheless, it concluded that federal projects for flood control, hydropower, and other purposes could be feasible in certain regions and would fill a void not satisfied by the private sector (Merritt, 1979: 48; U.S. Senate, 1912: 27; Holmes, 1979: 5). Today, it is obvious that projects from this era were conceived as site-specific responses to the particular needs of selected regions and were not undertaken with regard to systematically established national priorities based upon a political theory of the environment.

The first multipurpose programs, which emerged in the 1930s, were intended to rectify this economic development bias and to place water policy on a less uncertain footing. In the early part of that decade, conflicts raged between the Corps of Engineers and the newer Bureau of Reclamation, created at the turn of the century to address the particular concerns of farmers and homesteaders living in the arid West. These conflicts revolved around which agency should build what particular project in a given river basin as well as which agency's priorities (flood control and navigation in the case of the corps, or irrigation and cheap hydropower in the case of the bureau) should take precedence.

During this conflict, Franklin D. Roosevelt's interior secretary, Harold Ickes, fought for and won permission to establish a number of river basin interagency study groups. Although these planning bodies were given formal staffs, research and planning funds, and some powers of program review, they were sharply limited in their access to Congress, in their ability to veto uneconomic or environmentally questionable water projects, and in their control over planning objectives. The latter were reserved to the construction agencies. Nevertheless, this effort, a forerunner of river basin commissions, constituted the first significant attempt to go beyond a purely ad hoc concept of water resources policy, wherein justification for particular projects was based largely on perceived benefits accruing only to a few groups (Derthick, 1970: 135–36).

The next stage in the evolution of water resources development as a systematic, coherent body of public policy came about in the late 1950s. Federal planners became concerned with steadily deteriorating water quality from both point and nonpoint pollution sources and with the growing problem of regional drought, especially in the Northeast urban corridor. These concerns forced a metamorphosis of interagency study groups into full-fledged river basin commissions with well-funded staffs and presidentially appointed directors. This metamorphosis was designed to provide greater public visibility for their efforts (Derthick, 1970: 144–49).

By the early 1960s, many of these river basin commissions were displaying a significant proclivity to inject order and coordination into the planning process for water projects. The Delaware River Basin Commission was probably the most ambitious of these river basin commissions in this regard. While the U.S. Constitution allows states to establish joint bodies for a variety of planning purposes, including water resources development (Article I, section 10, clause 3), the commission, formed in response to flooding and in-stream flow depletion in the Delaware basin in the late 1950s and early 1960s, was the first to include the federal government as a partner. The commission has been remarkably effective in alleviating interstate conflicts created by the midsixties drought in the Northeast; in implementing common water quality standards for surface waters among the states of Delaware, New Jersey, New York, and Pennsylvania; and in coordinating the development of sewage treatment, municipal storage, and other water systems (Derthick, 1970; DRBC, 1961, 1978a, 1978b). However, there are constraints on the effectiveness of river basin commissions in changing the attitudes of water resources agencies and the general public.

First of all, the federal natural resources agencies governed in theory by these river basin commissions act like public works bureaus. This helps to explain why shifts in environmental attitudes in the academic, engineering, and political communities in the 1960s have not produced dramatic policy changes within these agencies. Water resources agencies have been slow to concede that nonstructural solutions to water problems, such as floodplain management, flood hazard warning systems, water conservation, and recreational management, are workable and beneficial (Mazmanian and Nienaber, 1979: 8–36; Cahn, 1978: 231–32). In the particular case of the Delaware River Basin Commission, this problem is exacerbated by the fact that the commission has not displaced or supplanted existing water resources agencies. It reviews proposals put forth by the Corps of Engineers and other agencies. In addition, because its decisions are contingent upon the consensus of semisovereign states and the Congress, it has not yet shown itself capable of articulating independent, regionally integrated goals.

Second, interagency coordinating commissions generally cannot resolve political differences among their component agencies. Water resources agencies generally differ about the primary purpose of federal water policy. Should they promote agricultural development upstream of a major water project? Should they provide flood control for downstream residents? Or should they provide hydropower to beneficiaries outside the region? Such conflicts, rooted in highly localized perspectives, constitute a major stumbling block in the establishment of a sound, ethical national water policy. As a result of these differences, river basin commissions provide little more than shopping lists of agency projects, instead of plans based on coherent priorities. This may explain why these commissions generate little public awareness of, or enthusiasm for, their efforts. It may also explain why the most ambitious of these commissions, the Delaware River Basin Commission, failed to respond accurately to market forces affecting water or to go beyond legalistic formalities in adhering to pollution standards (Wildavsky, 1979: 184–203; U.S. Senate, 1978b).

In response to these deficiencies, Congress created the Water Resources Council in 1961. This council was an interagency data-gathering and policy-screening body that worked closely with the Office of Management and Budget. It was empowered to "encourage the conservation, development, and utilization of water and related land resources of the United States on a comprehensive and coordinated basis" (WRC, 1978: 1). Furthermore, it was supposed to provide presidential-level supervision of water policy by assessing available economic and environmental information on all proposed plans and projects submitted by such federal agencies as the Corps of Engineers, the Bureau of Reclamation, and the river basin commissions.

In order to prevent the promotion of pet projects by water resources agencies and thus to eliminate piecemeal, incremental, and uncoordinated attacks upon water resources problems, state input was encouraged in the planning process. The Water Resources Council was supposed to formulate national policy by assembling a series of state water plans financed by special planning grants provided by the council itself. These grants would encourage the articulation of comprehensive goals by requiring states to integrate their assessments through the local river basin commissions. States were also encouraged to request the assistance of the Corps of Engineers or the Bureau of Reclamation in preparing detailed plans in order to gather basic data on the nature and location of water resources, demand patterns, and potential long-term problems within their borders.

In practice, however, the planning process of the Water Resources Council was a disappointment. Technical assistance from federal agencies to the states did not assure meaningful participation by citizens at the crucial point—the inception of planning by federal agencies. Public works bureaus continued to adhere to their own plans and to bypass instruments that would encourage public participation. Generally, these agencies did not look upon the plans of river basin commissions and states as guideposts for their own projects (Robie, 1980: 72). The fact that many water projects proposed by federal agencies after 1965 were altered or, in some instances, canceled, confirms this fact. In many instances, a project would proceed in the face of significant public opposition, which could have been anticipated had the planning process been followed in spirit. Instead, opposition by a state governor, at the point when a project was at an advanced stage of development, often forced federal agencies to suspend project plans (Corps of Engineers, 1979: 4–29).

As a result of these problems, and by its own admission, the Water Resources Council found no consensus on "an appropriate ideological basis for policy" (WRC, 1968: 1). Attempts to gain adherence to a variety of principles and standards for water resources planning—including guidelines for public participation, the use of benefit-cost analysis, and the consideration of alternative plans for the solution of water problems—have met with considerable opposition from the traditional beneficiaries of water projects and, in some instances, from Congress, water resources agencies, river basin commissions, and states. In the Far West, for example, if the public perceived that a desired project was rejected because of adherence to principles and standards, it would oppose the standards, themselves (Goslin, 1978; WRC, 1973).

Before the abolition of the Water Resources Council in 1981, its major achievement was the publication of two national water assessments. The first assessment relied wholly upon previously published federal data. State participation in both assessments consisted of projections of future demand and estimation of available water supply. Neither plan articulated any general philosophy about water resources development or natural resources management. Moreover, the council did not identify in either plan its own vision of the respective roles of the national and state governments in water resources policy making. It also failed to define the place of water resources development in an overall natural resources policy.

Events since the presidential election of 1980 have reversed the trend toward comprehensive planning and, ironically, underscore the failure of the Water Resources Council to foster a national water resources policy. In 1981, the council, which led the battle for rigor and consistency in water policy, was abolished. Had it been retained, a process for forcing a meeting of the minds on the appropriate goals for U.S. water policy might have been achieved. The council was invested with the authority to compel justifications for new projects conforming to the broad public interest. Moreover, it required the incorporation of broad regional issues and the participation of a variety of stakeholders in policy making. It also recognized the synergistic relationship among all natural resources and began to prioritize goals such as regional equity and environmental protection.

In 1982, compliance with the principles and standards designed to integrate efficiency, equity, environmental quality, and regional economic development into the formal project-planning process was made voluntary (Conservation Foundation, 1984: 17; *Environmental Reporter*, 1981: 540). While no water resources policy participant has publicly called for a return to ad hoc policy making, no alternative criteria to confront serious water resources problems has yet been entertained.

Water Policy as Gratuitous: A Theory of Policy Choice in the Absence of a Political Philosophy

An ethically defensible democratic policy is one that obligates decision makers to carefully weigh the impacts of their decisions upon society as a whole. Current water policies place no obligation upon beneficiaries to weigh the impact of decisions upon the broad range of human needs and environmental resources. They also place little obligation upon those same beneficiaries to repay benefactors for policies from which they derive benefit. They thus do not originate from decision-making rules that conform to our intuitive desire for justice. I argue that such policies are gratuitous; they are based upon the assumption that it is justifiable for rational, free individuals to refuse to allow the needs of society to restrict their use of certain resources.

A policy that permits certain people to demand benefits from government without paying for them, without rewarding those who do pay for them, without respecting the fragile, depletable character of natural resources is a gratuitous policy. While natural resources policies have often been criticized as capricious, a gratuitous policy may or may not be capricious. Policy makers are often highly methodical in weighing benefits and costs, in trying to satisfy the preferences of various groups, and even in stating how a policy satisfies multipurpose objectives.

Carefully formulated policies may still be gratuitous, however. By ignoring the issues of equity and by attempting to placate every interest, the result often is a policy without any strings attached. Eric Uslaner, in a recent study of American energy policy, characterizes such placating of interests as a "preference for policy inaction" (Uslaner, 1989: 1). The cause of this preference is that members of Congress try to accommodate the demands of constituents and interest groups for cheap, abundant energy. The resulting policy makes it difficult, especially during a crisis of supply, to convince citizens to pay more for energy, to accept greater lifestyle regimentation in order to conserve energy, or to agree to centralized control of resources, even if such control might ensure energy supply for all of society, now and into the future (Uslaner, 1989). While Uslaner characterizes such a policy as a structuring of preferences designed to produce a minimal winning coalition for consensus building in politics, he clearly has in mind a concept similar to that of gratuitous policy.

The concept of gratuitous policy is also similar to the problem of the free rider depicted in social choice literature on decision making and exemplified by the writings of Mancur Olson (1965). Olson contends that the free rider—an individual who refuses to join a union or who contends that he or she should be taxed only for the value of actual services received from government—subscribes to an ethically inappropriate position. This is true for two reasons. First, while an individual may be incapable of seeing the value of the collective good provided through an institution he or she is a part of, the fact remains that certain goods can be provided only if institutions can raise the revenue and other resources to support them. Second, individuals generally have no incentive to sacrifice for the collective good unless compelled to. Thus, a certain compulsory sacrifice of liberty may be necessary to ensure that goods vital to a stable, secure life are provided to all who need them. When free riders operate with impunity, insufficient resources are acquired to provide for the collective good in an efficient and equitable manner (Olson, 1965: 88–96).

In natural resources policy, political scientists often attribute gratuitousness to two factors, separately or in combination: (1) the fragmented, decentralized structure of natural resources policy making, exemplified by the placement of responsibility in several agencies, and (2) the venerable tradition of antistatism in American political culture, which prevents the concentration of authority in any single group but at the same time inhibits coherent policies that protect the environment and promote the prudent use of resources.

While both of these factors are valid explanations for bad policy, they are symptoms of policy irrationality, not its cause. The cause of this irrationality is the willingness to rank individual economic liberty—the power to be acquisitive—above the broad range of human needs. An optimal public policy would maximize the range of alternatives under consideration and provide lucid, scrutable information about all alternatives. It would hold policy makers accountable for the consequences of their decisions and would assure adequate time and methods for deliberation about all relevant social goals. Let us examine the first of the traditional explanations of gratuitous policy to illustrate this point.

Institutional Fragmentation and the Lack of Policy Choice

The impact of institutional fragmentation upon U.S. water policy is well understood. The problems encountered by the Water Resources Council and river basin commissions were anticipated by numerous investigative panels, study groups, and commissions long before our current water crisis. In 1955, one of the most highly regarded of these panels concluded:

> The greatest single weakness in the federal government's activities in the field of water resources development is the lack of cooperation and coordination of the federal agencies with each other and with the states and local interests. . . . The federal interest has been expressed in different laws empowering different agencies to pursue particular programs for different purposes. (President's Advisory Commission, 1955: 2)

This lack of overall coordination persisted well into the 1960s. It prompted Hubert Marshall, reflecting upon Congress's role in natural resources policy, to suggest that it also inhibits the careful weighing of alternatives:

> One of the requirements of rational choice is that decision makers have the opportunity to consider alternative proposals that may better accomplish specified goals or may accomplish them at less cost. . . . The jurisdictional jealousies of the several construction agencies make dispassionate consideration of alternatives all but impossible. (Marshall, 1978: 408)

These "jurisdictional jealousies" have prompted calls for reorganization of the administration of water resources management in order to eliminate or reduce interagency conflict and policy inconsistency. It was partly in response to such critiques that President Lyndon Johnson convened the National Water Commission in 1967 in an attempt to broadly assess the social, ecological, and economic aspects of water policy.

While the commission, whose work terminated in 1974, focused upon the need for reorganization, it was not an administrative umbrella for policy. Nevertheless, its charter constituted a significant concession to the principle of coordination. Proclaiming itself "free of commitment to any agency or program," the commission studied the effects of water law on economic growth and lobbied for reconsideration of large-scale impoundments that diminish species diversity, deteriorate riverine habitat, and create environmental imbalances that undermine the economic objectives for which such projects are undertaken (NWC, 1969: 2, 57–59).

Despite all of these efforts, it is apparent that calls for reorganization fell largely on deaf ears. In 1985, the Conservation Foundation, reporting on the status of a national water policy under the Reagan administration, summarized the causes of administrative fragmentation in the following way:

> All sides of the iron triangle—legislatures, bureaucracies, and interest groups—seek to fit new programs into the mold of existing processes, legislative jurisdictions, and agencies. . . . These different interests have succeeded in splitting water development authority among different federal agencies . . . each of which caters to the desires of its particular constituency. This fragmentation of power is often duplicated in practice, if not by administrative structure, at the state and local levels—in part, stimulated by a need to mirror the federal structure of grants and mandatory programs. (Conservation Foundation, 1984: 17)

Like many critics before it, the Conservation Foundation called for policy coordination, coherence, and rigorous benefit-cost analysis. The failure of reorganization to take hold and to achieve these goals reflects a deeper problem infrequently addressed by water policy analysts. Neither reorganization nor administrative integration alone will solve water resources problems.

First, in the absence of value consensus on the objectives of policy, centralization only heightens and intensifies conflict. A careful study of the character and administrative ideology of water resources agencies suggests that every administrative entity possesses its own organizational philosophy, which, in the particular case of the Corps of Engineers and Bureau of Reclamation, is rooted as much in the period in which it was formed as in the training and socialization of its personnel (Clarke and McCool, 1985: 13–45; Warne, 1973). This organizational philosophy resists change or the imposition of new values. For example, while the Corps of Engineers is broadly skilled in the science of water resources management, its basic approach to water resources development is a dogged insistence that regional economic growth and national integration and security are appropriate goals of natural resources development. Moreover, the corps believes that it has the proper balance between civic action skills and discipline required to achieve these goals in a nonpartisan fashion.

The differing philosophies held by agencies constitute competing approaches to policy. Even if a particular approach appeals to only a relatively narrow constituency, and even if a new organization is created to serve as an integrating, coordinating entity, this striving to fulfill individual goals persists. This is one reason why U.S. water policy has been incoherent. The problem is not that water resources agencies cannot be reorganized; it is that each agency seeks to maintain support from its constituency regardless of where it is administratively located (Marshall, 1978: 411).

The development of the Pick-Sloan Missouri River basin project, discussed in chapter 4, exemplifies this problem. Jurisdiction for water resources management in this region was shared by both the Corps of Engineers and the Bureau of Reclamation, and they could not agree on the optimal development of its water resources. Congress opted to allow both agencies to develop separate plans and then urged the integration of these plans after project construction by establishing review boards that ironed out conflicts over reservoir management for flood control, hydropower, irrigation, and navigation. Recognition of the power of narrow constituencies led Congress to ban even the study of interbasin transfers for fear that merely studying such proposals would build political momentum among interest groups and agency staff for the development of the transfers.

Second, if agencies with different mandates were brought under one umbrella agency (for example, if the Corps of Engineers and the Bureau of Reclamation were placed in a single federal department of natural resources) the values held by the individuals working for each agency would tend only to be sharpened and exacerbated. Ironically, this same tendency is revealed in reverse by the splitting up of the Atomic Energy Commission into the Nuclear Regulatory Commission and the Energy Research and Development Administration (the forerunner of the Department of Energy) in 1974. The Nuclear Regulatory Commission continued to favor development of nuclear power because its personnel, all former employees of the Atomic Energy Commission, supported nuclear industry self-regulation and the expansion of nuclear power (Ford, 1984).

The result of this conflict within umbrella groups is that component agencies will either persist in their original objectives, a centrifugal tendency, or else look to top political leadership to guide and initiate policy. The latter option is more likely if component agencies have lost their legitimacy through pursuing unpopular policies. The latter option may resolve conflicts only temporarily and in an ad hoc fashion. Different policies may prevail under different administrations, and a change of administration may bring an abrupt shift in policy—which in the case of natural resources impedes the comprehensive, long-term planning essential for their prudent management.

This is exemplified in the transition from the Carter to the Reagan presidencies. This transition had a profound impact upon the politics of the Water Resources Council, the river basin commissions, and the construction agencies. The Carter administration sought to bolster the principles and standards under which water projects are justified by encouraging nonstructural tools for abating flood damages and alleviating water supply problems (e.g., floodplain management and water conservation). His administration also sought a more systematic use of ecological impact studies in water resources planning.

Just as momentum for this view was achieved within the Water Resources Council and the river basin commissions, a new administration came to power that was not only deeply indebted to the interests of water-thirsty western states but also committed to slashing domestic spending and weakening the influence of environmentalists (Caulfield, 1984: 223–24). The result was twofold. First, the process by which water policy was formulated became further fragmented. Second, federal indecisiveness over such policy areas as cost sharing and new construction starts increased the anxiety of states that were trying to solve pressing water problems but were unable to afford solutions by themselves. While no one questions the legitimacy of political control by the administration in office, the practical problem with abrupt shifts in policy is that, unless states know how much federal support they can count on for new project starts and for what types of projects, they are reluctant to do anything at all.

Third and finally, even if administrative reorganization could alleviate interagency conflict and create a genuinely unified water policy, that unified policy might be counterproductive of rational choice. As Gilbert White has noted, a viable water policy has multiple objectives, and does not exclude for the sake of unity the single objectives of any participating agency. Even at the risk of heightening conflict, rational management of water resources should heighten, not limit, debate over alternatives for reaching these objectives. While reorganization may integrate water policy, it may also remove countervailing pressures that promote flexibility, experiment, and innovation (White, 1969: 32). Say what one will about the short-sightedness of single-purpose projects, such as dams built exclusively for flood control or hydropower, their narrow objectives make them efficient because they can be speedily erected. Moreover, they are politically popular precisely because they benefit narrow rather than broad constituencies. Unfortunately, their speed and their narrowness increase the chance of irreversible environmental damage. As we shall see, the best way to avoid such damage is to increase, not diminish, administrative pluralism, while simultaneously harnessing that pluralism to an environmental ethic.

Antistatism and American Environmental Policy

There is a long-standing tradition in American society of resisting government intrusion in natural resources management. This resistance stems from our heritage of individualism, the myth of the frontier, regional and ethnic diversity, and enthusiasm for private enterprise.[1] it affects popular attitudes toward environmental policy in several ways.

Americans generally favor environmental disruption if it brings economic progress or the optimization of economic efficiency (usually defined as maximizing the yields from land and water resources for present and future generations). However, they generally oppose environmental disruption that is perceived as denying local access to, or control over, natural resources. Put another way, public support for any given environmental policy depends upon the benefits derived locally. In the case of water policy, local beneficiaries are thought of as only those living in the region where a project is to be constructed, not those who reside in the larger geographical area affected by the project. By the same token, equity is thought of as fairness to those local residents directly enduring hardships, such as loss of land, when these projects are constructed (Sheinbaum, 1983). This ignores the fact that others, who may live outside the local area, may also endure hardship.

Civil servants invested with authority to regulate natural resources are generally viewed, not as generators of wealth or as contributors to the betterment of the state, but as squanderers of resources and, at times, dishonest (Abramavitz, 1980). In certain regions, this perception is compounded by an anti-outsider complex (Schoenbaum, 1979; McConnell, 1966: 196–245).

As a result, plans for water projects may stir powerful local resentment, especially if their benefits are not perceived as accruing to residents or if they are viewed as an assault upon a region's ability to manage its own resources competently. Thus, for a water policy based upon sound economic and equity criteria to be publicly acceptable, it must be sellable within these constraints.

From the standpoint of water policy reform, antistatism prompts two distinct challenges that are difficult to reconcile. The first challenge is to counter the dominance of the so-called iron triangle of legislative committee, bureaucratic agency, and interest group in the formulation of natural resources decisions. This triangle results from a resistance to authority being concentrated in either a strong executive or a centralized legislative system controlled by party discipline. This resistance manifests in environmental policy as (1) piecemeal, incremental policies, (2) oversight by innumerable subcommittees, and (3) a network of mutual benefits. The latter consists of voter support for congressional representatives in exchange for legislation and budget allocations favoring constituent interest groups.

Reform of the iron triangle will require articulation of policies that are relevant and comprehensible to average people concerned with the socioeconomic and environmental impacts of natural resources developments on their daily lives. This means that simply rejecting ditional pattern of natural resources policy making will not do, b Americans expect that natural resources policy will benefit re and local economic interests. Reforms thus far attempted have largely cosmetic. They have not forced water management agencies and interest groups to come to grips with the basic normative objectives of water policy—the enhancement of both nature and human life. While these reforms may have succeeded in bridling acquisitive self-interest, they do not offer alternative values, because the process of policy making does not illuminate or educate; it merely pits one faction against another in a test of strength in a controlled arena.

The second challenge is to make policy that is perceived as fair to people in the locality affected—that is, to counter the prevailing notion of individualism. For example, while a national scheme to divert water from river basins in water-rich areas to arid regions might be sensible for promoting national development, it would generate considerable local opposition in the water-rich areas, which might lead to demands for regional compensation. The articulation of a broad public interest is difficult in an antistatist society, which defines democracy not as a society organized by principles of deliberation and consensus about what is fair, but as a society that satisfies the sometimes disparate preferences of the majority, regardless of cost.

For contemporary water policy, as we shall see, the prevailing power structure and belief system underlie our present water resources dilemma. Established policy-making institutions refuse to introduce bold plans to solve pressing water crises, while at the same time they resist attempts at reorganization for fear of losing their power base. They perceive that doing nothing, while an ineffective solution to environmental problems, is at least unlikely to offend any established stakeholder.

Toward an Environmental Ethic: Rudiments for a Political Theory of Water

A central thesis of this book is that an ethically defensible natural resources policy is one that satisfies a broad range of human needs, from survival and biological exigency to an enlightened existence in harmony with one's inner character, with others, and with nature. Implicit in this assumption is that a theory of justice should encompass natural resources as well as people. This is so for two reasons. In order to ensure the satisfaction of this range of human needs, the teleological development of people requires an enlightened regard for the distribution, use, and potential for abuse of natural resources. In addition, na-

ture is intrinsically valuable in its own right because of its own telos,
or purpose. Every natural resource has a place in the unity and order of
the physical world.

My view, similar to that of Aldo Leopold, John Muir, and other classic
environmental philosophers, is that a balance of nature is not only important for nurturing the biophysical qualities of ecology necessary to
sustaining life but is essential to human beings, in particular, because
of the psychological rejuvenating effects of natural balance (Leopold,
1966: 176ff; Muir, 1970).

Contemporary political psychologists, as well as political philosophers, have long recognized that each person's capacity for justice is
based at least partly on a supportive context provided by nature and
society (Cochran, 1977: 546; Bay, 1978; Kohlberg, 1970). Nature endows
each of us with the specific capacity to satisfy our needs through our
intelligence, our mechanical instincts, and our physical makeup. It also
shapes our capacity for moral reasoning, which evolves through many
stages from childhood to adulthood (Kohlberg, 1970, 1971, 1981; Maslow, 1968, 1954). In order to balance our basic needs and capacities,
however, we also require a socially supportive context that coexists
with nature. Such a context is characterized, many of these same philosophers and psychologists tell us, by bonds of fellowship based upon
a sense of being rooted in a physical place as well as in a temporal
society.

This argument has been advanced in diverse, yet strikingly parallel
ways. For example, it has been argued that our ontological incomplete-
ness as infants requires us to seek authenticity—the fulfillment of our
innermost proclivities—through harmony with others and with nature
(Bay, 1978) and that life in a highly fragmented, industrialized society
results in alienation and estrangement from nature and society and a
breakdown in civility and social bonds (Simon, 1960; Macpherson,
1978). In any event, this developmental, communitarian aspect of human behavior is thought to establish a cognitively defensible basis for
morality.

Conversely, the failure to achieve ontological completeness results in
inner feelings of being victims of injustice, a feeling often based on real
mistreatment. According to contemporary philosophers and psychologists such as Abraham Maslow, Lawrence Kohlberg, and C. B. Macpherson, this feeling prevents us from living an examined life as active
citizens conscious of the impact and consequences of our actions upon
others and the larger world. These contemporary philosophers and psychologists draw upon the classic roots of the understanding of this problem, exemplified by the writings of Plato and Aristotle (Plato, *Republic*,
book 10; Aristotle, *Nichomachean Ethics*, books 2, 3, and 4). Following

the teachings of this classical tradition, contemporary philosophers and psychologists contend that persons are morally incomplete at birth; that obedience to moral norms and values thus emerges developmentally; that extreme egoism is unnatural and found only in individuals whose cognitive development has been stunted; and that a commitment to the welfare of society requires a sense of authenticity acquired through participation in the affairs of society. Patterns of moral development thus may underlie deficiencies in the decision-making institutions of society that hinder the attainment of this supportive context and produce alienation and estrangement from nature and ourselves.

The impulse to develop one aspect of our personality at the expense of others—for example, the biophysical (appetitive) part at the expense of the rational (reflective) and the emotional or aesthetic (spiritous)—is one cause of the failure to lead an examined life (Plato, *Republic*). Likewise, the failure to utilize, distribute, and sustain natural resources in a balanced way is both a symptom of our failure to develop harmony within our souls (appetitive people disregard the fragility of nature) and a cause of injustice. By denying others fair use and access to natural resources, we deny to them the opportunity to fulfill their needs. We may also upset the balance of nature and possibly produce irreversible disruption of food chains, the atmosphere, and the sustainability of all forms of life. *Thus, the first rudiment of an environmental ethic is a relationship with nature that nurtures our teleological development.*

Justice entails the fulfillment of balance and harmony within one self and in society and the preservation of natural resources. A specific system for making public policy is required to achieve these goals. This system would have two major characteristics: (1) an awareness of the multiple consequences of government actions, not just economic efficiency or aesthetic quality, and (2) a contractarian notion of decision making, in which each individual agrees to a basic constitutional framework for allocating and managing natural resources appropriate to the availability of the resources and the needs of society.

In a liberal, democratic society, a simple endowment of nature with rights and liberties would not suffice to provide this environmental ethic or satisfactorily encompass multiple consequences of decisions. The reason for this is analyzed by Bruce Ackerman. As Ackerman notes, natural resources cannot advance their own power or raise legitimate claims. Natural resources do not, in other words, have rights that they can claim against human society. The relation between natural resources and citizens is authoritarian, and natural resources must rely for protection upon the policy choices of citizens, who in a liberal society do have claims against one another (Ackerman, 1980: 70, 101–28).

What this suggests is that the most fruitful avenue for protecting nature in a liberal society is through some version of a social contract, which, as will be seen momentarily, has other advantages as well. For a political theory of the environment, the most useful feature of the contractarian approach is avoidance of the naturalistic fallacy—the false identification of a value judgment with a factual one (Frankena, 1963: 82). Instead of inducing proper ethical behavior by means of observations about nature and society and thereby justifying political norms for the use of water, I utilize a social contract approach to describe how rational, reasonable individuals may agree on the distribution of water or other natural resources. *Thus, the second rudiment of an environmental ethic is a social contract view of political society.*

Following Ronald Dworkin (1977), I view a contract as a model for establishing how reasonable people can establish principles for decision making that are fair and that conform to moral intuition. In short, a contract is based on the idea that just decisions encompass what is reasonably possible, given the scarcity or abundance of a natural resource, the political resources of public officials, and our very human needs to act on principle and not on faith alone.

In chapter 2, I explore the elements necessary for making rational decisions in water policy and expand this contractual, teleological theory of the environment. I consider the difficulties in reforming the ethics of policy in light of these elements. Chapter 2 establishes a theoretical framework that guides the critique of water policy throughout the book. Policy outcomes are set forth, and an approach to their partial justification, based upon public choice theory, is also elucidated. In addition, benefit-cost analysis and traditional conservationist approaches to water policy are initially evaluated within the stated objectives of this approach. Following this partial justification, the need for a social contract view of natural resources decision making is introduced in greater detail, using some of the principles of public choice theory and criticizing principles that fail to meet the test of the social contract.

Chapter 3 examines the absence of a justifiable policy framework both in American water law and in the approaches to planning by water officials. The failure of law and planning to effectively manage natural resources on behalf of a public good is related to the absence of an overarching set of policy values. It will be shown that water law does not place enough emphasis on responsibilities to nature and society and does not accommodate the character of water resources. It is shown that planning is insufficiently attuned to democratic participation.

Chapter 4 uses the Garrison diversion project in the northern Great Plains as a case study of competing policy values in water resources development. It considers whether or not such competing values can be reconciled and, if not, which values should take precedence. The issues of intergenerational justice, equity, and compensation are defined and related to the water policy framework developed in chapter 2.

Chapters 5, 6, and 7 examine the implications of gratuitous policy-making in water resources management from the standpoint of, respectively, structural reform of the process by which water policy is made, competing definitions and conceptualizations of conservation, and the use and misuse of benefit-cost analysis in water resources development. Additional case studies are introduced as they are appropriate to specific theoretical issues, including the case of the ill-fated Blue Ridge Project in the New River valley of North Carolina, Virginia, and West Virginia.

Chapter 8 discusses the reasons why water and other natural resources policies traditionally fail to conform to the tenets of democratic theory. It focuses on the dominance of elitism in policymaking, as exemplified by the historical experience of the Corps of Engineers. In the formulation of water policy, the self-interested values of narrow political subsystems have dominated. In the implementation of water policy, the technocratic approaches of engineers and planners have had greater legitimacy than the broader, sometimes more aesthetic and less systematic, viewpoints of the general public.

Finally, chapter 9 introduces a framework for placing rational choice at the forefront of policy values in natural resources management. This framework is based on an approach termed regional contractualism. Essentially, I offer a way of integrating the natural characteristics of water with the political constraints dictated by human use. This framework is predicated upon accurate assessment of social needs, prescribed rights and duties for all water resources users within a designated water resources region, and an environmental ethic that dictates prudent resource use and respect for all living things.

Comparisons with the water resources management systems of other societies are offered as a means of assessing the viability of this framework. Furthermore, the regional contract argues that all natural resources policies, in order to be democratic, must define the obligations of those benefiting from resource use and the manner in which policy costs should be allocated. It is also necessary to anticipate the probable impacts of policies on natural systems.

2   Ethics and U.S. Water Policy

When the well's dry, we know the worth of water.
—BENJAMIN FRANKLIN

*We have acted as if water were like air—free, so omnipresent as
to exist beyond our conscious thought; so unquestionably necessary to life on this planet that it would be foolish to spend any
time or energy thinking about it.*
—FRED POWLEDGE, *Water*

The Components of an Ethical Environmental Policy

Water problems are the result of misguided and misdirected human
choices. They are not the product of physical or technical limitations
of the resource itself. All the fresh water there ever was still exists on
this earth. Overdevelopment of arid regions, pollution, and failure to
plan for drought have made water resources unavailable in particular
places and at particular times. Failure to appreciate the implications of
this simple fact has directly contributed to an impending water crisis
in the United States. In short, regional, national, and local disputes over
water stem from the way political, legal, and social institutions manage
it (Conservation Foundation, 1984: 365).

Our current water crisis revolves around demand exceeding supply—
especially in the generally arid but rapidly growing Far West—and the
quality of available supply becoming diminished nationwide by pollution. In the latter instance, nonpoint contamination of water caused by
agriculture and storm water runoff is inadequately encompassed by current regulatory policy. In some instances, air pollution through acid
precipitation damages lakes and streams, making the burning of coal a

key source of water pollution. Moreover, demand and quality concerns extend equally to ground and surface waters and are compounded by the relative absence of a national policy for the former (Gianessi et al., 1986; Stanfield, 1985; Smith, Alexander, and Wolman, 1987). Studies of these issues suggest the need to rethink our basic attitudes about water as a commodity to be exploited for individual gratification with little regard for the consequences of our actions.

In this chapter, it is argued that in order to meet the challenges of this crisis, we must first understand that natural resources policy in the United States has been based upon values that maximize short-term exploitive gain and minimize equity. These values have encouraged practices that impose negative environmental impacts upon water and related land resources. They have also discouraged alternative solutions to water problems that are less costly and potentially more beneficial to society as a whole. Thus, in order to address these problems, a way must be found to encompass values that maximize long-term social benefit in water resources policy.

Policy Outcomes as Justifications for Environmental Policy

The U.S. system of water management is a combination of state and local water laws and national policies shaped by regional pressures, the now familiar distributive politics pattern (Lowi, 1979). This pattern inadequately incorporates concerns over justice and environmental sustainability for three reasons. First, the structure of natural resources decision making in the United States inhibits the incorporation of these values. The traditionally weak state capacity of public bureaucracies— the result of antistatist public attitudes and political fragmentation— has made agreement on policy values over water and other natural resources nearly impossible to attain (Skocpol and Finegold, 1982).

Second, since water policy has been largely directed toward regional economic development, it has also been politically gratuitous or, in other words, based upon the assumption that it is justifiable for individuals to ignore societywide goals.

It has been assumed that such problems of implementation could be mitigated by better planning before construction proceeded. Planning would clarify the relationship between beneficiaries and benefactors; would design mechanisms for long-term payback, which would make projects relatively painless to undertake; and while not necessarily conceding that resources are fragile, would study the environmental impacts of a project to mitigate their most serious effects. The major problem with this assumption is that the planning profession has no single set of ethical principles and, by its own admission, expects to be guided by goals articulated by citizens in the political arena (Burke and Heaney, 1975). Unless these goals are clearly articulated, planning can only impact upon policy after critical decisions are formulated concerning who benefits from, and who pays for, particular projects and programs.

If planners are asked to proceed from a limited set of objectives, such as increasing regional water supply, they will only design and build dams, waterworks, and hydroelectric plants and will leave ecological, social, and economic questions unanswered (R. Wilson, 1973: viii; NWC, 1973: 366). This is why planners and engineers traditionally view natural resources policy in pragmatic and incremental, rather than holistic, terms. Simply stated, they are ill equipped by training and demeanor to solve ethical problems. Their closely detailed, technical work produces anonymity and inhibits moral responsibility for the consequences of decisions. Thus, if ethical values are to be incorporated into natural resources policy, they must be articulated in the political arena.

A third inhibitor of ethical policy is the fact that, even if policy makers could agree on rules for formulating equitable natural resources decisions, the criteria for selecting specific policies would still have to be elucidated. This is an especially formidable task. In water policy, different but equally desirable goals may conflict with one another. For example, a dam to provide water for irrigation may have to be built on highly productive bottomlands. If the farmers living on this land gained title from ancestors who received federal land grants, their removal from this land may violate a promise given "in perpetuity." Unless these farmers are removed from the impoundment area, however, cheap irrigation water for a larger number of farmers cannot be brought about. For water resources agencies, one question generated by such a conflict is, Which goal is more important, providing water to many people or upholding a commitment made to a few? In actuality, since water resources agencies have been traditionally concerned mostly with economic gains, they have tended to ignore noneconomic issues, such as distributive justice or the environmental impacts of their efforts.

Normative political theorists often distinguish between meliorative and preemptory criteria in selecting public policies (Braybrooke and Lindblom, 1963; Frankena, 1963; Beatley, 1989). In natural resources policy, preemptory values encompass deontological principles. A deontological principle asserts that what is good or right is determined by the intrinsic properties of an action. Promises, commitments, and obligations are based on preemptory values, because they are made without duress or compulsion. Moreover, those to whom they are made fully expect they will be carried out (Frankena, 1963: 19–21). Examples of preemptory issues in public policy are fulfilling promises made by government to various groups, upholding individual civil rights and liberties, and obeying canons of fairness. These political imperatives may be explicitly stated in constitutions. On the other hand, citizens may value them implicitly because of the weight of tradition or political culture or, as shall be seen, because of implicit or explicit agreements made among citizens and government (Rawls, 1971). Meliorative values refer to the measurable consequences of policy, such as benefits, costs, and risks to various groups. Meliorative concerns encompass choices among policies designed to enhance, promote, or hinder health, opportunity, welfare, and other issues (Braybrooke and Lindblom, 1963: 166, 212).

When policy makers try to address both values in the same public policy, conflicts often arise over the priorities that should be assigned to them. Moreover, if implicit as well as explicit promises are entertained, there may arise conflicts over promises made to groups that stand on opposite sides of a natural resources or land use issue (Beatley, 1989). In the case of my previous example, one question raised by the building of this hypothetical dam is, Which value should be protected, the meliorative gains accruing to farmers from cheap irrigation or the preemptory commitment of upholding a land grant promised to a particular group?

The building of a water project might be an exchange designed to fulfill an implicit promise made to farmers that their children would be compensated. Moreover, this implicit promise may conflict with meliorative concerns over environmental quality to a wider region or even another political society. While no promise is sacred, as Timothy Beatley points out, in the making of natural resources decisions, governments risk their credibility and legitimacy if they break clear, consistent, and explicit promises. The very foundation of land use and other long-term environmental decisions would then be called into question. Citizens would not trust the word of government. While reminding us that there may be perfectly good reasons for breaking such promises—for example, to protect irreplaceable natural objects or to preserve features of the natural environment that sustain ecological balance—in all cases, governments must attempt to weigh the consequences of both decision criteria (Beatley, 1989). In chapter 4 we examine the Garrison diversion project, which exemplifies this very problem, in the context of two conflicts, one between the United States and Canada and one between environmentalists and water project beneficiaries.

Some political philosophers argue that the concept of public choice is one way to decide such conflicts and to arrive at ethically justifiable political decisions. Essentially, public choice theorists argue that there really is no cognitively defensible way of choosing between meliorative and preemptory considerations in public policy. Three reasons are given. First, the justness or rationality of political principles may be nothing more than passionately held preferences with no independent philosophical standing (Chisholm, 1966: 15–16). Second, even if limited consensus is attained on the rules for making decisions—for example, constitutional amendments, legislative procedures, the consideration and weighing of alternatives to meet an objective (C. Anderson, 1979: 716–17; Kalleberg and Preston, 1975; Rawls, 1971)—this would not necessarily help us choose specific policies. Third, assuming that problems of cognitive status and ethical criteria could be resolved, the character of pluralistic societies would still inhibit consistent policy implementation. The capacity of bureaucracies to solve social and environmental problems varies by the level of economic development of societies and is partly shaped by bureaucratic competition and government fragmentation (Waterbury, 1979: 100–17; Lowi, 1979; Skocpol and Finegold, 1982).

Public choice theory's answer to these dilemmas is as follows. First, taking as its point of departure analytical investigations into the character of ethical judgments (Taylor, 1961; Toulmin, 1950; Griffiths, 1958), public choice theorists presume that people have the capacity to make commitments to which they can be bound due to their ability to distinguish the consequences of various alternatives.

Second, political decisions are a special type of commitment, which obligate decision makers to explain their rationale for policies. These decisions cannot be merely prudent, because they have consequences that shape and constrain the choices of others as well as oneself. Thus, to aspire to high political office in a democracy compels one to accept the responsibility to defend policies by reference to some concept of a public good. It is the obligation of democratic governments to defend policies by mirroring peoples' wishes. It is not the obligation of citizens to justify why they do not like them. One of the proclaimed ethical advantages of the American democratic tradition, which has its roots in the notion that the most qualified elites should be placed into positions of authority, is that elected officials recognize their obligation to sort out from the many preferences articulated by citizens those that conform to a true public good. These officials are placed into positions of authority because of this obligation and are held accountable if policies go awry.

Third, within political restraints, policy makers are free to choose different policies, are cognizant of the consequences of any policy, and consequently are able to distinguish between the needs of a polity and their own personal desires. While policy makers often predicate political decisions on the hope of getting reelected, it would be ethically inappropriate to make policy decisions on the basis of self-interest, antici-pation of personal enrichment, whim, or caprice. To do any of these things might obstruct citizens' right to oppose government edict, to debate alternative policies, and to ensure that decisions are being made honestly and lawfully (C. Anderson, 1979; Dror, 1968: 159–69).

The freedom of elected decision makers also obliges them to recog-nize the ethical responsibilities of their power. It is reasonable to expect them to make decisions that conform to a public interest and that are consistent with lawful rights, canons of fairness, and socially acceptable standards of efficiency (C. Anderson, 1979: 713). Moreover, they should realize that any policy can be justified, and criticized, by reference to several criteria, each of which may be desirable to different groups. Thus, to say that a policy is rational must mean more than that it serves the greatest good of the greatest number of citizens, since this would meet only one possible criterion of a good public policy—namely, the consequences of decisions—and not necessarily its conformance with promises, obligations, or past commitments. Having established the cri-teria by which public choice theorists would address these dilemmas, we turn to the manner by which they would make ethical environmen-tal and natural resources decisions.

The Public Choice Approach to an Environmental Policy

In a democracy, elected officials charged with making natural resources policy must satisfy constituents who demand practical solutions to flooding, drought, and water supply problems. Bureaucracies managing these same issues must live within established budgets, over which they have only limited control. They must also endure legislative committee oversight and respond, every four to eight years, to changes in presiden-tial direction. Even courts, which have increasingly played an important role in environmental litigation, must operate within the parameters of constitutional justification, the separation of powers, and the preroga-tives of Congress and the president to establish or eliminate programs.

The proliferation of different policy-making institutions often leads to the predominance of constituency and bureaucratic goals in water policy. The fragmentation of policy responsibility inherent in this con-stellation of institutions also makes it difficult to discern a clear public interest over and above the interests of various regional or bureaucratic constituencies. This compounds the problem of reconciling meliorative and preemptory criteria, because, at any given time, agencies may be on different sides of a natural resources issue.

How can these two problems be overcome? One commonly proposed solution in the case of water policy is more centralized control over policy through the establishment of hierarchical policy regimes. Unfortunately, bureaucratic hierarchies generate their own inefficiencies, are resistant to change, and worst of all, provide inadequate feedback on their own conformance with desired social goals. This appears to be especially true among very large agencies wedded to traditional patterns of solving problems (Bennis, 1966: 1–15).

In water policy, this problem is exemplified by the politics of the Corps of Engineers and the Bureau of Reclamation, which have often resisted attempts to change their original missions or to open their decision-making processes to public scrutiny. It is also illustrated by the adversarial and sometimes combative relationship these agencies had with the Water Resources Council and river basin commissions. For this reason, a second proposed solution—public choice theory—has been offered by political scientists and is beginning to receive serious attention in the policy community.

Public choice theory, the application of economics to political science, was developed by economists and other policy analysts concerned with natural resources issues. Its relevance clearly extends (and has been applied) to several policy areas. The particular public choice school I have drawn upon is that which takes its point of departure from environmental concerns. Its central focus is the relation between the character of a resource and the technology utilized for its exploitation (Sproule-Jones, 1982; Young, 1982; Ostrom and Ostrom, 1971). Proponents of this approach predicate that the cost, abundance, disposition, and interdependency of a natural resource should ultimately determine the appropriate (or optimal, meaning economically most efficient) arrangements for its management.

According to Mark Sproule-Jones and Oran Young, two of the foremost proponents for this approach, the assessment of a natural resources policy must focus on the systems of delivery to consumers. Ultimately, the goal of these delivery systems is to respond to consumer preferences by operating under the most cost effective decision-making institutions, instead of under hierarchically structured bureaucracies, which have little regard for the impact of their decisions on human needs and natural resources. User fees, service charges, or voucher payments effectively register public preferences on environmental policies. Mechanisms to ensure equity among varying users' ability to pay must, of course, also be established (Sproule-Jones, 1982; Young, 1982; Ostrom and Ostrom, 1971). While user fees can be regressive, public choice theorists contend that there are two assurances to protect against this. First, public choice schemes have long dealt with the inequity of fee-paying systems by using such adjustments as credits and rebates. Second, since one test of a good policy is its ability to reconcile efficiency and equity, a regressive user fee structure would not be tolerated, at least in principle.

Moreover, by comparing the performance of alternative systems, political scientists can weigh the relative advantages of public versus private enterprises or government regulations versus free markets. Young, whose research focuses on specific measures of provision system performance, contends that successful achievement can be gauged by reference to five criteria held in high esteem in industrialized polities. These measures, and their implications for water policy, are depicted in table 2.1.

These five performance measures are predicated upon two assumptions, the first of which is empirical, though with normative implications, while the second is clearly normative: (1) individuals seek to maximize their preferences in a competitive market characterized by scarcity, and (2) the proper role of the state is "to avoid deep intrusions" in the economic arena (Sproule-Jones, 1982: 794, 800). The former assumption is based upon observation of consumer behavior. The latter is derived from the approaches' contention that every effort to eliminate inefficiency should be encouraged. Young further suggests that his public choice framework should be viewed as an institutional perspective, which places a deontological conception of property rights at the core of the set of rules governing any natural resources regime (Young, 1982: 10, 15).

Because natural resources are unevenly distributed, and because there are numerous possible arrangements for any given provision system, the success of any natural resources regime varies according to the character and cost of the exploitation of a resource and a polity's level of development. In theory, a natural resources regime that encompasses a geographical area appropriate to the resource and a value system in close conformity with that of its larger polity will allocate the resource in a structurally efficient manner, in line with the standards of Pareto optimality.

Public choice theorists contend that their approach overcomes the dilemmas caused by fragmentation, provides a framework for defining the public interest in natural resources policy, and reconciles meliorative and preemptory values. This is so for three reasons. First of all, natural resources and their location and accessibility constitute irreducible facts about the world. These facts establish unambiguous parameters for choosing public policies. Since decisions relating to exploitation of natural resources in a public choice system are determined by individual preferences viewed as rational responses to "the perceptions and incentives of institutional arrangements," the locus of decision making

Table 2.1 Performance Measures of Natural Resources Regimes

Measure	Definition	Examples	Pertinent Issues for Water Policy
Allocative efficiency	Net economic benefits occurring from a policy	Any macroeconomic gain to society: increased timber harvests, greater yields from fisheries, etc.	Net gains in water supply, hydroelectric power, flood protection
Equity	Distributive fairness: how benefits are allocated among various groups	Protection of lower socioeconomic groups, protection of future generations, balancing of public and private sectors	Balancing regional development, repaying groups for losses of land, using government to redistribute wealth through TVA-type projects
Noneconomic values	Desired social goods not captured by calculations of efficiency	Humane treatment of animals, pollution control, aesthetic preservation	Clean, usable water, preservation of wild rivers
Transaction costs	Costs of doing business: ratio of costs to operate regime versus benefits of policy outcomes	Operation and maintenance of any policy: costs of rules, regulations, tangible public works, etc.	Payback of water project, operation and maintenance of waterworks, support of or opposition to conservation, irrigation laws

Table 2.1 (continued)

Measure	Definition	Examples	Pertinent Issues for Water Policy
Feasibility	Conformance of a regime with economic and social systems	Initial public acceptability, costs of gaining public compliance with demands of regime's rules, stability of regime. (Is it long lasting?)	Public support of or opposition to dams. (Will agencies manage projects as they promised, indefinitely?)

Source: Adapted from Young, 1982, pp. 119–30.

is always the individual consumer (Sproule-Jones, 1982: 792, 794). Because individual responses can be measured with a high degree of certainty, and because the performance measures cited by public choice theorists constitute those most frequently cited by individuals themselves, the cumulative preferences of individuals constitute scrutable, politically viable guides to policies that are consistent with a democratic consensus.

Second, public choice theory successfully reconciles meliorative and preemptory concerns. Young's framework contains both consequential policy criteria (allocative efficiency, transaction costs, and noneconomic values) and preemptory ethical imperatives (equity and feasibility). An optimal policy is one in which both criteria are encompassed in order to maximize benefits while minimizing social costs (Young, 1982: 120). Reconciling these modified utilitarian criteria is not without its difficulties, as will be seen at the end of this chapter.

Third, public choice theorists believe they have solved the problems associated with policy implementation without reliance upon inefficient, undemocratic hierarchies. Neither property-rights-based systems nor publicly owned systems of natural resources management are assumed to have intrinsic value. The appropriateness of a particular regime is gauged by its benefit to users over time. Unlike social welfare analyses of policy performance, which focus solely on microeconomic concepts of efficiency, public choice theory views natural resources as public goods, which by their very character must be commonly pooled for users to derive advantage from them. This is much along the lines of Mancur Olson's notion that institutions may have to compel conjoint support of services that are not directly and equally received by everyone, in order to provide the service to those who do receive them (Olson, 1965). It is simply impossible for each individual to obtain all the necessary resources by him or herself. Moreover, even if it could be done, conflicts over competing claims would be virtually impossible to resolve.

For water policy, this suggests that proper allocation of benefits and costs must be determined within a comprehensive water management system that reconciles political boundaries with regional sources. It also suggests that the appropriate boundaries for the management of water resources may have to transcend state or even national boundaries, as shall be discussed momentarily. Appropriate institutional arrangements should not be bound by considerations of nationalism or tradition.

There are three other characteristics of public choice theories relevant for the management of natural resources. First, in contrast to orthodox public administration theory, which emphasizes centralization, public choice theory entertains alternatives that stress democratic collectives of decision makers arranged like utilities, each possessing a high degree of independence (Ostrom and Ostrom, 1971: 212). One problem with this assumption, of course, is its emphasis upon majoritarian preferences as a key to policy evaluation, a subject addressed later in this chapter. In theory, this should maximize the opportunities for public participation in natural resources management.

Second, the criteria for public choice (i.e., the goals of public policy) are interdependent. In order for a policy to be equitable (fair in the way its benefits are distributed or allocated), it must allocate benefits to different classes, races, genders, and regions while remaining sensitive to the rights of future generations. This suggests that the computation of the transaction costs of water policy (those entailed in the operation and maintenance of dams, hydroelectric plants, and irrigation works, for example) is extraordinarily complex.

Generally, public works agencies compute these costs by factoring them out over an arbitrary fifty-year amortization period. Water resources planners commonly compute this amortization using discount rates based on the predicted worth of money. The assumption here is that the ultimate value of a water project is determined by inflation. In fact, however, this method does not fully compensate for the opportunities foregone by later generations, who will lose the monetary value of the resources beneath an impoundment, once a dam is built.

Along the same line of reasoning, in order to be politically feasible a policy must be affordable. In other words, feasibility and efficiency are determined by two separate measures of economic cost: the level of modernization of a society and the capacity of a government to mobilize resources. Some natural resources remain constant; some are depleted over time. However, political arrangements for their management may optimize their prudent exploitation at a certain stage of development. This could be true regardless of the scarcity or abundance of the resource or the economic sophistication of a society. For example, political scientists often argue that a river basin can be managed in a more coordinated, systematic way by a comprehensive, politically independent agency than by several public works agencies.

However, at a certain stage of a nation-state's development, such ideal arrangements may overextend the government personnel. The experience of the Nasser regime in Egypt in the early 1950s illustrates this dilemma. From the standpoint of long-term river basin planning, it made the most sense to manage the Nile River's resources through a comprehensive, transnational basin authority, encompassing Egypt and the Sudan. However, a young, revolutionary regime opted to invest its limited monetary resources in a popular and grandiose engineering scheme undertaken within a single nation. The Aswan High Dam, the product of this scheme, has been accused of generating environmental problems that far outweigh the economic problems it was designed to resolve. Nevertheless, at the time it was erected, it was probably the most feasible scheme the regime could have come up with, especially given the constraints of nationalism and the need for a popular catalyst to unify the Egyptian people around the goals of the revolution (Waterbury, 1979: 110–117).

Third and finally, public choice theory depends on the support of diverse groups. In the United States, the process by which natural resources policy is made is highly fragmented and pluralistic. However, despite this pluralism, the process is inaccessible to diverse viewpoints, because the desires of strategically placed interests take precedence over the needs of weaker, disadvantaged groups. (We shall see this phenomenon in our analysis of case studies, beginning in chapter 4.) This phenomenon explains the lack of equity in water policy despite the fact that public participation often appears broadly based. Public choice theorists believe they can provide a vehicle for meaningful public participation. This vehicle would provide a way to assess the issues important to the public and to decide them in a way that overcomes the power imbalance.

To public choice theorists, the essence of just decision making is open-endedness, respect for freedom of expression, and encouragement of diverse views. Policies should accommodate conflicting goals, such as economic growth and environmental preservation. This requires minimizing transaction costs (those entailed in operating a user system), since the less money spent on delivering policy, the more money there is for satisfying the needs of participating groups. By consciously minimizing these costs while registering the preferences of all consumers, public choice theory increases the chances that a broad range of interests in natural resources policy will be addressed.

Does public choice theory adequately account for the deficiencies in U.S. water policy? Does it provide a viable alternative to prevailing policy? Or does it merely prompt further problems by its emphasis upon efficiency?

Efficiency as Justification for an Environmental Policy

The core value of public choice theory is efficiency. Consequently, public choice theorists suggest that reform of natural resources policy rests upon changes in political authority to make possible a free, unrestricted market. To some extent, this message has gotten through—but with misplaced interpretations. For example, narrow values of efficiency emphasize reorganization of government agencies as a panacea for water policy fragmentation. As should be apparent from the discussion of public choice theory and of resistance to structural reform, water problems are not problems of organization. They are caused by inappropriate guidelines for policy. Multiple-purpose projects serving several interests heighten value conflict and sharpen the lack of agency coordination, but they do not in themselves cause these ambiguities. Let us examine two of the most common attempts to address these problems in light of the lessons of public choice theory.

Conservation and Preservation

In recent years, critics of water policy have focused on the need for policies to encourage prudent use of water and to minimize practices that pollute and deplete it. Many of these critics are merely reviving an older approach to the management of water resources, an approach labeled *conservation*. This older approach was frequently invoked during the nineteenth century, when many of the fiercest water resources battles were raging in places such as California's Owens Valley and Tuolumne River. Unfortunately, the term *conservation* ranges in meaning from the exploitation of nature on behalf of efficiency to a humble acknowledgment of our moral limits as members of an intricate, natural web (Hays, 1958: 40–45; Leopold, 1966).

Conservation properly refers to the management of natural resources in such a way as to assure the production of maximum sustainable yields for present and future generations. As defined by proponents of scientific resource management such as Gifford Pinchot (1865–1946), conserving a resource means maximizing its efficient use while minimizing the transaction costs entailed in its management. This is accomplished by limiting exploitation to a level sustainable by the resource's natural processes of recuperation.

Preservationists, on the other hand, assert that the exploitation of nature ought to be guided by a value system that transcends instrumental human needs. John Muir (1838–1914), arguably the best known early American preservationist, defined appropriate exploitation, especially of water, in sacred, almost religious terms. Muir suggested that his personal campaign to prevent the damming of the Tuolumne River in Yosemite Valley, California, was rooted in aesthetic truths impermeable to scientific scrutiny and only understandable to the heart (Muir, 1970: 28–33).

More recently, philosophers such as Tom Regan and Paul Taylor have defended preservation on Kantian grounds. They suggest that all living things, including flora and fauna, should be treated as ends in themselves and have rights that should not be violated for short-term human gain (Regan, 1983; Taylor, 1981). According to the preservationist ethic, the principal criterion of a natural resources policy should be the protection of noneconomic values (the beauty of a free-flowing, white-water river, for example). It also implies that the concept of equity should embrace relationships among all living things, not just people. A preservationist would contend that allocation of water should be based on the needs of flora and fauna in both the region from which the water is being transferred and the region to which it is being delivered. Water laws should encompass the minimal water needs of plants, animals, and people. A serious problem with this contention is the difficulty in attributing to plants and animals the same rights we attribute to people, since flora and fauna are unable to advance their own claims against society.

Both bases for preservation point to the need to consider the process of natural ecosystems apart from calculations of economic efficiency. Thus, both are consistent with public choice views, which suggest that those who manage water resources should seek conformity between the political and natural worlds. The policy implications of both views are discussed in detail in chapter 6 in a case study of the New River project.

At this point, it is necessary to consider why a shift from development to conservation or preservation of water resources will not make us better able to manage water problems. First, the meaning of *conservation* is ambiguous, shifting, and often elusive. Second, both conservation and preservation have been depicted by their proponents in a fashion far too romantic and emotional to guide practical policy. Third, the question of what instruments are optimal for carrying out the objectives of conservation or development must still be answered. Fourth, prior to selecting such instruments, the necessity for government intervention must be established.

Conservation and preservation differ in their degree of optimism regarding the sustainability of nature in the face of human impacts. Conservation values water as an extrinsic commodity, preservation thinks of it as having intrinsic value. This contrast underscores the role of rational fallibility in defending public policies toward nature.

It is important that agreement over the value of water be established before institutional arrangements are developed, or policy instruments inappropriate to long-term management goals may be inadvertently selected. While this may be excusable in some situations, as in the case of the Aswan Dam, it is less justifiable in a developed polity, which has the bureaucratic ability and political will to make long-term decisions.

Drawbacks of Benefit-Cost Analysis

The principal drawbacks of public choice theory are (1) it presumes that the self-interest of individuals is supreme and that individuals wish to maximize economic benefit and lessen economic costs, and (2) it mandates that, regardless of other concerns, deep intrusion by the state in natural resources policy should be avoided. Both of these drawbacks partly explain the reliance upon benefit-cost analysis in water policy.

Some attribute the origin of formal benefit-cost analyses of construction of water projects to the Flood Control Act of 1936, which required that the Corps of Engineers assess benefits and costs in river basin improvements (Conservation Foundation, 1984: 40). Others say its first meaningful use occurred after the creation of the Water Resources Council in the 1960s and the adoption of standards guiding the definition and calculation of benefits and costs (Mazmanian and Nienaber, 1979: 13–16). In either case, benefit-cost analysis has become a tool for narrowing alternative choices in water policy by reference to explicit criteria and goals. Reliance upon this tool is symptomatic of the lack of any agreed upon method to go beyond the concept of the greatest good for the greatest number. While economists who advocate benefit-cost analysis have long recognized the limitations of this concept, water project advocates have reified the concept into a cognitively defensible, normative standard (Rowen, 1977: 553).

Benefit-cost analysis has two ethical shortcomings. First, it often ignores questions of equity and distributive justice. As noted by John Rawls (1971), it is necessary in assessing the efficiency of a political decision to recognize that there are at least two separate dimensions by which one may compare economic benefit. On the other hand, we may compare a particular strategy for providing a public good with an alternative designed to provide the same good. This comparison, though rarely done by government agencies, might help decision makers allocate a good in the most economical manner.

On the other hand, we may compare individual effects of the overall allocation of goods in a society—including the accumulated effect of a particular policy, a measure Rawls called structural efficiency. It refers to the allocation of goods that, if changed to make one person better off, would not make another worse off. Structural efficiency in water resources policy would ask if a reallocation of water from one region to another could improve one region without bringing harm to another.

Somewhat ironically, water resources agencies often defend project benefits in regional terms, as if the residents living adjacent to a water project have, implicitly, special claim to the water. While it is widely conceded that water resources exploitation may produce benefits outside a single region, and despite the fact that all citizens may bear the costs of improvements of the resource, this practice usually fails to meet the test of structural efficiency.

Second, benefit-cost analyses often fail to incorporate in their assessment the so-called noneconomic values of water resources. These noneconomic values include the aesthetic and sublime qualities of a wild and scenic river or a species of wildlife.

In recent years, novel methods of social preference assessment have been developed to incorporate such concerns in policy decisions. These methods are effective only if policy makers are prepared to actually go out and ask people what values they want incorporated in water policy. Although some water resources planners have undertaken to do this in recent years, the use of these methodologies is neither universal nor without drawbacks.

The following examples of such social preference assessment methodologies illustrate this point. Recreational planners have in recent years tried to calculate the demand of rafters for white-water streams to prove that undeveloped white-water streams may still generate considerable economic benefits. However, recreational managers have discovered that, without restrictions on river use, overcrowding, noise, and littering degrade the landscape and reduce its aesthetic pleasure. Simply stated, the perception of white-water rafting as cost-free increases its popularity. Thus, without some kind of regulation, opportunity costs to potential users and to the government agencies that manage the white-water resources are also increased (Berry, Cox, and Wolff, 1983). This suggests that benefit-cost analyses need to assess opportunity costs in computing the benefits to society of white-water preservation. It also suggests that, in comparing alternatives for water resources management, the benefits and costs of nondevelopment still require some sort of metric to be fully understood.

Another example of social preference assessment is afforded by recent attempts by some agencies to gauge public preferences for river basin management along a whole spectrum of issues. These issues range from benefit estimation to social and environmental impact, relocation of groups, public involvement in decision making, and even technology transfer of the benefits of water projects to other community activities. A framework developed by Jerry Delli Priscoli and his associates in the Corps of Engineers represents one of the most ambitious of such attempts (Priscoli, 1981). While significant effort has been expended in developing a profile of public concerns to be utilized for water planning in Corps of Engineers' districts, in many cases planners have had to rely upon projections of demographic trends compiled by agencies that are themselves "assumption based and value driven" (Priscoli, 1981: 17).

Social preference assessment is also used for scenic resources. Richard Chenoweth and his colleagues at the University of Wisconsin at Madison employed two methodologies to encompass aesthetic values.[1] These techniques were developed and applied in support of Wisconsin's Scenic Resources Trust. One technique is visitor-employed photography, the other is image-capture technology. Both techniques provide empirically derived, publicly ascertainable facts about peoples' preferences regarding physical landscapes. These preferences can then be used to guide decision makers in the design and development of scenic corridors along river valleys, in mountain areas, and in other aesthetically valuable places (Chenoweth and Niemann, 1988; Chenoweth and Pardee, 1988).

Chenoweth, a psychologist working in the field of landscape architecture, has found that, when people were asked to photograph elements of a landscape that added to or detracted from the scenic beauty (during a trip down the Wisconsin River from Prairie du Sac to Prairie du Chien), a substantial consensus in aesthetic preferences was displayed. When replicated among visitors in other scenic areas, the technique yielded similar results (Chenoweth and Niemann, 1988).

Image-capture technology is a computer-simulation-derived methodology for addressing the same issues. Representations of the landscape are converted into digitized units, captured by a computer, and modified by the viewer in order to change or modify the landscape (Chenoweth, 1989a). The most important implication of such manipulation of simulated landscapes is that would-be landscape modifiers and other intervenors could simulate the landscape they propose and provide government agencies and environmental groups with a legally binding document, holding them to agreed upon impacts and landscape modification (Chenoweth and Pardee, 1988; Chenoweth, 1989a, 1989b).

However, policy makers must agree ahead of time that public rights to scenic beauty are, in and of themselves, protectable rights, even if no other economic or noneconomic impacts can be demonstrated. A series of Wisconsin ordinances and regulations protect such rights, but the degree to which other states or federal agencies recognize such rights varies considerably (Chenoweth, Tlusty, Niemann, 1982).

As a result of such techniques, planners have become apprised of the need to assess non-property-based values in decision making. These values include psychological trauma and other behavioral impacts from water projects, which are not measured by traditional benefit-cost techniques. The curious thing about these values is that they can be quantified, thus blurring the distinction between economic and noneconomic concerns. An example cited by Priscoli is the translation into dollars of degrees of impairment endured by those whose homes are flooded, using Veterans Administration payments for comparable disabilities (Priscoli, 1981: 16). An example cited by Chenoweth and Niemann (1988) relates to what some economists refer to as contingent valuation, the assignment of an economic value to a preference. Chenoweth notes that the combination of photographic content and visitor survey data from the Wisconsin River trips can be used by policy makers to quantify visual preferences, estimate how much visitors value the experiences, and even derive means for establishing how aesthetic resources measurably benefit mental health.

As these examples indicate, economic efficiency relates to a whole array of benefits by which people declare themselves better off. Since public choice analysis assumes that the foremost goal of government-sponsored water projects is to produce gains that exceed costs for a majority of citizens, policy makers are obligated to clearly define gains. This should not be left to water resources engineers or planners, however, because they are not trained to elucidate social preferences but to design instruments to satisfy those preferences.

The lack of an agreed upon framework for prioritizing and defining gains encourages the quantification of benefits and costs as a means of minimizing raids upon the federal treasury. While weighing benefits and costs may place a simple methodological ceiling on government expenditures, it does not do much more than this. It does not, as some of its proponents argue, prove that citizens are made better off than before through more jobs, higher incomes, greater recreational opportunities, cheaper food, or less expensive electricity.

Critics of benefit-cost analysis in the context of water policy have often singled out this rationalization for special discussion. S. V. Ceriacy-Wantrup has noted that, even if the "standard [of benefit-cost analysis] is impure relative to an ideal conceived through economic theory it . . . serves a worthwhile purpose, to restrain the abuse of economic arguments in the political process" (Ceriacy-Wantrup, 1964: 10). Other economists concede that, instead of simply calling for the methodology's abandonment, critics should consider ways to employ it more effectively and within a larger framework of values. Otto Eckstein, a longstanding critic of the abuses of benefit-cost theory by water resources agencies, exemplifies this approach. Eckstein suggests that ratios favoring benefits need to be set high enough to accommodate the social cost of capital raised by taxation and to assure high quality projects (Eckstein, 1958: 281). On the surface, this sounds like an idiosyncratic argument advocating no more than refinement of a hackneyed, overused quantitative tool. Upon closer analysis, however, Eckstein has hit the normative problem of benefit-cost analysis squarely on the mark.

To accomplish what Eckstein wishes, policy makers would have to justify benefits by reference to the costs borne by groups hit hardest by taxation. In other words, incorporated into the computation of the benefits and costs of building a dam must be the obligations to society of the dam's beneficiaries and the rights of those affected by the dam, whose preferences are not assessed.

In addition, Eckstein (1958) believes that benefits should be defined in the broadest possible sense, that is, as gains to all of society, not merely the few. If regional gain is the principal motive for a water project, then policy makers would be compelled to explain how benefits would satisfy the needs of many regions. There are several ways this could be done.

Policy makers could argue that a water project is required to repay people for losses of lands. The Garrison diversion project is an excellent example of this dilemma, as we shall see. It could also be argued that a water project is necessary to compensate residents of a region for burdens sustained in other areas. Building irrigation projects for westerners to compensate them for having to buy manufactured goods at prices that benefit easterners is an example.

The third criticism of benefit-cost analysis in water policy is exemplified by the criticisms of Irving Fox, who suggests that the goal of policy should be to achieve a "reasonable approximation of a social optimum" that balances efficiency and equity. In order to achieve this optimum, policy makers need to understand the political motivations of people who exploit natural resources. Citing the settlement of the West and the subsequent development of its water resources, Fox says that traditional benefit-cost calculations do not effectively encompass the motivations of early American settlers.

According to benefit-cost theory, the actions of those who settled the frontier should be reducible to a set of calculations that proves that the benefits of moving westward outweighed the costs of migration. In fact, settlers were often motivated by a sense of adventure, by restlessness, and by a willingness to gamble that success would come despite likely hardships (Fox, 1966: 284). Could crops be grown on arid, windswept plains? Could white settlers establish permanent settlements in places where native Americans lived only nomadically? The answers to these questions are not registered in benefit-cost approaches to natural resources decision making.

All of these criticisms raise the questions, How should the specific objectives of efficiency be defined? and What is a policy efficient for? The answers lie in the process by which natural resources decisions are made, which is a concern of public choice theorists but one often ignored by water resources agencies. Under the simplest circumstance, the assessment of efficiency varies in accordance with the preferences of the group. Under the most difficult of circumstances, even if the preferences of a majority could be ascertained, one cannot assume that majoritarian preference encompasses the range of criteria needed for making decisions in a democracy. Unfortunately, proponents of water resources development have often used a brand of democratic theory that relies on utilitarian tradition. This tradition ignores both the fact that not all preferences are appropriate for the protection of the rights of citizens or for the protection of nature and the fact that the beneficiaries of development have obligations to society.

If this utilitarian, sometimes gratuitous, concept of democracy is carried to an extreme, it forces illogical policy choices. For example, economic efficiency is variously defined as the cumulative preferences of the majority or as the greatest good for the greatest number. These criteria are not necessarily synonymous. The former implies that the beneficiaries participated in making policy. A policy made in the latter way can provide the greatest amount of good to everyone and the least loss to anyone, yet be opposed by a majority of citizens. A policy can be simultaneously efficient and undemocratic, in both the narrow pluralistic sense used by many proponents of water resources development and in the broader sense being argued for here.

While many water projects have increased the net satisfaction and economic productivity of the entire United States, it is not necessarily true that a majority of people in any particular region explicitly favored them, even if they benefited from them. In most cases, the tacit consent of citizens—one criterion for measuring conformance with democratic tenets—was rarely obtained before construction proceeded. Would residents of the upper Colorado River basin have approved construction of Glen Canyon Dam if they had known that water losses to evaporation and seepage from Lake Powell would appreciably diminish usable water supply in that region? Would they have consented to using Lee's Ferry, the site of the project, as the dividing line between the upper and lower Colorado River basins for purposes of allocating water among western states had they known that the choice was determined by engineering convenience and not user benefit?

Even if a majority of those directly affected by a project in a particular region did favor a certain water project, this would not prove that the project was efficient. To assume it did would be to confuse policy process with outcome. Advocates of water projects often confuse efficiency with the outcomes of a free market in order to rationalize obtaining benefits to their regions from government expenditure (Conservation Foundation, 1984: 5). In actuality, the imperfections of a free market might cause the demands of a certain group to go unnoticed or unanswered because it lacks advocates to defend its cause before Congress. This ideological confusion is encouraged by the so-called distributive politics pattern of decision making, which dominates the making of water policy.

From the standpoint of the goals of public choice theory, this practice begs the question of who should participate in making water resources decisions. Prior decisions in this area most often represent the preferences of privileged elites, not those of the average citizen. Moreover, while lack of consent does not necessarily denote lack of benefit, in the Glen Canyon case, had citizens known of the consequences of the project ahead of time, would they have chosen this project? One must go beyond public choice theory to answer this question.

Gratuitous Policy and Public Choice Theory

Public choice theorists criticize natural resources policies for not being responsive to public demands about a range of social and environmental concerns. They claim that policy is gratuitous, or formulated without regard for the rights of those who pay and without obligations to those who benefit. In other words, it legitimizes the free rider discussed by Mancur Olson and others.

This free rider problem is present in all U.S. land and water policies. The problem is exemplified by agricultural policy, which is formulated by the iron triangle of commodity and farm groups, congressional representatives from farm belt states, and specialized bureaus within the U.S. Department of Agriculture. It is also illustrated by energy policy—so far as the United States can be said to have one—whose fragmentation is reinforced by the demands of beneficiary groups. Tightly knit subsystems for each major energy resource formulate independent subsidy-oriented decisions on research, development, exploration, price controls, and technology transfer. Nuclear policy, for example, is made separately from coal policy. If there is a common denominator shared by each subsystem, it is the supremacy of the physical and technical character of the resource in shaping the historical pattern of policy development (D. Davis, 1982; Uslaner, 1989). In this sense, policies partially conform to the expectations of public choice theory.

In order to reform this system, serve the needs of society, and create a policy able to respond effectively to impending water crises, a reorientation of the values of decision makers must occur. To public choice theorists, rational policy begins with the premise that individuals maximize their preferences within the constraints of a provision system sometimes characterized by scarcity. Scarcity, or the potential for it, constitutes an important condition of all natural resources, especially water.

Public choice theory has tried to accommodate contradictory preferences by suggesting ways to rank performance criteria (the goals of policy depicted in table 2.1). Public choice theorists who focus upon natural resources policy provide little guidance as to how this should be done. I contend that the inability to rank contradictory preferences is symptomatic of methods of policy evaluation that emphasize pure majoritarian preference. The solution—prioritizing goals by basing policy on equity and integrity—requires a process of deliberation not present in current decision-making frameworks for water policy. Public choice theory can help us understand what the preferences of citizens are, but decision makers must then utilize other methods for sorting out these preferences in order to produce ethically justified policies.

For example, since public choice theory assumes that optimal performance in any provision system is accomplished by addressing the preferences of different users, it sometimes further assumes that each criterion is relevant to all users. Hence, there is little need to prioritize goals. Urban dwellers concerned with water pollution will probably be satisfied if part of the federal water resources development budget, usually earmarked for irrigation projects in the rural West, is devoted to wastewater treatment plants for cities. This would be seen as equitable, since projects relevant to each region are being provided for. Likewise, if construction of a dam creates abundant storage of water for irrigation while generating large amounts of electricity, then virtually everyone can agree that such a project is efficient (but for different reasons). Moreover, since the power generated is relatively economical, urban consumers of the power may even overlook the fact that the charges they pay are used to repay the full costs of the nonhydroelectric features of the project: its irrigation, flood control, and recreational benefits. Under current policy, power customers, not farmers or other beneficiaries, subsidize these costs, reinforcing their gratuitous quality.[2]

The problem with the assumption that priorities need not be ranked is that, during periods of competing demand, a scarce resource may become even scarcer. If an upstream farmer cannot control pesticide runoff from his farm, drinking water quality in towns downstream of his farm will be adversely affected. Unfortunately, residents of these towns, not the farmer, are usually forced to pay for the restoration of water quality. Likewise, highly consumptive uses of water—to irrigate, to cool steam-generating power plants, or to make coal slurry—limit the water's secondary use. Perhaps the best way to prioritize competing uses would be to adopt the principle of reasonable fallibility: if an irreplaceable resource vital to the health of an ecosystem could be irreparably damaged, then the use should be excluded from consideration. Unfortunately, however, without specific sanctions against certain uses, the political subsystems that formulate water policy may be unable to resist accommodating even the most ridiculous of demands for water. Accounts of the ill-famed North American Water and Power Alliance illustrate this point.

The alliance was formulated by a southern California engineering firm to construct water impoundments in the Canadian Rockies principally for irrigation and power. Proposed in the early 1960s, it envisioned an incredibly complex series of canals, pumping stations, and interbasin transfer networks for irrigating western farms and ranches, augmenting navigational flow in the Great Lakes and the Mississippi River, and eventually reversing the stream of every major underutilized river in Canada and Alaska. While these projects were roundly criticized as an ecological boondoggle of unprecedented proportion, scaled-down versions of the alliance remain, in the opinion of some, viable alternatives to water supply and quality problems (Reisner, 1986: 452).

Water laws, by prioritizing need, have been the traditional mechanism for regulating demand and insuring supply. However, water laws in the United States have not assured equity or protected noneconomic values, because the laws often do not conform with the disposition of water resources. Oftentimes, the laws have encouraged consumption by imposing gratuitous criteria for water rights or have failed to account for the hidden costs of overuse and depletion or for the rights of those not living near a watercourse or an underground aquifer.

Because some people simply refuse to acknowledge the need for pooling resources when the resources are scarce, no law can solve water problems unless people voluntarily subscribe to an environmental ethic: a set of values that controls conflicting preferences by reducing demands for water, by changing expectations about its unlimitedness, and by accepting obligations toward each other as users.

Another problem acknowledged by public choice theory is the appropriate structure of natural resources decision making. Public choice theorists argue that an open system—one that responds axiomatically to individual preferences by establishing multiple, decentralized utilities joined together by user fees and other sanctions—can be democratic. Such a system would tie the obligations of beneficiaries to the concerns of benefactors (Sproule-Jones, 1982; Young, 1982). Unfortunately, there is no such system in water policy. A legitimate question is, Can such a system be practically established?

American water policy is currently decentralized in many respects. Each state has its own water laws; riparian doctrines prevail east of the Mississippi River, prior appropriation rights prevail west of it. Likewise, as the example of the Delaware River Basin Commission reveals, states and their citizens are free to create regional compacts to allocate water resources; to divide the costs of their management; to agree on the regulation of pollution and conservation and to the allocation of groundwater; and to establish decision-making tools able to respond quickly to technical problems. The problem with this system is that decentralization does not guarantee broad access to the process of decision making. Current water resources systems clearly deny decision-making access to some users, as we shall see in our analysis of Garrison diversion project and the Blue Ridge dam. The preferences of those who stand to lose their homes to a water impoundment are usually denied by the iron triangle of policy making, although they stand to lose land, jobs, and other economic opportunities.

Even when compensation is offered to policy losers, alternative uses of land and water resources are often denied permanently, since, once impounded, a river cannot be restored. Moreover, even if land could be reclaimed, there are few precedents for returning it to those who lost it or for restoring it to its original use.[3] Compounding this problem is the fact that so-called market restraints—increases or reductions of water demand by, say, farmers who purchase water from the Bureau of Reclamation—are inexact barometers for forcing consideration of alternatives. Market factors in water resources decision making are constrained by water rights, which are often based on fixed entitlements or by settlement patterns shaped during a region's early history.

Finally, contrary to public choice theory's assumption that a natural resource and its technology are fixed, the historical pattern of a resource's development and exploitation is partly determined by political culture and frequently shapes popular acceptance of arrangements for its management. The experience of the Tennessee Valley Authority reveals, for example, that the lack of significant interest in developing the water resources of the middle South by the Corps of Engineers and other federal agencies created a policy vacuum easily filled by a grass roots agency, which worked with, not against, established local interests (Selznick, 1966).

In the United States, popular mistrust of bureaucracy, the adversarial character of natural resources decision making, and until relatively recently, the assumption that environmental impacts were mitigative by better planning, have shaped a regulatory climate for water policy only modestly supportive of coherent, integrated guidance by a single agency, or even by multiple, regionally based instruments accessible to many interests. In chapter 3, it is suggested that the absence of such support is exemplified by the unique character of water law, the ambivalent role of planners in formulating water policy, and the limited consensus over ethical values found in both water law and water policy. While public choice theory may remain a viable point of departure for some of the issues encompassed by an environmental ethic, it is not enough. Provisional systems must be established that are better adapted to the character of natural resources and to the need for justice.

Expanding the Scope of an Environmental Ethic

A central thesis of this book is that an ethically defensible natural resources policy is one that satisfies a broad range of human needs, ranging from survival and biological exigency to an enlightened existence in harmony with one's inner character, others, and nature. The specific system for making a public policy that would achieve these goals, I believe, hinges upon a social contract among reasonable people, with some tangible elements to it.

Following Rawls (1971), I find the ideals of the classical tradition appropriate, because they address our foremost natural duty—to support just institutions, since those institutions benefit us. On the other hand, like Rawls, I find these ideals problematical. In actual societies, people are fundamentally self-interested and prudent. The parameters of U.S. water policy, for example, make it clear that stakeholders often calculate only their own short-term economic or other interest. While upon reflection they may aspire to justice, the station in life to which they are born biases them toward certain social arrangements. This is particularly true in the disposition of natural resources. If one is wealthy and has access to numerous resources, one is inclined to protect arrangements guiding the use and exploitation of those resources. If one is poor and has little chance of influencing the arrangement of power, one is likely to distrust preexisting laws and political arrangements protecting the use of and access to natural resources.

As a result, the social contract optimal to the management of natural resources would be based upon a "veil of ignorance" (Rawls, 1971). The contract's rights, duties, and obligations would constitute ethical responsibilities, which we would agree to even if we were ignorant of our station in life. Why would we agree to such an arrangement? Like Rawls, I believe we would do so because, as rational, reflective individuals, we know that, without such an agreement, the eventual disposition and distribution of resources could lead to intolerable disadvantages for some of us. The success of our individual ways of life is dependent upon this allocation and distribution of resources, particularly since we do not know where or when we shall be born.

Contract theorists argue as to whether contracts can be politically viable if they are merely ahistorical constructs, such as that which Thomas Hobbes (1588–1679) used to implore citizens to accept that living in a society and benefiting from the government obliged them to obey the Leviathan (Hobbes, 1957). Resolution of this debate is quite beyond the scope of our concerns here. Suffice it to say that there is no compelling reason why such a contract need be historical, like that of John Locke (1632–1704), who envisioned us literally sitting down and agreeing to form a civil society (Locke, 1963).

A contract could comprise tacit agreements based upon mutual understanding and logical deduction concerning the conditions necessary for justice.

While ahistorical, the contract would have historical characteristics. Its terms could be modified or renegotiated as conditions, such as inmigration to a region or periodic drought, warranted. There is nothing contradictory about this attempt to reconcile both historical and ahistorical components. As Bruce Ackerman (1980) notes, such a philosophical "muddling through" would be entirely consistent with a "principled agnosticism" characteristic of a democratic society. Principled agnosticism dictates that the best we can hope for in the resolution of conflicts over resources is that citizens agree to reason together and that they agree that any resolution reached will be tentative because of their collective uncertainty about the status of nature.

The ahistorical character of the social contract derives from the fact that rational, reflective individuals, contemplating how they should utilize natural resources, would place themselves in this Rawlsian "original position" before prescribing any policy that allocates water or provides a vehicle for its management. The reason they would do this is because, without first agreeing upon rules for fairness in the making of decisions, they would most likely make decisions based solely on specific, tangible, short-term ends, such as having enough water for farming. This would result in policies that would result, quite literally, in a state of war—all water users against each other—similar to that predicted by Hobbes in a generalized state of nature without common authority to adjudicate disputes.

We might find ourselves, like some westerners in the late nineteenth century, choosing a system for the allocation of water that assigns water rights to whoever finds and uses the water first. The only way newcomers can get access to water is by fighting others for it or buying the rights from those willing to sell. The basis of law under such a system is might makes right, rather than any principles of fairness. Some would be unable to live a dignified, meaningful existence. Others would abuse water to their own detriment and might soon exhaust the supply, as well as themselves.

An appropriate question to pose at this juncture might be, Why could not such a contractarian framework rely upon more libertarian approaches to justice, such as that of Robert Nozick (1974)? The answer is that Nozick's argument, and that of most other libertarians, fails to satisfactorily resolve the problem of prioritizing rights and values. Nozick takes as his point of departure the Lockean theory of private property, which grants inalienable rights to expropriation and use to those who mix their labor with nature. This position is untenable, because it denies the limits of nature. In addition, it equalizes all rights, values, and priorities and fails to provide guidance for the resolution of conflict among those values if, as in the case of natural resources, we have good reasons for making and defending our choices.

In chapter 3, we examine the tenets and principles of U.S. water law to better understand in what ways this body of law conforms, or fails to conform, with such a contractarian notion of justice.

3   Law, Engineering, and the Absence of Environmental Principles in Water Policy

Water Law and Environmental Ethics

Water law is one of the oldest methods for managing water resources in Western society (Powledge, 1982). It arose because informal cooperation over water rights, the avoidance of conflict over its allocation, and agreement over the values guiding both of these have been impossible to achieve.

In this chapter, I argue that water law has provided an inadequate basis for legitimizing rights and duties.

First, two different sets of water law predominate: one east and one west of the Mississippi River. While each set is supposed to reflect the varied abundance, disposition, and uses of water in these regions, neither encourages conservation or satisfactorily encompasses these natural characteristics of water very well. They do not discourage pollution, or encourage prudent use and reuse of water, or provide guidelines for effective management of groundwater resources, an increasingly important problem. Ideally, an effective water law should reconcile the social uses of water, as well as the legitimate rights of these users, with its natural disposition.

Second, until quite recently, American water law has overemphasized the protection of water users' rights to do what they want with water. This laissez-faire approach has diminished an appreciation for the economic and noneconomic value of water. Such ignorance has been compounded by conflicting legal jurisdictions and the absence of a centralized authority to settle conflicts. Too little attention has been given to each citizen's responsibility to assure the continuing high quality and availability of water. In short, water law does not optimize unwasteful use by reconciling the social uses of water with its availability.

The chronic failure of water law to articulate user responsibility and to deter conflict has contributed to regional crises involving surface water depletion, groundwater overdraft, point and nonpoint pollution, and unwise interbasin diversion. These crises have encouraged policy makers to seek to increase water supply rather than to control demand. In the absence of consensus over values governing water use, it is much easier to gain political agreement on the former than on the latter. This approach has contributed to the overuse of water and has generated demands for engineering solutions to provide more of it.

The failure of water law places extraordinary responsibility for implementing water policy in the hands of engineers. Unfortunately, engineers are inadequately trained to address ethical issues in environmental management. As a consequence, issues of equity, feasibility, transaction costs, noneconomic values, and public participation have been insufficiently incorporated in water policy. The conferring of water rights upon a few groups and the placement of authority for policy in the hands of an engineering elite have produced a water policy both undemocratic and unresponsive to environmental concerns.

Water Rights and Water Wrongs: Gratuitous Policy through Law

Water is regulated in most American states by one of two sets of laws: the riparian rights doctrine and the law of prior appropriation. Evolving through common law interpretation with relatively little statutory modification, the riparian rights doctrine establishes that surface water rights belong to those owning the land abutting the water. Each landowner is entitled to reasonable use of the watercourse adjacent to his or her property; this means a use contingent upon the total amount of water available in a watercourse and the uses made by others. A key assumption guiding riparian users is that water resources are plentiful for multiple uses. This is the principal reason why it predominates in states east of the Mississippi River.

About twenty states, mostly in the West and Midwest, employ some variation of the law of prior appropriation: the rights of the first user of a watercourse take precedence over those of subsequent upstream or downstream users. Thus, time rather than location determines justifiable use. Hawaii is a curious exception to both systems. Its water law is based on a combination of Polynesian custom, riparian doctrine, and statutory modification (WRC, 1968).

Since prior appropriation states lie in arid regions, a guiding assumption behind this doctrine is that water is scarce. As a result, water rights are more exclusive than under riparian doctrine, and they place the interests of established users over those of newcomers. One major difference between prior appropriation and riparian doctrine, resulting from the assumption of scarcity under the former, is that, although both evolved as court-centered laws, the former has been more amenable to statutory and administrative modification (R. Johnson, 1968: 197). So little was known about western water resources when pioneers settled the trans-Mississippi West that demands arose for laws to fit varying and unpredictable conditions.

Under both doctrines, allocation and management of groundwater have been problematical. Both riparian and prior appropriation states utilize a reasonable use doctrine. A landowner is entitled to as much groundwater as is reasonably necessary for domestic and other uses. However, a distinction is generally drawn between underground streams, or true aquifers, and percolating groundwater. In most instances, the former are treated like surface water. This means that the landowner is not entitled to unlimited use, because an underground stream may flow through the property of several users. Percolating groundwater, however, generally entitles a landowner to exclusive proprietary rights. Most states assume that groundwater is percolating unless proven otherwise by a particular litigant, which encourages groundwater overdraft. Thus individual property rights take precedence over sound environmental management practices (NWC, 1968).

As might appear obvious, the foremost policy problem in riparian doctrine is the relationship between water rights and land ownership. In most instances, the riparian owner is entitled to use water for any purpose he or she wishes, as long as the flow is not considerably diminished or the quality impaired (Davis and Cunningham, 1977). Traditionally, one problem arising from this doctrine has been determining reasonable and socially beneficial use. Water rights under riparian doctrine are not determined by the actual needs of the user or by some concept of fairness (what any individual would choose under a veil of ignorance). In essence, these water rights are gratuitous, because they do not oblige beneficiaries to pay for the benefits they receive. The more land one owns adjacent to a watercourse, the more power one has to shape water use in that region, with only limited obligation to pay for the consequences of one's actions. Moreover, failure to use the water does not diminish one's right to it.

During periods of stream flow depletion, some incentive for conservation is provided by allowing diversion of allotments from commercial livestock watering, irrigation, and other entrepreneurial uses to domestic and household use (Davis and Cunningham, 1977). Nevertheless, riparian doctrine fails to provide adequate water rights to those who do not own lands abutting the water.

As long ago as 1955, a Department of Agriculture economist, commenting on the impact of riparian law on agriculture, noted that the riparian system provides "shrinking" opportunities for water use and contributes to monopoly and disuse, because it "does not provide a quantitative guide to fair and dependable division of water supply" (Busby, 1955: 670). Moreover, because representation in water conflicts is usually limited to those with a direct stake in a dispute, riparian doctrine fails to "afford a basis for the public to participate in . . . the development of water use."

Unlike riparian doctrine, prior appropriation laws provide little basis for equitably distributing water in periods likely to produce user conflicts. During a drought, for example, junior users will get no water while senior users will be fully protected. It does not matter that some junior users may have an equal need for the water or that senior users would not rationally choose to allocate water in such a manner if they did not know ahead of time that they would indeed be the senior users. By contrast, in a riparian state in the throes of a drought, all users with claims to a watercourse would be forced to cut back on a pro rata basis, since the abutting watercourse would become depleted throughout its track.[1]

Three major equity and feasibility problems inherent in both doctrines reveal the disconformity between regional disposition of water and its social uses under U.S. water law. These are (1) balancing water availability with water use, (2) adequately protecting the quality and quantity of groundwater, and (3) transferring water rights.

Water Availability and Water Use

Neither riparian nor prior appropriation doctrine adequately balances water availability and use, because both doctrines assume that water resources in every region, even the arid West, are sufficiently abundant for several uses simultaneously. The riparian landowner is not held to any standardized measure of beneficial use. Instead, issues of appropriate use leading to contention are usually resolved by litigants in a court of law.

Traditionally, courts have refused to develop general principles and have settled conflicts case by case. One reason for this is that water rights in most riparian states have evolved as an adjunct of property laws. As a consequence, conflicts over water rights have been resolved not by reference to some standard of public interest but by reference to the presumed character of the water resource in dispute. For example, let us assume an instance where two landowners are party to a conflict over water use during a drought. Recall that under the practice of reasonable use each riparian owner is entitled to an amount of water sufficient for all necessary uses, limited only by total stream flow available at any given time. Allocation of rights can be satisfactorily established only by knowing how much water is available in a given stream. But how can this be determined? In practice, each individual's reasonable use depletes the total amount available at any given instant. This means that the volume of water in a river, creek, lake, or stream varies almost continuously.

Many courts resolve this conflict by using the natural flow doctrine. This doctrine permits each riparian owner rights to the stream as it supposedly existed in its natural state (prior to being developed, impounded, or diverted) and subject only to diminution by other riparian owners for such uses as drinking and household use (*Missouri Law Review*, 1954). The significance of this distinction is twofold. First, general reliance upon natural flow doctrine tends to encourage water conservation. Second, however, the decision to apply natural flow criteria is left to the discretion of individual courts. Thus, given the discretionary nature of this doctrine under riparian law, if one wants to encourage conservation, it would be necessary to pass specific enabling legislation. There is strong resistance to such legislation, for fear it would abridge property rights, but one critic suggests that this may be the only long-term way to resolve drought-inspired conflicts (Viessman, 1978).

For its part, prior appropriation doctrine seems to work fairly well when there is essential equality among uses and where quantities of water are small, numerous, and easily transferable, as in the West. However, where landholdings are few and large, a relative minority of proprietors may acquire a near monopoly over a region's water supply (V. Ostrom, 1971). This doctrine, like the riparian doctrine, also encourages wasteful use. Since water rights can be contested if the water isn't used, proprietors may use their appropriation up to the allowable limit, although they could conceivably manage their operations with less water. An infrequently noted consequence of the loss of water rights through nonuse is to exclude Hispanics and native Americans from making claims upon water in the West (Conservation Foundation, 1984: 392). These groups have obvious historic claims to water. However, they are unable to point to a record of recent use. In essence, prior appropriation doctrine is characterized by both inequity and environmental shortcomings.

The Political Science of Groundwater

Groundwater presents an unusual challenge to natural resources management because it is not only a significant source of water supply but also may equal as much as eight times the amount of fresh water in all lakes and rivers in the United States. Legal doctrines governing groundwater were once described by the National Water Commission as "a rather recent development, and a sporadic one" (NWC, 1968). More recently, the Council of State Governments expressed alarm at the fact that groundwater is regulated by "at least seven major federal environmental acts [and] administered by an average of five divisions in a typical state" (R. Brown, 1986: 402).

There was little concern with the allocation of groundwater as long as supplies were abundant and little was known about the subterranean world. However, in recent years groundwater has been regulated as more has been learned about its character, migration, source, rate of recharge, and benefits (NWC, 1968). The growth of regulation parallels the growth of significant depletion and pollution problems. The impact of these problems is graphically exemplified in a recent survey conducted by the Council of State Governments. The council asked state officials to rank natural resources concerns in order of urgency. All fifty states identified groundwater as a threatened resource, while 65 percent ranked it as the most threatened natural resource in their state (R. Brown, 1986: 403). State groundwater policy is depicted in table 3.1. Major federal laws pertaining to groundwater, the impact of which have been more recent and, as shall be seen, more controversial, are depicted in table 3.2.

In the American experience, the first groundwater laws were based upon court decisions that generally found that an owner of land was entitled to ownership of all the water under it, because it was deemed to be part of the soil. As a consequence, a landowner could not be held liable for any particular use he or she made of groundwater. This initial practice soon gave way to a doctrine of reasonable use, which, as in the case of surface water, meant that a landowner could be held liable if his or her use of, or interference with, an aquifer affected the welfare of others (R. Brown, 1986: 403).

Over time, other practices developed to refine and codify the resolution of conflicts. Many states developed a doctrine of correlative rights governing the withdrawal of water from an aquifer common to several landowners. Rights to withdrawal were divided in proportion to an in-

Table 3.1 Status of State Groundwater Protection Laws, 1986

State or Other Jurisdiction	State Statutes for Groundwater	Policy for Protecting Groundwater Quality	Policy under Development
Alabama	No	No	Yes
Alaska	No	No	No
Arizona	Yes	Yes	No
Arkansas	No	No	Yes
California	No	Yes	Yes
Colorado	No	No	Yes
Connecticut	No	Yes	No
Delaware	No	Yes	Yes
Florida	Yes	Yes	No
Georgia	Yes	Yes	No
Hawaii	No	Yes	Yes
Idaho	No	Yes	No
Illinois	No	No	Yes
Indiana	No	No	Yes
Iowa	No	No	Yes
Kansas	Yes	Yes	No
Kentucky	No	No	Yes
Louisiana	No	No	No
Maine	Yes	Yes	Yes
Maryland	No	No	No
Massachusetts	No	Yes	No
Michigan	No	Yes	Yes
Minnesota	No	Yes	Yes
Mississippi	No	No	Yes
Missouri	No	No	Yes
Montana	No	Yes	No
Nebraska	No	No	Yes
Nevada	No	Yes	No
New Hampshire	No	Yes	No
New Jersey	Yes	Yes	Yes
New Mexico	Yes	Yes	No
New York	Yes	Yes	No
North Carolina	No	Yes	No
North Dakota	No	No	Yes
Ohio	No	No	Yes
Oklahoma	Yes	Yes	No
Oregon	No	Yes	No

Table 3.1 (continued)

State or Other Jurisdiction	State Statutes for Groundwater	Policy for Protecting Groundwater Quality	Policy under Development
Pennsylvania	No	No	Yes
Rhode Island	No	No	Yes
South Carolina	No	No	Yes
South Dakota	No	No	Yes
Tennessee	No	No	Yes
Texas	No	No	No
Utah	No	Yes	Yes
Vermont	No	Yes	No
Virginia	Yes	No	No
Washington	No	Yes	Yes
West Virginia	No	No	Yes
Wisconsin	Yes	Yes	No
Wyoming	Yes	Yes	No
Puerto Rico	No	No	No
Virgin Islands	No	No	Yes

Source: Adapted from Office of Groundwater Protection, 1985, p. 406.

dividual's total land holdings over an aquifer. From the standpoint of equity, it was presumed that the more land one owned, the greater one's need was for water, especially for agriculture and livestock watering. Unfortunately, such an argument remains viable only so long as the region remains rural and agrarian. In the West, some states applied a variation of the prior appropriation doctrine to groundwater. This meant that rights to groundwater could be acquired only by withdrawal for beneficial use (R. Brown, 1986).

In all cases, however, two major questions remained largely unanswered by these practices. First, Should aquifers be mined until they are totally exhausted? In some regions of the United States, such as the Ogallala aquifer region of the central plains, this practice is already pervasive. Some argue that groundwater is a mineral like any other and that this practice is, consequently, no cause for alarm.

If groundwater is depleted, one of two things might occur: the economic character of a region might change to one less reliant on consumptive uses of water; or another source of supply might be located. In either case, it is generally assumed that the demand of water users in a free market will shape the decision. If the cost of irrigation water remains low, depletion is likely to occur, and pressure for construction of surface water impoundments will arise. On the other hand, high prices for irrigation water withdrawal should encourage water conservation (Reisner, 1981).

The second question is, Can ground and surface water resources be managed as an integrated whole in order to control pollution? It is widely known that nonpoint pollution flowing into rivulets and streams, especially from farm pesticide runoff, can seriously contaminate groundwater. However, the hydrologic mechanics of this relation remain little understood on a site-specific basis (see, for example, U.S. House of Representatives, 1983; Stokes et al., 1989). To compound matters, pollution and depletion have in some instances been inadvertently subsidized by federal agricultural policies encouraging intensive farming. Such policies led to groundwater overdraft and neglect of the impacts of pesticide runoff.

As shown by table 3.2, the Safe Drinking Water Act of 1974 and the amendments of 1986 are two of the most ambitious federal acts protecting groundwater. These acts were intended to protect aquifers from contamination. They establish drinking water standards for surface and groundwaters and procedures for state enforcement. They also provide maximum contamination levels for groundwater, regulate underground injection wells used by industry for pumping wastes deep underground, and provide the Environmental Protection Agency with authority to implement site-specific restrictions for so-called sole-source aquifers at the wellhead. These latter provisions are enforced by the Office of Groundwater Protection within the EPA, which effectively constitutes a national groundwater agency. The EPA considers sole-source aquifers to be essential municipal drinking water supplies, which require special forms of technical assistance to assure purity (Office of Groundwater Protection, 1986: 1–4; Mosher, 1984b).

Gaps remain in the scope and enforceability of these laws. These gaps reflect the inability of traditional water law to reconcile the natural character of water with its social uses and, thus, to articulate an environmental ethic. First, the 1974 Safe Drinking Water Act did not explicitly link surface water and groundwater regulation. The improper management of surface water can contaminate groundwater, and groundwater contamination, while difficult enough to prevent, is almost impossible to alleviate once it occurs.

Furthermore, regulations controlling the disposal of hazardous waste apply only to the few existing deep-injection and brine disposal wells, and there is considerable variation among states in the way these regulations are implemented (Conservation Foundation, 1984: 391). This

Table 3.2 Major Federal Laws Governing Groundwater

Act and Year	Major Regulatory Functions for Groundwater
Clean Water Act, 1972	(1) Elimination of discharge of all known pollutants in nation's water by 1985 (deadline since extended by Congress) (2) Establishment of uniform, enforceable national standards (3) Establishment of national permit program for point-source discharges (4) Establishment of statewide and areawide planning and management programs to implement feasible methods for obtaining clean water
Safe Drinking Water Act, 1974	(1) Protection of underground sources of drinking water and regulation of contaminant levels in public drinking water systems; primary authority to the states; EPA to share costs of enforcement (2) EPA supervision over sole-source aquifers and state adherence to rules requiring underground injection control systems to insure drinking water quality in conformance with federal standards (3) Federal grants to states to carry out public water system supervision programs and underground water protection programs
Resource Conservation and Recovery Act, 1976	(1) Prohibition of discharge of contaminants in a manner that would allow them to enter any water—including groundwater (2) Cradle-to-grave management of solid waste disposal facilities; monitoring of hazardous wastes to deter groundwater contamination; permit system to avoid siting of such facilities over sole-source aquifers
Clean Water Act, 1977	(1) Federal conformance with state standards for surface and groundwater quality as well as instream flow (2) Uniform enforceable national standards

Table 3.2 (continued)

Act and Year	Major Regulatory Functions for Groundwater
Comprehensive Environmental Response Compensation, and Liability Act (Superfund Act), 1980	(1) EPA authority to clean up abandoned solid waste sites, monitor facilities, provide assistance to states for emergency response, and participate in cost-sharing activities facilitating these efforts; prevention of substances from spills designated as toxic or hazardous under other federal laws from leaking into groundwater
Safe Drinking Water Act Amendments, 1986	(1) Strengthening of the Safe Drinking Water Act by outlining restrictions on underground inspection of hazardous waste (2) Establishment of a sole-source aquifer demonstration program within states and communities (3) Establishment of a state-supervised program to develop wellhead protection areas to prevent contaminants from entering groundwater used as a public water system
Superfund Amendments and Reauthorization Act, 1986	(1) Strengthening of the Superfund Act provisions pertaining to groundwater by providing greater regulation over leaking underground petroleum tanks and greater technical assistance for emergency response; establishment of uniform inventory format for identification of toxic substances that might enter groundwater

Sources: Freedman, 1987; Mosher 1984b.

was precisely why the 1986 amendments to the Safe Drinking Water Act were passed. The amendments outline restrictions on underground waste injection, establish a sole-source aquifer demonstration program, and compel the states to develop wellhead protection programs. In practice, the precise definition of a wellhead protection area is left to the determination of states, and inconsistencies among states remain in the way they manage the law.

Some states define wellhead protection areas as lying within a few hundred feet of a well, a practice that makes for easier enforcement but does not assure optimum groundwater protection. Other states chart the perimeters of the protection areas several miles distant from the wellhead, a practice that maximizes the protected area but exacerbates the problem of enforcement and restricts private property rights (Office of Groundwater Protection, 1986: 2). While it is far too early to tell if such variation in implementation will make the objectives of the groundwater protection acts difficult to accomplish, inconsistency at the state level follows the pattern of state resistance to the Clean Water Act of 1972. Under this act, the first comprehensive water pollution law passed by Congress, the EPA was given limited authority to protect groundwater, as noted in table 3.2. The EPA could issue planning funds to states for developing waste management plans aimed at averting groundwater contamination. In practice, most states rejected the planning funds as undue interference in state land use policy (Mosher, 1984b: 224).

In essence, the inertia of traditional water rights doctrines has prevented the success of comprehensive groundwater protection. Because resistance to federal intrusion in this area has been sparked by traditional property right prerogatives, upon which most state water laws are based, effective reform is likely to emanate only from the states themselves. This appears to be precisely what is occurring.

An example is afforded by the experience of Madison, Wisconsin. Recognition of nonpoint pollution as a pervasive source of groundwater contamination led the state of Wisconsin to enact its own model nonpoint pollution controls, which involve land use planning and new farming practices. The city of Madison responded by placing a soccer field on the downhill side of a shopping mall. When it rains, runoff from the mall collects in the soccer field, which acts as a holding pond until the water evaporates, preventing the polluted runoff from contaminating nearby streams or percolating into aquifers (Stanfield, 1985: 1880).

Federal and state policies to prevent groundwater depletion are at an even earlier stage than policies to prevent groundwater pollution. For example, it has been estimated that the Ogallala aquifer, a vast underground natural reservoir in the central plains heavily used by farmers, is losing 14 million acre-feet of water each year through irrigation, an amount equal to the average flow of the entire Colorado River main stem. Accurate groundwater pricing is necessary to halt this trend, but conflicting jurisdictions, overlapping claims to groundwater, and the lack of a comprehensive regulatory framework have thus far deterred such action (Mosher, 1984a: 164).

One notable exception to the prevailing policies is Arizona's pioneering 1980 Groundwater Management Act, which "represents the closest thing to a comprehensive regulatory approach" yet attempted in this field (Conservation Foundation, 1984: 393). The act allows a single state agency to inventory groundwater, establishes long-range goals for sustained yields, and allows the state to allocate water deliveries. These goals are ambitious, and the capacity of the state government to implement the act's provisions fall far short of the act's objectives (Conservation Foundation, 1984: 393). Moreover, imports of Colorado River water through the recently completed central Arizona project are still needed to meet growing demands.

Transferring and Allocating Water Rights

The transference of water rights under riparian and prior appropriation doctrines is especially contentious as the economic character of a region changes. The initial allocation of rights, while perhaps justified by the economic conditions prevailing when a region is first settled (a utilitarian concept of rights), may make no sense at all if those conditions change. Unfortunately, since both doctrines tend to establish rights on a semipermanent basis, changes in law are likely to be resisted strongly when new interests without a stake in the legal status quo arise.

Except in the case of interstate compacts such as the Delaware River Basin Commission, which must be ratified by Congress, regulation of water supply is left up to states. Most riparian and some prior appropriation states exert permitting controls, which give state departments of natural resources or similar agencies greater control over water allocation and quality than would otherwise be permitted. However, most conflicts over rights are still settled by litigation.

It will be recalled that many states vacillate from case to case between natural flow and reasonable use doctrines. Natural flow doctrine holds that the riparian owner is entitled to the full, natural flow of a watercourse, subject only to diminution through natural uses by other riparian owners. Reasonable use doctrine entitles each riparian owner to make a reasonable use of the water in light of the conventional practice in the state (NWC, 1968: 422).

Many courts in states using the reasonable use doctrine have simply conceded that what is reasonable is a question of fact to be determined from the circumstances of a particular case. This is the prevailing attitude in many midwestern states, for example (NWC, 1968). The problem is complicated by the practice of interbasin diversion, which causes conflicts across regions. Before turning to that problem, however, there is one more concern related to the transfer of water rights that exemplifies the disconformity of water law and the disposition and quantity of water: diffused surface water.

Diffused surface water is rain or snow melt not confined to a watercourse but spread out over vast areas. It is locally allocated by rules different from those applied to rivers or streams. States have been concerned not only with how this water resource is utilized but also with how it should be disposed of. It is sometimes considered a nuisance (NWC, 1968). Two practices tend to predominate. Under the common law rule, diffused surface waters are considered a common enemy, which any landowner is entitled to divert or obstruct to protect his or her property. Under the civil law rule, diffused surface waters are assumed to flow in an approximation of a channel. In practice, this means that low-lying lands are the natural recipients of the flow.

By the 1960s, common law and civil law doctrines effectively merged, with the balance of change in favor of civil law rule (NWC, 1968). Most courts maintain that a landowner cannot negligently or unreasonably divert surface water in such a way as to harm a neighbor. On the other hand, the civil law rule has been modified in most cases to allow landowners to obstruct or divert upland drainage (NWC, 1968). The significance of these changes is that courts now strive to promote reasonable use of land and water in ways that will protect individual rights.

In almost no case is consideration given to broad environmental or social criteria. Thus, issues such as nonpoint runoff pollution, the impact of diffused waters upon wetland habitat or migratory wildlife, or future water shortages have been virtually ignored in attempts to settle conflicts over diffused surface waters. This is one reason why state wetland protection policies have inadequately encompassed environmental concerns.

Water Law and Environmental Philosophy: Debates over Diversion

In the United States, water law constitutes one of the last significant bastions of state authority in natural resources policy. State laws define the nature and limit of water rights and, for the most part, govern land use policies that shape water use. Nevertheless, federal authority clearly takes precedence in the event of conflicts, especially between states. As a practical matter, according to an 1824 case, *Gibbons vs. Ogden*, all surface waters in the United States are effectively subject to federal regulation.

Under the commerce clause of the U.S. Constitution, Congress has the power to regulate interstate and foreign commerce (Article I, section 8). From the standpoint of water rights, this fact has a dual significance. First, navigation has been held by the courts to be a function of commerce subject to congressional regulation. Thus, navigable rivers may be dredged, diverted, dammed, widened, and otherwise modified to serve this function. Nonnavigable tributaries of navigable streams may also be regulated. The reason for this is that depletion or diversion of these tributaries could impact upon the navigability of their main stems.

Second, the commerce clause permits regulation of water resources for reasons other than navigation. While the full scope of this power has rarely been exercised, in principle it means that any water use having a bearing upon interstate commerce could be regulated by the federal government. A provocative and increasingly important area of water law, which reveals the implications of this power, is federal proprietary rights and interbasin diversion.

As has been seen, the federal government has traditionally deferred to states in the regulation of ground and surface water supplies. A 1982 U.S. Supreme Court decision, *Sporhase v. Nebraska*, radically modified this practice. In this case, the Court ruled that a Nebraska law limiting exports of water out of state (in this instance, to a litigant who owned some land in Colorado) was an unconstitutional restriction of the federal commerce clause (Conservation Foundation, 1984: 383–87; Neumann, 1985).

Sporhase's significance is nearly incalculable. It could radically alter states' authority to halt transfers of water from farms to cities. Since considerable resistance to the development of alternative water supplies is growing, states cannot rely on such development as a way of avoiding the need for water transfers. In addition, one irony of *Sporhase* is that the litigant in this case wished to divert water from Nebraska to Colorado precisely because Colorado law barred him from drilling in the heavily overdrawn Ogallala aquifer.

Finally, subsequent to *Sporhase*, Congress and the Great Lakes basin states (Illinois, Indiana, Michigan, Minnesota, Ohio, New York, Pennsylvania, and Wisconsin) have expressed a desire to explicitly prohibit interbasin transfers of water without their mutual consent (Conservation Foundation, 1984). In short, in the wake of *Sporhase*, conflicts between competing uses of water have grown, water has become scarcer, and market forces have driven up the price of water (such as urban area offers to purchase water supplies from other states). Since there is no single, comprehensive system of regulation able to challenge traditional rights-based claims, such conflicts will continue to give rise to alternatives based on the augmentation of water supply rather than the limiting of water demand. A post-*Sporhase* case study that exemplifies this dilemma is the Yampa River diversion scheme.

The Yampa is the largest untamed tributary of the Colorado River in the state of Colorado. A developer with water rights in the Yampa valley has offered a plan to build a large impoundment on the Yampa and sell the water to San Diego, California. Thus far, neither proponents nor opponents of this privately financed scheme place much confidence in chances for actual construction. And the state of Arizona's legal claims to Colorado River water threaten the success of the scheme. Nevertheless, the idea behind the plan remains perniciously attractive throughout the West. It is likely that future attempts to accomplish a similar objective will be undertaken somewhere.

The plan to export Yampa River water to southern California has gained favor among two regional groups. The first are the residents of San Diego, who live 1,400 miles from the potential supply. The second are Yampa valley residents, who are suffering from economic depression with the failure of the oil shale industry, and others who have no current need for the water but could receive a price for its sale to California at least five times what they would receive from federally subsidized projects (Simison, 1984).

The ramifications of this plan are numerous. Colorado officials fear that permitting such sales would compromise future availability of water for the state's own needs. Ironically, some environmentalists support the plan, despite the fact that its development would dam the state's longest free-flowing river and create its largest human-made reservoir. Because the price of the project's water would be expensive, it is reasoned that the project "would create an incentive for investments to use its water more efficiently" (Simison, 1984).

Finally, a series of compacts governing allocation of the Colorado River's waters, as well as those of its principal tributaries, may pose an insurmountable obstacle to the project's construction. This fact not only exemplifies the power of water law to allocate supply and to adjudicate changes in the status quo but also, and more importantly, underscores why traditional water conflicts are more easily resolved by augmenting supply than by limiting demand. In short, even recent changes in U.S. water law such as the *Sporhase* decision and the 1986 amendments to the Safe Drinking Water Act have not altered this reality. They have not changed deep-seated attitudes toward water as a form of private property to be exploited and developed in a gratuitous manner.

Water Resources Development and the Ethical Responsibility of Engineers and Planners

It is easier to resolve water rights conflicts by increasing supply rather than by compelling people through regulation to reduce their demand. This is why structural solutions to water problems—such as building dams—are popular. Despite a litany of environmental concerns over impoundments, dam building continues. This means that enormous authority for making water resources decisions has been given to engineers and planners. This is important for several reasons.

First, engineers and planners have talents that lend themselves to solving a number of water resources problems, including flood control, flat-water recreation, hydroelectric power, and navigation improvement. As a result, their influence pervades not one but several water resources issues. The important point, however, is that technology is politically neutral. Even though engineers and planners dominate decision making on these issues, their decisions can be democratic if they result from a broad-based decision-making process and if these experts can be held accountable for their decisions.

Second, despite the fact that water resources agencies traditionally dominated by engineers and planners have significantly changed their objectives in recent years, meaningful mechanisms for enhancing public participation have not followed. The attitudes of engineers and planners have only appeared to change because federal budget cuts, the using up of good dam sites, and the opposition of environmental groups have led to the failure to build new dams. This has occurred over the objections of engineers, not because of their support for these objectives. Water resources agencies still resist even a cautious view of the environmental impacts of water resources developments. This resistance stems from the fact that the agencies that employ these engineers and planners have constructed some of the world's greatest monuments to technology. They possess a strong sense of mission and will not readily admit ecological mistakes committed in the past.

Third, public confidence in the building of dams and other structural measures as a viable solution to water and other natural resources problems has varied in direct proportion to public confidence in technology. In recent years, public trust in engineers has declined and, with it, public confidence in agencies such as the Corps of Engineers and Bureau of Reclamation as stewards of water policy. This decline in trust has inhibited the search for novel solutions to water problems, because the American public is ambivalent toward technology.

This ambivalence stems at least partly from recent energy and environmental disasters. The very names Three Mile Island, Bhopal, Chernobyl, and Teton Dam connote the impossibility of an accident-free or errorless technology. These names also generate skepticism toward government agencies that have promoted the illusion that such an accident-free technology can be developed. By their very nature, technologies designed to modify, control, or exploit the environment are prone to accidents or are laden with risks to the ecosphere and the public's health and general welfare. Public apprehension toward these technologies can be alleviated only if these risks are seen as mitigable. Moreover, this mitigation generally requires public participation in identifying such risks, because the public's apprehensions about risks, even when realistic, constitute a barrier to accepting potentially hazardous technologies that may be beneficial in some other ways. Engineers alone cannot identify these risks; the public must tell them what they are (Perrow, 1984).

While Americans are increasingly skeptical of technology, they continue to place considerable faith in the marketplace to solve natural resources problems. For water policy, this means that distrust of public agencies has been compounded by a hostility to government intervention in the field of natural resources. The result has been a love-hate outlook toward government and a belief that public apprehensions over risk and environmental impact cannot be satisfactorily mitigated by public institutions.

If public agencies can solve natural resources problems with technically elegant panaceas, then the public will accept government intervention. But if a problem cannot be solved through simple engineering, or if the engineering solution is itself risk laden, then government is likely to encourage changes in law and public attitudes, to force conservation of resources, to raise their price, and to restrict their development. Attempts to do this rarely curry political favor to the same degree that monuments to technology have in the past (see, for example, Worster, 1985).

Americans are increasingly distrustful of technology because they distrust its management. Since these managers often formulate decisions in secret and tend to perceive the benefits of technology as high and the risks as low and easily manageable, the general public is reluctant to follow their recommendations. To mitigate this distrust requires overcoming two separate but related obstacles: (1) a lack of confidence in the technical competence of engineers who work for government, and (2) distrust in their professional integrity. A certain amount of skepticism and even distrust is healthy for a democracy. It encourages accountability of decision makers to the public, for example. However, at a certain point, distrust leads to an erosion of confidence in political authority and a reluctance to invest public officials with the power to make hard choices. Overcoming this extreme form of distrust requires changing public perceptions of engineers, improving means for holding the latter accountable to public desires, and reeducating engineers to be more attuned to legitimate public concerns.

Democratic Values and Public Opposition toward Engineering Solutions in Water Policy

In an era of growing technological sophistication, specialization, and complexity, important political decisions affecting the environment are increasingly made by select groups of experts who are only indirectly accountable to the general public. Examples include such controversial fields as nuclear power and hazardous waste regulation. The secluded work of these specialists generates a distance between citizen and government, reducing citizens' opportunity to influence the outcome of decisions critical to their health, welfare, and quality of life (Barber, 1984; Mansbridge, 1983). Unless this lack of accountability is eliminated, the result can be a profound sense of political alienation, posing a significant challenge to democratic theory and to hopes for developing an environmental ethic. The problem is not that the majority of citizens are locked out of decision making but that the process of decision making discourages thoughtful, imaginative ideas that might lead to environmentally and socially conscious decisions. The key to rectifying this problem is making the process of decision making less secluded and less secretive so it will be accountable and accessible.

One reflection of this lack of accountability in water policy is increased public opposition toward large-scale water projects. The failure of billions of dollars worth of investments in massive water projects to solve water shortages, prevent floods, or solve groundwater or pollution problems has nurtured public opposition toward continued pursuit of these policies. Some of this opposition is due to inflated expectations of what was achievable. However, some of it is the result of inflated promises. In addition, there has arisen a growing public preference for small-scale solutions to natural resources problems, which inflict fewer irreversible environmental impacts (Brunner, 1980).

This preference stands in marked contrast to public attitudes displayed during the Great Depression, when massive engineering achievements like the Hoover and Grand Coulee dams symbolized the power of harnessed science to satisfy a number of democratic aspirations, such as economic growth, regional development, and cheap energy. The great winged statues gracing Hoover Dam's entrance exemplified an optimistic attitude toward large-scale engineering projects, which today appears quaint. One thing these statues symbolized was the triumph of democratic aspirations through the accomplishments of civil engineering. This artistic symbolism stands in marked contrast to the contemporary view held by many environmentalists, that technology is inherently undemocratic. In fact, technology is politically neutral. Its application can be democratic if choices over its implementation result from a broad-based decision-making process and if its practitioners can be held accountable for their decisions.

Why is it difficult to develop democratic accountability among engineers responsible for implementing policy? And why does the public distrust engineers? First, engineers and planners are perceived by the public as sharing an elitist view of decision making. This elitist view is often biased toward development, is antipreservationist, and oftentimes ignores the workings of natural systems (Burke and Heaney, 1975: 2). Moreover, this outlook forms a barrier to an environmental ethic by closing the deliberations over the use of water resources. Debate over strategy is often limited to the structural solutions to water resources problems, which has served to maintain concentration of authority in the hands of engineers (Dickson, 1981; Region 7, 1980).

This closed process of decision making is not unique to water resources management. Many government agencies responsible for natural resources or energy policies, especially those policies that pose a risk to the environment or public welfare, operate under an ethos of secrecy, closed deliberation, and hierarchical command. As a consequence, engineers and planners employed by these agencies often resist opening their records of decision to public scrutiny.[2]

Second, engineering approaches to natural resources problems tend to inhibit democratic decision making by rarely considering nonstructural alternatives, such as better management of floodplains, public education about conservation, or how white-water recreation may be accommodated. In short, water resources problems are rarely viewed as requiring more effective management of the resource, negotiation between interests with legitimate stakes in the results of a decision, or accommodation of different social values. Instead, they are viewed as technical challenges to be resolved through purely technical means.

A recent water resources conflict that illustrates this problem is the ill-fated Blue Ridge hydropower project. The Blue Ridge project was a proposal for a pump storage hydropower plant on the New River and would have been located in both North Carolina and Virginia. A license for this project, originally granted to a private utility, was remanded by the Federal Power Commission in 1976 as a result of the collaborative effort of environmentalists, scenic river advocates, and local residents opposed to the project.

The basic reason for this project's failure was the rise of two recent, interconnected trends, which exemplify public distrust in the competence and integrity of engineering solutions to water and energy problems. First, the project was economically unviable without heavy government subsidy from agencies dominated by engineers and planners, especially the Federal Power Commission and the Corps of Engineers, both of which pushed hard for the project. These agencies recommended approval of the Blue Ridge project with little input from the affected public. Second, the project was vulnerable because its purpose (to generate electricity during peak demand periods and to consume energy during periods of low demand in order to refill an upstream reservoir) was difficult for the public to comprehend. In essence, the entire project was viewed by the agencies as too complex and esoteric to marshal significant popular support (Schoenbaum, 1979; Feldman, 1987b).

The coalition opposed to the Blue Ridge project was able to successfully target the sensibility of powerful local groups that were consulted neither about the fate of the New River nor about the need for a project providing peak power for the benefit of outsiders. The power company responsible for initiating the project was placed on the political defensive because it failed to consider alternatives to a pump storage reservoir. These alternatives, such as energy conservation or construction of a coal-fired steam plant, might have been considered had the utility explored various options with the region's residents.

A third criticism of the engineering approach to water problems is that it negates individual responsibility for policy implementation. Engineers tend to work anonymously, not in an attempt to avert ethical responsibility but through a conscious decision to place scientific principle over personal gratification in the solution of technical problems (R. Wilson, 1973; Dubos, 1980). Unfortunately, while well-intended, this practice has often produced an unconscious disdain for public involvement in water resources decisions.

Raymond Wilson, a sociologist who has had the opportunity to survey this attitude, suggests that the disdain for public participation among water planners results from their attempt to proceed from clear-cut objectives: "Elitism was the rule in planning [because] members of the lay public were considered ignorant, uninformed, and as having no standing to participate in planning. [As a result], water planning . . . took place within rigidly defined boundaries" (R. Wilson, 1973: ix).

Implicit in Wilson's observation is a fourth reason why the social and environmental impacts of water projects are ignored. Engineers and planners share an optimistic outlook toward nature's recuperative powers. They believe that development and exploitation of nature is almost always good, and they often point to critical periods in American history when the development of water projects generated enormous benefits to the public. Again, Wilson's survey of water resources planners is instructive:

> Most planners' images of nature and the environment [are] pragmatic, rarely going beyond physical attributes. Nature and water [are] valued for their contribution to man in terms of their resource potential rather than for the metaphysical benefits they may provide. . . . The future world envisioned by planners is a conservative

one. The horizons are generally less than 25 years. . . .
Optimism about the availability of resources is strong.
Existing technology and institutions are seen as being
adequate to meet most future problems. (R. Wilson,
1973: 167)

What is interesting about this claim is that, in practice, it is articulated on two different, yet equally persuasive levels. The first is the
tangible level of the material benefits accruing from water resources
projects. The second level is the impact of these projects on restoring
public confidence during periods of national crisis.

In regard to the latter, the observations of William Warne, a former
Bureau of Reclamation engineer, are especially apt. In Warne's view,
giant dams such as Hoover and Grand Coulee inspired the American
public during the Great Depression. As public cynicism about economic
"laws" grew, the solidity, permanence, and simplicity of the great engineering achievements of the New Deal increased public confidence in
the ability of government and restored public trust in its ability to solve
unemployment (Warne, 1973: 37). Conversely, when public confidence
in engineering solutions wanes, usually during periods of economic nor-
malcy, so does public confidence in the agencies for which engineers
work. Unfortunately, because the authority upon which these agencies
rely for their power are well established, reform is difficult to introduce.

Where does the solution lie? Are engineers and water resources planners to blame for failures in water policy? In their defense, it must be
noted that these individuals are not one-dimensional technocrats concerned only with narrow, technical problems. They believe that their
achievements are humanitarian and progressive. What makes engineering solutions noble, in the view of many engineers, is precisely the fact
that they *are* permanent. Once built, water projects not only alleviate
the practical problems for which they were constructed but allow society
to turn its attention to other problems. In short, most engineers think
of themselves as concerned with broad social issues. During the so-
called golden age of engineering, from about 1850 to 1950, engineers
achieved some of the greatest technical feats in history. Many came to
believe they were social revolutionaries, unlocking a potential for social
change and progress hitherto undreamed of.

According to Samuel Florman, an engineer and observer of this age,
this revolutionary vision stemmed from several sources. There was
the elementary pleasure of solving problems, the satisfaction of releas-
ing the common person from drudgery, and the more profound belief
that achievements in the mechanical, electrical, and civil engineering
arts

> would tend to make all men more nearly equal, thus
> making the engineer an agent in the realization of the
> democratic dream. . . . [The common man] would inevit-
> ably become more educated, cultured, and ennobled, and
> this improvement in the race would also be to the credit
> of the engineering profession. Improved human beings, of
> course, would have to be happier human beings. (Flor-
> man, 1976: 2)

In this view, technology was a panacea for the world's problems. Engineers could not be, nor should they strive to be, impartial or detached
about their work, because the future of society depended upon them.
Since the 1950s, the public has grown weary of the immodest promises
of technology. Environmental pressures, the dawn of the nuclear age, a
fear that science has given us the technical means for instant mass
suicide without the political means to avert it, and a loss of faith in
many professions has produced a decline in esteem for engineers.

In the case of water policy, it has grown increasingly apparent that
even small-scale engineering solutions to natural resources problems
can generate irreversible impacts and may cause new problems not
amenable to engineering solutions (Deudney, 1981). These problems include increased water salinity through intensive irrigation; significant
water temperature differences downstream of an impoundment, which
adversely affect aquatic life; bank erosion; siltation and the resulting
restriction of water-borne nutrients; and conversely, reservoir eutrophi-
cation through an increase of nitrogenous compounds from pesticide
runoff. Additional problems include the raising of groundwater levels,
extinction of some types of biota, an increase in rates of water evaporation and water seepage, and in some areas, earthquakes from the sheer
weight of impoundments. Partly as a result of such impacts, many people question the positive visions promoted by these technologies and
blame engineers, rightly or wrongly, for their negative impacts (Deudney,
1981: 11–17). What can be done about this?

In the first place, the basic problem is a distinctly political one. Our
understanding of nature and of ourselves has simply not kept pace with
our knowledge of science and technology. We know how to manipulate
some things in this world, but we have had an extraordinarily difficult
time deciding why we should manipulate them and understanding why
they often resist manipulation (Bennett, 1987: 45–83). The political
realm has often deferred to "experts" the major value decisions pertaining to the exploitation of the environment, because it has not been
possible to reach political consensus.

There is an irony and a hypocrisy in all of this. If, as Florman notes, engineers can be faulted for failing to recognize that "life is complex" and for putting their faith "in efficiency and progress" at any cost (Florman, 1976: 27), political leaders can be faulted for a graver sin: the failure to "look at the total picture . . . to calculate the cumulative effect of many new technological developments" on the environment (Florman, 1976: 33).

In short, what is needed are environmental principles to evaluate alternative approaches to natural resources problems. Purely environmental impacts of water projects constitute only one issue such an ethic should encompass. Other problems include the socioeconomic impacts of sudden increases in hydroelectricity in developing nations, for example, when the premature establishment of energy intensive industry upsets the politics and culture of a country.

In addition, the goals of water resources development must be transparent and scrutable in order to enhance public participation, like the environmental reforms of the 1970s. The National Environmental Policy Act, for example, encouraged an assessment of the impacts of decisions. The starting point for these changes must be a political framework within which decisions can be made democratically. At one time, these were precisely the tasks of water laws. Is there a better alternative?

Decision Rules for a Social Contract of Water

Every use of water cannot be accommodated in all places at the same time. Merely prioritizing water uses is of little help. Certain uses of water are simply inappropriate, because they serve no genuine social needs. Lawn sprinkling in Phoenix, Arizona, may be desired by some and even prioritized in such a way as to be permitted during low demand times for more important uses. But what social good is served by it?

I postulate two criteria as a point of departure toward implementing an environmental ethic. First, policy goals and objectives should be articulated through regionally based political-hydrological frameworks. This suggestion will be pursued in greater depth in chapter 9. The implications of the lack of such a framework is exemplified by the Garrison diversion project, discussed in chapter 4. Second, competing values should be accommodated within a social contract framework for decision making.

Regional Contractualism: Think Globally, Act Regionally

If we could begin with real, discernible needs based upon our intuitive concepts of justice (clean, safe, fairly abundant water priced affordably so as to cover the cost of supply and transit), we would soon realize that a regional hydrological framework supplanting existing water law

Figure 3.1 Water Resources Regions of the United States Used in River Basin Planning by the Water Resources Council

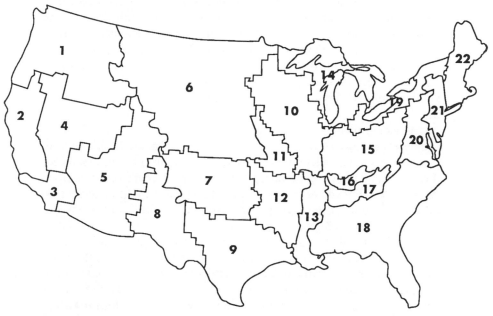

1	Pacific Northwest	9	Western Gulf	16	Cumberland
2	Central Pacific	10	Upper Mississippi	17	Tennessee
3	South Pacific	11	Lower Missouri	18	Southeast
4	Great Basin	12	Lower Arkansas Red	19	Eastern Great Lakes
5	Colorado River		and White	20	Chesapeake Bay
6	Upper Missouri	13	Lower Mississippi	21	Delaware and Hudson
7	Upper Arkansas Red	14	Western Great Lakes	22	New England
8	Upper Rio Grande	15	Ohio River		
	and Pecos				

Source: Mather, 1984: 7.

would make sense. This framework could maximize conformity between (1) a supply of resources adequate for people's self-development and their enlightened existence, and (2) the natural disposition of water and related land resources in a given region. The regions could be defined by the water resources planning basins outlined by the Water Resources Council in the 1960s and 1970s (see figure 3.1).

The regions could be organized within a nationwide system of self-sustaining water management authorities, which would address needs on the basis of a social contract guided by three principles:

1. Residents of a water resources region would be bound together by certain rights and duties. Among these rights and duties are expectations of fair and equal treatment regarding water use and payment of the costs entailed in that use. No one should utilize water resources in such a manner as to jeopardize the rights of other users or the needs of flora and fauna dependent upon it. Rules would be based upon what would benefit the least-well-off person in society under a veil of ignorance.

2. Regional boundaries for each political-hydrological region should be determined by a combination of hydrological characteristics and historic settlement patterns related to water. As was seen in our discussion of riparian and prior appropriation doctrines, both characteristics influenced the establishment of water laws. The problem is that these laws failed to conform fully to the natural amount, quality, and disposition of water in these regions.

3. Decision-making rules, designed to assure equity and political equality among all users, would establish the priorities for allocation, the management of water resources, and the criteria for construction projects and for modifications to river basins and groundwater resources. This part of the social contract for water will require formulating a formal, constitutional basis for allocation. Following the contractarian approach of Rawls (1971), each participant would recommend policies for water use based upon structural efficiency; water would be allocated according to rules that, if changed in order to make one person better off, would not result in making another worse off. Moreover, following the tenets of our own stated desire to avoid gratuitous policy, beneficiaries would recognize their obligations to benefactors and would be willing to pay to support such policies. In essence, decision makers would agree ahead of time that self-interest is not an appropriate metric for evaluating the appropriateness of policies.

Part of what I am suggesting is a variant of the river basin compact idea, exemplified by the Delaware River Basin Commission. The shortcomings of river basin compacts can be overcome by extending the compacts to every region, investing them with powers traditionally held by federal public works agencies, and financing them through a pay-as-you-go system of funding supported by water user taxes deposited in special basinwide accounts. In chapter 9, we shall examine an example of a river basin compact in another developed country (France) in order to elucidate the manner in which such a system could be applied to the United States.

Benefits, Costs, and the Burden of Equity

Water policy is made in an environment of command decisions not determined by the whims of the marketplace. Aside from the "imperfections" of nature, such as the lack of water in some regions where it is needed and the overabundance of it in others at the wrong times, practical constraints limit changes in policy. Prior allocations of water to various regions, long-term commitments made to certain groups (promises of federal irrigation water made to Dakota Territory settlers, for example, are discussed in chapter 4), and the unmitigable impacts of environmentally misguided practices (groundwater contamination through deep-injection wells, for example) all constrain present-day policy makers' efforts.

To optimize public preferences in the allocation of water, each political-hydrological region should be viewed as a group of consumers who pool their resources for mutual benefit. If water resources are viewed in such a manner, then the delivery systems for water resources become somewhat analogous to self-sustaining, publicly owned utilities. Their operation would be characterized by the following features.

1. Optimal management of water resources would be gauged by the system's conformity to structural efficiency: equity, ecological harmony, economic and political feasibility, and the minimizing of transaction costs. Because these criteria vary regionally depending on climatic factors and social ones, they would be subject to varying weights in different locales. It would be the task of basin authorities to establish fair weights for these criteria.

2. Users would be guided by an awareness that all natural resources are interdependent. This interdependency would shape the types of technologies applied to the development and exploitation of water resources. Thus, instead of engineers deciding how water shall be allocated and managed, the entire relevant public would express their views through a user-guided system of decision making.

3. The fees necessary to support any construction project or management scheme would come from the users themselves and be managed by the user-guided system. Otherwise, water users might opt for the most expensive environmental modifications. Moreover, users would understand the real costs of water pollution and depletion by recognizing it as a function of resource interdependency.

Thus a purely technocratic outlook toward water resources would be discouraged, issues other than economic efficiency could be incorporated in decision making, and a goodness of fit between the demands of water users and the ability of water and related land resources to sustain these demands would be assured. Criteria for this fit would include the inherent value of the resource to the viability of the natural environment, its irreplaceability, and its importance to the ecological character of the region. The serious flaws of the Garrison diversion project would have been prevented if such a framework had been used. More to the point, had such a framework existed, policy makers might have steered clear of many of the controversies now associated with it.

4 The Great Plains Garrison Diversion Project and the Search for an Environmental Ethic

It's time for all North Dakotans to get solidly behind this project. We should let our Congressional delegation, our state officials and our legislators know that we need and want this project . . . that Missouri River water is the birthright of everyone in North Dakota. We already have waited too long for it—and have seen the benefits that we could have and should have received literally go down the drain.
—BOARD OF DIRECTORS, GARRISON DIVERSION
CONSERVANCY DISTRICT

Water required to feed the Garrison system will be drawn from the Missouri River via a complex series of canals, pumps, and reservoirs. . . . [Its] waste waters will then be flushed into Manitoba's lakes through the Red and Souris river systems. Promoters of Garrison claim its benefits far exceed its cost. However, Canadians will be the ones who end up paying most dearly for the diversion while gaining none of its benefits.
—ACTION COMMITTEE AGAINST GARRISON

Birthrights in Water Policy: An Overview of the Garrison Diversion Project

The Garrison diversion project, a component of the massive Pick-Sloan project for development of the water resources of the Missouri River basin, was authorized by Congress in 1965. It is one of the largest and most expensive public works projects ever undertaken in the United States. When completed, it will probably be the last major federal irrigation scheme in the West.

Its principal purposes are (1) to irrigate some 250,000 acres of arable land in North Dakota, (2) to provide water for municipal and industrial use to fourteen communities, and (3) to enhance recreational opportunities and fish and game programs within and adjacent to the canals and reservoirs resulting from its construction. The project is supposed to be financed by hydropower sales and other revenues from the use of Lake Sakakawea, created when the Garrison Dam was completed in 1956 (IJC, 1977: 1–117; Corps of Engineers, 1972: F-2; see also An Act

to Make Certain Provisions in Connection with the Construction of
the Garrison Diversion Unit, 79 stat. 433).

Environmental litigation, international opposition, and federal budget
cuts have led to a sharp reduction in the size and scope of the Garrison
diversion project since 1984. Its irrigable acreage has been reduced by
over 50 percent, a principal feeder reservoir crucial to the project's original design has been eliminated, and provision of municipal and indus-

Table 4.1 Project Data on the Garrison Diversion Project as Originally
Proposed (250,000 acres under irrigation)

Project Feature	Project Data
WATER SUPPLY SOURCE	
Garrison Dam with Lake Sakakawea	Capacity, 24,355,000 acre-feet
MAIN SUPPLY WORKS	
Snake Creek pumping plant	Capacity, 2,050 cubic feet per second
McClusky Canal	Length, 73.6 miles, capacity, 1,950 cubic feet per second
REGULATING RESERVOIRS	
Lonetree	Area, 32,980 acres; conservation storage, 280,000 acre-feet
Jamestown	Area, 2,100 acres; conservation storage, 28,000 acre-feet
Taayer	Area, 1,440 acres; conservation storage, 28,500 acre-feet
OTHER SUPPLY CANALS	
Velva	Length, 84.3 miles; initial-end capacity, 2,000–160 cubic feet per second
New Rockford	Length, 52.3 miles; initial-end capacity, 1,600–1,100 cubic feet per second
Warwick	Length, 55.1 miles; initial-end capacity, 770–75 cubic feet per second
James River feeder	Length, 4.3 miles; initial-end capacity, 450 cubic feet per second
Oakes	Length, 11.3 miles; initial-end capacity, 320 cubic feet per second
Devil's Lake feeder	Length, 9.4 miles; initial end capacity, 400 cubic feet per second
DISTRIBUTION CANALS	
Open canals	193 miles
Buried pipelines	444 miles

Table 4.1 (continued)

Project Feature	Project Data
DRAINS	
Open drains	358 miles
Buried pipe drains	1,662 miles
IRRIGABLE LANDS	
Oakes	45,980 acres
LaMoure	13,350 acres
Warwick-McVille	47,220 acres
Karlsruhe	12,200 acres
Lincoln Valley	6,515 acres
Middle Souris	103,800 acres
New Rockford	20,935 acres

Source: GDCD, 1986.
Note: See figure 4.1 for location of project features.

Figure 4.1 The Garrison Diversion Project: Location of Principal Works and Other Components

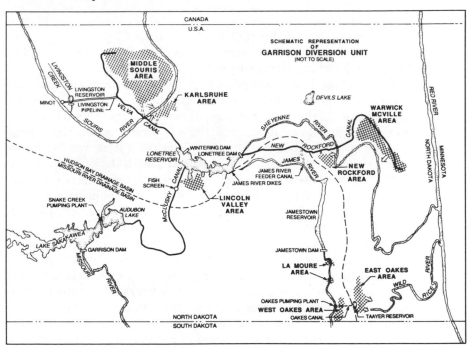

Source: Bureau of Reclamation, 1983.

trial water delivery systems has been moved from second to first priority by recommendation of a study commission appointed by Congress. Despite these apparent setbacks, the Garrison project illustrates the consequences of the lack of a coherent environmental ethic in American water policy. These consequences are twofold. First, its impacts transcend the boundaries of one country and cannot be encompassed by a single set of national laws, and there is little agreement between those two countries (the United States and Canada) over what values should guide transboundary water resources development. Second, proponents and opponents argue their respective cases in different terms, the former arguing in terms of compensation for promises and commitments (a deontological argument), while the latter postulates that harm exceeds benefits (a utilitarian position).

When completed, the Garrison project will divert water from the Missouri River behind Garrison Dam into a series of stair-step-like conduits. Return flows will eventually enter the Hudson Bay drainage system at several points, including the Souris River in northwestern North Dakota and the Sheyenne River in the eastern part of the state. From the Sheyenne, water would flow into the Red River of the North by way of the Warwick Canal, the dividing line between Minnesota and North Dakota, and from there into Canada's Lake Winnipeg, and eventually into the Hudson Bay (IJC, 1977: 12). Table 4.1 provides basic data on the Garrison diversion project. Figures 4.1 and 4.2 show the location of proposed and completed components of the project.

Criticisms of the Garrison project revolve around the negative impacts these return flows would have upon Canadian fisheries, flood levels, and the economy. In the opinion of many Canadians, especially those living in the province of Manitoba, these impacts, which include the possible transfer of Missouri River biota into Canadian waters, were supposed to be averted by the Boundary Waters Treaty with the United States in 1909. This treaty was designed to prevent the contamination, diversion, or degradation of the Souris, Sheyenne, Red, and Pembina rivers, which are used by both the United States and Canada (Loch et al., 1979: 1–39; M DNR, 1982).

There have also been criticisms of the project within the United States. The Sierra Club and the National Audubon Society have expressed concern over the project's impacts upon North Dakota wildlife in areas adjacent to feeder canals and storage works. More recently, there have been broader criticisms of the project's primary purpose, agricultural irrigation. Some have questioned the appropriateness of irrigating cropland to produce additional grain in a region that suffers from depressed farm commodity prices caused by overproduction.

There is also skepticism over the need for more municipal water for North Dakota communities that have not grown significantly in recent

Figure 4.2   The Garrison Diversion Project in Its Geographical Setting

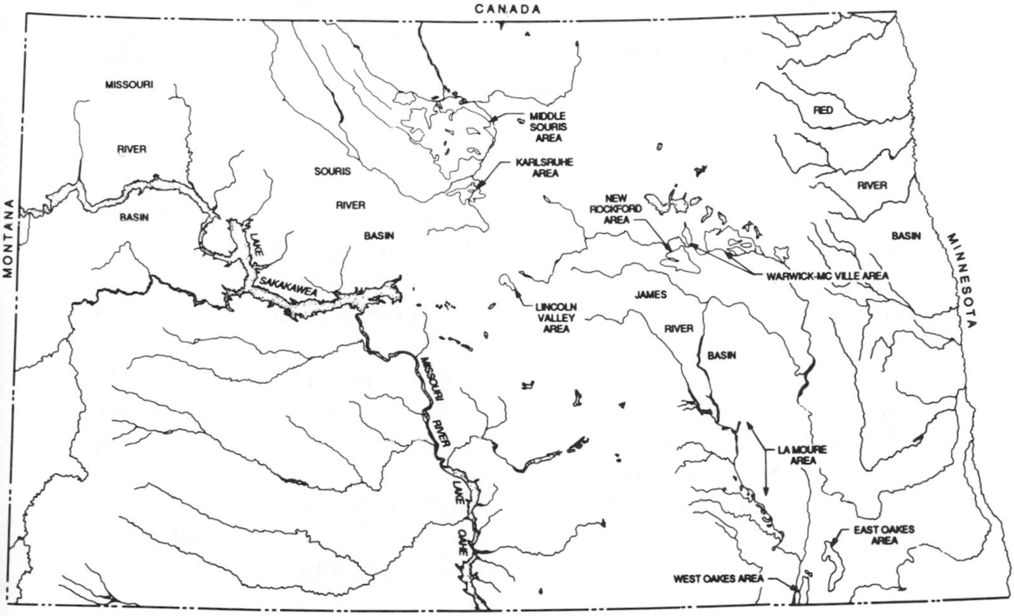

Source: Bureau of Reclamation, 1983.

years and that, in some instances, have lost population. Moreover, down-stream states that claim water rights to the Missouri River through prior settlement (in many instances, by reference to appropriation laws) have grave misgivings over threats to their water supply. Finally, a general anti-pork-barrel attitude displayed by some members of Congress and the Carter and Reagan administrations has eroded funding for the Garrison project, reducing the project's original size (Peterson, 1984; Corps of Engineers, 1972: 9).

What makes the Garrison project unique? How does it display the difficulty in developing an environmental ethic in water policy? From a purely engineering vantage point, the project is not unique at all. Similar river basin diversion schemes have been constructed in other parts of the American West. Many of these schemes overcame far greater technical obstacles, such as tunneling through high mountain ranges in the case of the Colorado River–Big Thompson project. Others have been larger in scope and encompassed far greater acreage, such as the Grand Coulee–Columbia River project in the state of Washington.[1] What makes the Garrison different is that it sharply elucidates the competing values in water policy.

The issues generating contention in the Garrison dispute revolve around regional equity, intergenerational justice, equal treatment of disadvantaged groups, and the balance between economic and noneconomic values. In addition, the project affects two separate countries with very different water laws, environmental concerns, and political resources.

Finally, ethical points of view adopted by proponents of the project have sometimes favored the welfare of persons while proving injurious to nature. For example, a small portion of the lands used for diversion and storage works lies in critical wildlife habitat, which may be irreplaceable. Moreover, the return flow from irrigated farms, while designed to maximize water efficiency, may introduce biota and dissolved minerals and salts injurious to Canadian fisheries.

The Hudson Bay and Missouri River watersheds have been separated for over 10,000 years. In that time, each watershed has developed unique flora and fauna. Many fish and fish parasites found in Lake Sakakawea, for example, have no counterpart in Lake Winnipeg. Thus, the Garrison project underscores the difficulty in establishing and implementing an environmental ethic, because no single ethical criterion to settle this dispute can possibly encompass all of the ramifications of the project.

Preemptory Goals in the Garrison Diversion Project: Promises and Commitments as Just Compensation

In natural resources policy, preemptory values encompass ethical imperatives referred to by philosophers as deontological principles. A deontological principle asserts that what is right is independent of what is good for a particular person. It asserts that what is morally obligatory is determined not by the social or economic consequences it brings about (e.g., a greater good for the many) but by the intrinsic character and expectations entailed in a promise or commitment. Promises, commitments, and obligations are made without duress and compulsion. Those to whom they are made expect they will be carried out (Frankena, 1963: 19–21). According to those who adopt preemptory principles in public policy, to hinge one's keeping of a promise upon the expectation of receiving tangible economic gains is wrong because it reduces ethical decisions to egoism and self-interest (Frankena, 1963: 19–21).

If a public works agency promises to provide alternate habitats for ducks and geese to replace habitats flooded out by an impoundment, for example, and then reneges on this promise after the project is completed, this would be morally wrong under preemptory principles. The original commitment would then seem to have been made solely to alleviate opposition to the project. Only if evidence emerged to suggest that the original commitment was impossible to fulfill or would produce undesirable consequences, would there be good reasons for overriding the preemptory principle (Beatley, 1989).

A second example, particularly relevant to the Garrison project, would be a promise by government to provide water and power to residents of a region who lost their land to a water project. If such a commitment was made in order to persuade area residents to accept the project, then the commitment would be especially binding if (1) the commitment was public, freely acknowledged, and not made under duress or coercion by the residents and (2) both parties (the government and the residents) understood that compensation was a fair exchange for something rightfully belonging to these residents.

In public policy, we call such deontological thinking *preemptory* because it is assumed that these commitments literally preempt, or take precedence over, the goal-directed, nonmoral benefits such policies are intended to bring about, such as producing more electricity, irrigating more farmland, preventing flooding, and so forth. To predicate an ethical decision on social or economic benefits is to justify one's actions by what are termed *meliorative* principles. A distinction between these two principles as applied to public policy is offered by Braybrooke and Lindblom (1963):

> Meliorative concerns lead analysts . . . to consider policies as in varying degrees promoting or hindering health, education, opportunity, and so on. . . . They happen to be derivative from properties of individual persons. . . . There are some moral judgments that . . . seem to have force independent of utilitarian considerations and seem to withstand utilitarian criticism in cases of conflict. These judgments are . . . preemptory [and include such things as to] keep promises, and [to] not make the community miserable for the happiness of one. (pp. 166, 212)

Most proponents of the Garrison diversion project argue that the project's basic goals are preemptory. All Pick-Sloan dams, including the Garrison, were built on arable lands in the upper Missouri River basin taken from farmers in exchange for an implicit promise that future generations would be compensated. Compensation was supposed to come in the form of cheap irrigation water in order to grow row crops and speciality crops, such as corn, potatoes, sugar beets, beans, and vegetables. Due to limited rainfall in this region as well as heavy reliance upon groundwater,[2] this appeared to be an equitable exchange for the loss of arable lands, especially since these highly profitable crops cannot normally be grown on the high plains. Moreover, inexpensive hydropower to fuel economic growth would provide electricity for farms and inspire new industries to relocate to North Dakota.

Critics of the Garrison project often assume that such quaint notions of compensation for unjust losses of land are held by only a few project advocates with recollections of the disastrous effects of the dust bowl of the 1930s. After a congressionally appointed panel proposed reducing the size and scope of the Garrison project in 1984, for example, one writer for the *New York Times* intimated that a few old-timers, some bearing shredded news accounts of farm foreclosures from the depression era, felt betrayed by "broken promises" (Peterson, 1984). In fact, the issue of just compensation has never been more central than it is today. Two factors that lay dormant during that earlier era are very potent in today's water controversies: native American rights and imbalances in regional water resources development.

Regional, Ethnic, and Intergenerational Justice in the Garrison Diversion Project

When the federal government promised to develop the resources of the Missouri River for the economic benefit of North Dakota and surrounding states, part of that promise was made to Indian reservations that had lost river bottomlands to Lake Sakakawea. Out of approximately 560,000 total acres lost to the Garrison and Oahe dams, almost 300,000 acres lay on these reservations (J. Johnson et al., 1962: 3). In the past, the tribes residing on these reservations (The Arikara, Hidatsa, and Mandan), now referred to as the Three Affiliated Tribes, as well as the independent Standing Rock Sioux tribe, were powerless to stop the construction of Garrison Dam and unable to compel the federal government to deliver promised benefits from the project after it was completed.

Legislation pending before Congress could appropriate nearly $200 million for the construction of irrigation and municipal water projects on the reservation and for the replacement of a school, hospital, and other facilities lost when Lake Sakakawea was filled. North Dakota's lone congressional representative, who supports this compensation measure, exemplifies the sway such intergenerational and ethnic claims still hold. Referring to the recommendations of a joint congressional committee, which endorsed this compensation package, Representative Byron Dorgan stated:

> This report, which comes from a great deal of work and a great deal of analysis, is important to those of us in North Dakota, and particularly to [these Indian tribes]. . . . We're waiting for the fulfillment of the promise, the second half of the promise . . . that if North Dakota ac-

> cepted a flood that comes and stays forever, the Federal
> Government promised to allow the use of waters behind
> that flood for economic development and for municipal
> water systems in North Dakota. Part of that promise
> was a promise to the Indian reservations. (U.S. Senate,
> 1987: 2)

The likelihood of such a measure being passed remains open to contention for three reasons. First, the money for this compensation pack-
age would come from the same hydropower revenues ostensibly earmarked to repay the cost of the project itself. Rural electric cooperatives
are opposed to this proposal because it could lead to pressures to raise
electric rates. Second, the Bureau of Indian Affairs opposes compensation by congressional enactment, because a small compensatory payment was made to these tribes for the cost of their relocation in the
early 1950s when the Garrison Dam was built. Third, some observers,
including North Dakota's senior senator, see the need for substantiation
of tribal claims that reservation residents were coerced into accepting
this initial compensation offer (Brasher, 1988).

While native American claims are relatively new and still building
support, the unresolved issue of regional equity has courted greater favor
from most North Dakotans. The area encompassed by the Pick-Sloan
project includes dams built on the Missouri main stem and its tributaries in four states. Direct and indirect economic benefits in the form
of irrigated acreage, hydropower, flood control, and recreation serve six
more states. States affected by Pick-Sloan include Colorado, Idaho, Iowa,
Kansas, Missouri, Montana, Nebraska, North Dakota, South Dakota,
and Wyoming.

Except in North Dakota, most of the original components of the Pick-
Sloan project have been built, and the residents of these other nine states
have been reaping economic benefits in the form of irrigation and hydropower. Some Garrison proponents charge that this unfinished state
of affairs slights North Dakota. Moreover, it is sometimes charged that
the only reason North Dakota has not reaped the promised benefits of
Pick-Sloan is because federal budget cuts have disproportionately affected the northern plains. Exemplifying such claims are the observations of former North Dakota governor William Guy, a principle advocate of the Garrison project and a long-time promoter of its benefits:

> The 10-state benefits embodied in the Pick-Sloan plan
> painted a glowing picture of the future for North Da-
> kota. But as the years have passed and other states re-
> ceived their benefits, North Dakota has been abandoned

as we strive to achieve the mitigation benefits promised
us in the Pick-Sloan plan. (*Fargo Forum*, 1983a)

In an article written for the Garrison Conservancy District, a local
organization formed to establish grassroots support for water diversion,
Guy goes on to detail some of these lost benefits. Noting that North
Dakota uses only 40 percent of Garrison's hydropower due to federal
policies mandating the sale of electricity to public bodies and municipalities (most electric utilities in North Dakota are investor owned and
ineligible to receive this power), Guy criticizes the fact that Minnesota,
"a state that contributed nothing to Pick-Sloan," should receive the bulk
of electricity from Garrison. Likewise, Guy notes that, while not one
single acre of North Dakota farmland is irrigated as a result of Pick-
Sloan, over 700,000 acres have been irrigated in Colorado, Kansas, Montana, and Wyoming.

The Garrison project's implicit and explicit promises for compensation have deeper roots than commitments made to farmers, ranchers,
and Indian reservations during the 1940s. In the 1880s, Congress allegedly promised adequate irrigation water for the homesteads of Dakota
Territory settlers. In 1887, settlers in west central North Dakota gained
permission from Congress to divert Missouri River water to provide
irrigation in order to stabilize agricultural production and to attract
settlers (J. Johnson et al., 1962; Red River Valley Historical Society,
1981: 12–13; Oettig, 1977: 38). In the minutes of the North Dakota
Constitutional Convention of 1889, explicit references were made to the
desirability of water diversion for irrigation (Red River Valley Historical
Society, 1981). Article 11, section 3 of that document states: "all flowing streams and natural watercourses shall forever remain the property
of the state for mining, irrigating, and manufacturing purposes" (GDCD,
1986: 2).

What makes this commitment appear especially binding to many
North Dakotans is the fact that state water laws have been the traditional means for establishing an equitable division of water resources.
External considerations, other than maintaining water quality and supply, do not affect the regulation of water flowing under or through the
state's boundaries. North Dakota's constitutional mandate was inspired
by the same erratic precipitation patterns that prevail in other parts of
the West—patterns that have compelled many western states to adopt
appropriation laws to allocate scarce water supplies. As a consequence,
when the Bureau of Reclamation proposed the diversion of water from
Lake Sakakawea to irrigate North Dakota farms under the Pick-Sloan
plan approved in 1944, many North Dakotans believed that this project's benefits represented a birthright granted in exchange for acts of
settlement committed by their ancestors.

Serious discussion of the diversion of Missouri River water grew out of the loss of arable lands and farm income resulting from the construction of the Garrison Dam. North Dakota's loss of 560,000 acres of farmland to Oahe and Garrison dams was supposed to provide downstream flood protection for other states (J. Johnson et al., 1962: 2; U.S. Senate, 1987: 2). What exacerbated this loss were the controversial origins of Pick-Sloan itself.

Pick-Sloan and the Garrison Diversion Project: Bureaucratic Fragmentation and Water Policy

Pick-Sloan was a compromise plan for water resources development between two rival agencies, the Corps of Engineers and the smaller Bureau of Reclamation. Originally, the bureau saw irrigation as the primary purpose of main-stem dam construction along the upper Missouri. To Congress, however, as well as to the Corps of Engineers, impetus for the project was provided by concerns with (1) controlling for floods downstream of North Dakota and Montana, (2) improving navigation for Iowa, Kansas, Missouri, Nebraska, and South Dakota, and (3) providing hydropower to fuel regional growth (Cass, 1981). Reconciling these goals has proven difficult, because it has never been clear exactly what the powers of each agency were to be in carrying out these goals, what priority was to be accorded each goal, and how beneficiaries were to compensate benefactors—those who paid for, and those who lost lands to, Pick-Sloan.

Congress decided that each of the main-stem dams composing Pick-Sloan (Big Bend, Fort Peck, Fort Randall, Garrison, Lewis and Clark, and Oahe) would be built by the Corps of Engineers primarily for flood control and the improvement of navigation on the lower Missouri–Mississippi river system. The Bureau of Reclamation, whose original interest in main-stem development was for irrigation and hydropower (the latter as a means of repaying irrigation costs), would share in the operation of these projects. A jointly managed reservoir control center in Omaha, Nebraska, is currently charged with accommodating, on a daily basis, the contrasting goals of both agencies and their clientele.

In pursuit of these different objectives, an interagency agreement has been implemented to allow power production, navigation, irrigation, and flood control to be placed on an equal footing in project operation. Through constant consultation and coordination, the Corps of Engineers determines how much water to release from each project to serve all purposes, while the Bureau of Reclamation selects hourly loadings of releases to meet electrical demand.

Prior to 1977, the bureau was further charged with the responsibility for selling Pick-Sloan power through a regional power-marketing agency serving the upper Missouri basin (the Western Area Power Administration). This agency is invested with final determination of electrical sales and is now part of the Department of Energy. Nevertheless, the bureau still decides overall load management in conjunction with the corps and the Power Administration (Corps of Engineers, 1973; Energy Reorganization Act of 1977).

All of these activities constituted the economic justification for Pick-Sloan. Because no single goal took precedence over any other, operational conflicts over new and established projects arose. For example, the Bureau of Reclamation hoped that hydropower sales would subsidize the entire plan, especially the irrigation component. When studies showed that irrigation was less cost effective than previously thought, support for the Garrison diversion project diminished further. As far as the corps and downstream states were concerned, the project's flood control, navigation, and hydropower benefits had been exploited (McConnell, 1966: 224; Hart, 1957).

This is exemplified by Garrison's initial troubles in getting on the policy agenda. One year before the Garrison Dam was completed, in 1955, the state of North Dakota created the Garrison Conservancy District to work with the Bureau of Reclamation in arranging plans to divert water for agriculture and municipal use to a twenty-five county area. The cost ineffectiveness of irrigation projects underlay the repeated failure in Congress of water diversion plans for Lake Sakakawea. In 1957 and again in 1959, the Bureau of Reclamation put forth water diversion plans for central and eastern North Dakota that could not meet the benefit-cost ratio requirements of the Flood Control Act of 1936.

The benefit-cost deficit was only overcome in 1962 and, then, only because of a curious policy adopted by the bureau. In other regions of the Far West, the bureau had practiced a basin account transfer for computing benefits and costs, which allowed power revenues to be shifted to irrigation account ledgers. This transfer inflated the value of project benefits and provided a means for subsidizing irrigation. In 1962, the bureau submitted a revised Garrison diversion scheme, stressing the nonirrigation benefits of the project, including industrial, municipal, and recreational benefits. The benefit-cost ratio using this formula was 1.67 to 1 (Red River Valley Historical Society, 1981). This project was authorized by Congress in 1965. While initial economic objections were overcome, however, unanticipated environmental impacts from connections between the Missouri and Hudson Bay drainage systems, intrinsic to the project's design, would generate conflict with Canada. This would further underscore the project's inability to reconcile different sets of values.

Meliorative Justifications and the Greater Good of People and Nature: Foreign Biota and Foreign Policy in the Garrison Diversion Project

Critics of the Garrison project have been animated mostly by meliorative concerns. They have argued that the choice to accept or reject the project should be driven by a straightforward, unbiased comparison of the costs, benefits, and risks of the project and not by reference to promises or commitments made at a time when the long-term environmental and economic impacts of large-scale water projects were insufficiently understood. This criticism falls squarely within the general characteristic of meliorative justifications identified by Braybrooke and Lindblom (1963): "Judgments about accepting or rejecting choices hinge upon comparison with alternatives. ... With a meliorative rule, it makes no sense to give an answer to the question, is the policy right or wrong? until alternatives have been identified and investigated" (150, 158).

Even if Garrison could have been initially justified by reference to some implicit commitment made to farmers, ranchers, and native Americans long ago, these critics charge, the lack of economic and environmental justification for the project today negates these arguments. There is no need to produce more food. Besides, much irrigable acreage in other parts of the United States has been taken out of cultivation. A more efficient and less environmentally disruptive way to grow more food would be to place this other acreage under cultivation again.

Moreover, these critics argue, the project's cost-benefit ratio is no longer favorable: the project is now much more expensive than originally anticipated due to environmental modifications to prevent Missouri River biota from entering Canadian waters. In addition, a reduction in the project's size has reduced anticipated benefits (Bureau of Reclamation, 1983).[3] In short, the project's dubious economic benefits and probable negative environmental impacts preclude the necessity for challenging project proponents' birthright claims.

There is an intriguing twist on this whole issue of meliorative versus preemptory concerns, which complicates matters further. Regardless of any benefits to North Dakota agriculture, industry, municipalities, or recreation from the Garrison project, respect for the Boundary Waters Treaty of 1909, the water laws on both sides of the international boundary, and the assurances of unencumbered use of water given to all parties in the region should preempt American rights to the exclusive economic benefits of the Missouri and its tributaries. This is the es-

Figure 4.3 Transboundary Waters Affected by the Garrison Division Project

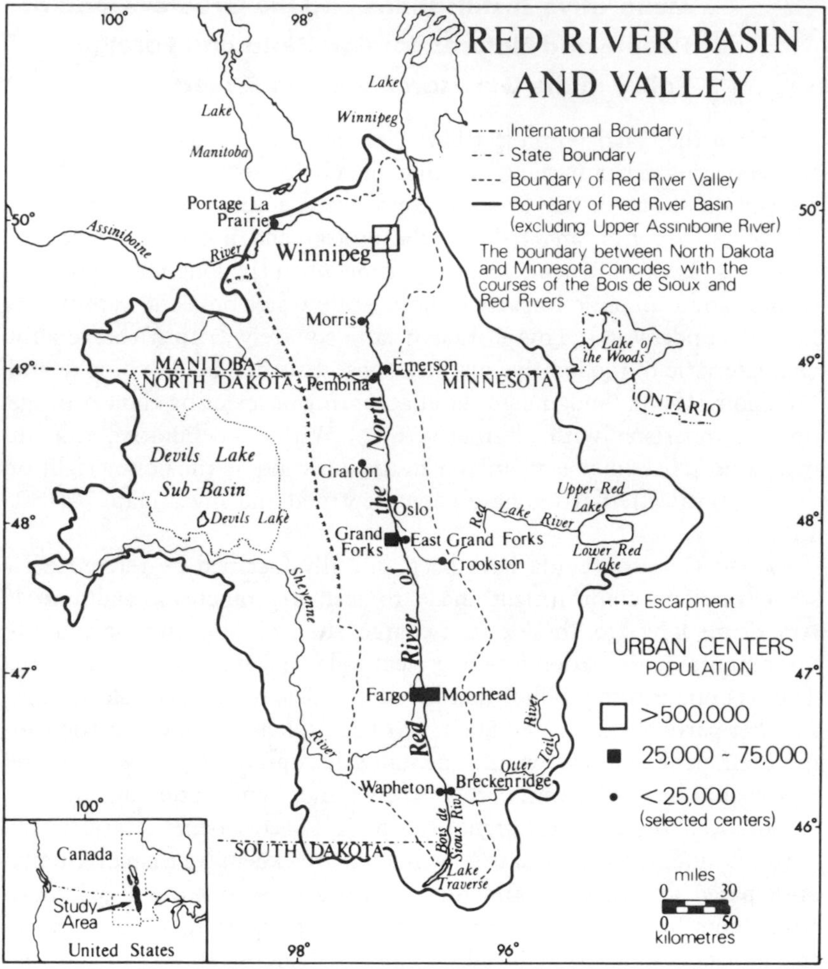

Source: Freshwater Foundation, 1985.

sence of Canada's formal opposition to the project (IJC, 1977: 9; IGDSB, 1976: 205). The boundary waters under contention in this dispute are shown in figure 4.3. The map focuses upon the Red River portion of the project's affected area.

One Canadian critic of the Garrison project, a former representative to a special Garrison study commission, contends that U.S. environmental law should prohibit construction of the project unless alternatives to water diversion are thoroughly debated, as required by the

National Environmental Policy Act of 1969. However, since passage of the act, no comprehensive review of the merits of the Garrison diversion project has been undertaken. The act has been used only to force modifications of features that could impose gross environmental impacts. It has not been used to find fault with the original premises of the project or to consider alternatives that might achieve the same goals without interbasin diversion. This controversy reveals how international factors complicate debates over the value of meliorative and preemptory management of natural resources.

International Resources Regimes and the Garrison Diversion Project: Was This Problem Avoidable?

In chapter 2, it was suggested that a public choice approach to managing natural resources offers some insights into how to develop cost-effective methods for their exploitation and at the same time minimize injurious environmental impacts and equitably represent the interests of common users. Prior to the Garrison project, long before Pick-Sloan, and much earlier than the coveting of the water resources of the Missouri basin by the Corps of Engineers and the Bureau of Reclamation, a well-organized resource regime, the International Joint Commission, governed a part of the Missouri basin. The commission, formalized by the 1909 Boundary Waters Treaty, was established in 1911 by the United States and Canada to minimize environmental degradation of their transboundary waters. It represented both nations' interests equitably. The commission stated what types of activities were to be avoided, was consulted on long-range planning, and studied and catalogued the resources within its jurisdiction. Like most mechanisms established by international agreement, however, the commission has no enforcement powers. Nevertheless, it has been a means for averting problems of mutual concern.

The commission is evidence that mechanisms for managing water resources encompassing large regions and diverse cultures are viable. Such mechanisms can manage resources coherently and comprehensively by transcending international boundaries. Canada's claims that the Garrison diversion project violates the Boundary Waters Treaty is based upon article 4 of this agreement—an explicit directive that prohibits harmful action to waters shared by both nations: "the waters herein defined as boundary waters and flowing across the boundary shall not be polluted on either side to the injury of health or property on the other" (IJC, 1977: 1).

The International Joint Commission, composed of three Americans and three Canadians, is charged with the "adjustment and settlement

of all questions" pertaining to boundary waters (Rieve, 1981: 14). The
commission has been given the almost unprecedented authority (a reflection of the traditionally amicable relationship between the United
States and Canada) to adjudicate water resources conflicts falling outside the jurisdiction of either country. In short, it constitutes a transnational river basin authority, based upon the principle that no action
by citizens of one country affecting shared water resources shall be
permitted if they infringe upon the welfare or rights of citizens of the
other country. The commission's role in the Garrison controversy began
three years after construction began.

In April 1970, the government of Canada transmitted its concerns in
an aide memoire to the U.S. Department of State. Canada's major concerns were that (1) the leaching of soil could degrade the water quality
of the Assiniboine, Red, and Souris rivers, affecting Lake Winnipeg and
the province of Manitoba, (2) return flows from irrigated farms, in pass-
ing through the Hudson River drainage system, would increase both
flood levels and the frequency of flooding along the Red River, and (3)
Garrison water conveyance systems, by providing a direct connection
between the Missouri and Hudson Bay drainage basins, might introduce
foreign biota (fish, fish eggs, parasites, and diseases) into Manitoba
waters. On the basis of subsequent reports by the Bureau of Reclamation, Canada reiterated its concerns in October 1971 (IJC, 1977: 2, 7).

Initially, no formal complaint was lodged with the International Joint
Commission. Canada counted upon the goodwill of Washington to address these issues in a less formal and more direct manner, since the
project was still in its incipient stage. Between 1970 and 1975, however,
two events occurred that changed the texture and tone of the conflict.
First, support for the project within North Dakota eroded. Project support was centered within the Garrison Conservancy District, headquartered at Carrington, North Dakota; however, North Dakotans
outside this area who stood to lose additional land to the diversion
project or who felt susceptible to pollution from irrigation runoff began
to oppose the project. Many of these opponents banded together in 1972
and formed the Committee to Save North Dakota, which filed judicial
actions in an attempt to halt the diversion. Other groups, more broadly
based and in some cases without links to the immediately affected
region, also began to take action against the project. The best known
of these groups is the National Audubon Society, which filed suit in
1976 to stop the diversion project because of its impacts upon the breeding and migratory areas of rare and endangered waterfowl (Rieve, 1981:
14).

A second development affecting the status of the Garrison project
occurred in 1973. Growing impatience with Washington's failure to

respond to Canadian apprehensions over the project led the Canadian Embassy in Washington to request formally that the matter be taken up by the International Joint Commission. The embassy informed the U.S. Department of State that "the proposed project would run counter to the obligations assumed by the United States under Article IV of the Boundary Waters Treaty of 1909" (Rieve, 1981: 14). In 1974, the Department of State announced its intention "to comply with its obligations to Canada not to pollute waters crossing the boundary, [and to cease] construction potentially affecting waters flowing into Canada . . . unless it is clear that this obligation will be met" (Rieve, 1981: 14). Thus, it initially appeared that the United States would lay the matter to rest by refusing to go ahead with the project unless Canada's concerns were resolved.

In 1975, both countries jointly called the machinery of the Joint Commission into operation to see what could be done to meet Canada's concerns. In October, the commission appointed the International Garrison Diversion Unit Study Board to investigate Canada's concerns and to estimate the project's impacts and the costs of alleviating them. It also looked into current water quality conditions throughout the transboundary region affected by the project.

The Study Board's conclusions were unsettling and controversial. Eight public hearings were held in the span of less than one year in order to expedite answers to the biota transfer problem, while simultaneously meeting Bureau of Reclamation concerns that project construction not be unduly delayed. No new field investigations were held; committees formed to study various aspects of the Garrison project, composed of American and Canadian scientists, could examine and evaluate only existing data (GDCD, 1986: 3). Following the release of the study in January 1977, the United States agreed to cease construction of a key Garrison component, the Lonetree Reservoir located on the Sheyenne River (GDCD, 1986: 15), despite the fact that the Bureau of Reclamation insisted that development of the reservoir would not violate the 1909 Boundary Waters Treaty. The agreement was an attempt to show Canadians that something was being done about biota transfer while addressing U.S. concerns that whatever was done would be relatively inexpensive.

Unfortunately from the Bureau of Reclamation's perspective, the major findings of the Study Board's report supported Canada's view that Garrison diversion's impacts could be potentially devastating to Manitoba: "the construction and operation of the GDU as envisaged would cause injury to health and property in Canada as a result of adverse impacts on the water quality and biological resources in Manitoba" (IJC, 1977: 3). The Joint Commission recommended that direct connections between drainage basins be eliminated and that less saline soils be irrigated. The report also urged further research to verify predicted water quality and quantity of return flows from the project and to determine the ultimate fate of nitrogen in the Souris River before any irrigation proceeded. Most controversial of all, the Study Board concluded that absolutely "no construction of that portion of GDU which affects waters flowing into Canada" should take place (IJC, 1977: 4).

The immediate upshot of the study was that the Bureau of Reclamation was forced back to the drawing board to come up with a plan to prevent biota transfer. A major structural modification offered by the bureau was the addition of a fish screen to inhibit the transfer of biota into the McCluskey Canal portion of the diversion project, a critical passage between the Souris and Missouri rivers. In fact, as if anticipating the Study Board's findings, the Bureau of Reclamation had first introduced the fish screen idea in 1975.

The Joint Commission cautioned that a fish screen or any other structural solution, alone, would be ineffective against transference of biota. It urged two modifications: (1) an extensive sand filtration system to remove biota missed by the McCluskey Canal screen, and (2) a series of storage ponds and plastic shields in and adjacent to the Velva Canal. The first would prevent any Missouri River water from Lake Sakakawea from entering the Sheyenne, Souris, or Wild Rice rivers (and thus into the Red River of the North); the second would mitigate seepage of return flows and, thus, would further minimize biota or saline transfers into the Hudson Bay drainage system (IJC, 1977: 66–67). In 1978 and again in 1980, Congress appropriated funds for these modifications, as well as for other features of the project, while simultaneously specifying that no funds be spent on project features not directly affecting Canada.

The Study Board's final report came to an unsettling conclusion about biota transfer. Regardless of preventive measures, the risk of biota introduction and contamination would remain high and its consequences would be largely unmitigable. Even if all the proposed modifications to prevent the transfer of biota were implemented, the risks of biota transfer would remain so great and the transfer so potentially adverse in its impacts that even a totally closed system might not solve the problem. Such a system "does not provide a sufficient guarantee against an occurrence" (IJC, 1977: 109).

The present status of the Garrison diversion project remains precarious. The government of Manitoba remains adamant in its opposition to the project on grounds that, until "appropriate water quality agreements" are negotiated and problems relating to biota transfers are resolved, it could not endorse these project changes and would oppose further construction (MDNR, 1982: 16). American groups opposed to all or part of the project have engaged in intense litigation to stop completion of the project. The focus of most of these efforts is the issue of whether or not irrigation should remain a principal purpose of the project. Finally, the ultimate size, scope, and even likelihood of completion of the Garrison diversion project remain uncertain.

A study commission convened in 1984 at congressional urging recommended a significant reduction in the project. While most court challenges lodged by environmental groups, revolving around Bureau of Reclamation conformance with the environmental impact process, have been settled in court (*Fargo Forum*, 1982a), uncertain funding by Congress has all but killed the Garrison project for the time being. The Bush administration, concerned with the budget deficit and, like its predecessor, uncommitted to a national water policy, has failed to move the project off center.

Toward a Resolution of the Dispute: Points of Contention and Their Normative Implications

In plowing through the vast record of arguments put forth by proponents and opponents of the Garrison diversion project, one is struck most of all by the fact that both sides are far apart because problems depicted by one are simply not viewed as problems by the other. The ethical values dividing the parties to this dispute are simply irreconcilable without them coming to grips with a fundamental question: Which values should be ranked most important in settling this dispute, and why?

Practically speaking, this division is reflected by the absence of agreement over the relevance of the Boundary Waters Treaty to this dispute. While the governments of Canada and Manitoba claim that the Garrison project violates the treaty, the United States has not conceded this argument. Proponents of the project interpret the treaty and the machinery of the Joint Commission as never intending to preclude development of the water resources of the upper Missouri basin (GDCD, 1986: 3).

Partial Solutions to the Garrison Diversion Controversy:
Why They Haven't Worked

SCIENTIFIC SCRUTINY AS NORMATIVE METHODOLOGY. Normative theorists frequently suggest that one means of resolving public policy disputes about technological impacts is by obtaining consensus on the rules for political discourse. If parties to a dispute can come to an agreement over the means for defining the problem and for establishing evidence of its severity, then it should be possible to agree on appropriate procedures for finding a solution.

One principle in the conduct of science is that a commitment to rational inquiry commits one to accepting the consequences of that inquiry, regardless of its effects upon one's self-interest. A scientific approach compels acceptance of research findings even at the risk of exposing errors of judgment, political bias, or prejudice. In the context of Garrison, this implies that agreement upon rules for impartial, detached, dispassionate discourse should at least obtain consensus upon whether or not there actually is a biota transfer that poses nonmitigable risk.

Unfortunately, while this goal is easy to define, it is difficult to achieve. Ethical discourse cannot submit to an empirical test of validity or reliability in the same way that scientific discourse can (MacRae, 1971). Even if policy makers can agree on rules for formulating equitable policies, or policies that meet other criteria for ethical decision making, the bases for making specific decisions would still need to be laid out. Garrison is an excellent illustration of why it is difficult to define these criteria in a manner satisfactory to all parties.

In this case, participants in the dispute have differing perceptions of what constitutes an acceptable risk. Those subscribing to a meliorative approach try to weigh the probability or the consequences of biota transfer against economic gains. Those guided by preemptory values categorically oppose accepting the risk from biota transfer, however small, on grounds that no one should be made to endure a hazard without his or her consent. This claim, cited by social contract theorists, ranges from the view that entities endowed with free will have rights they can exercise against society when they are threatened to the view that all living things are endowed with moral equality (Ackerman, 1980; Dworkin, 1977; Walzer, 1983; Regan, 1983).

This is why, although biologists may be able to describe in precise mathematical formulations the risks to Canadian fisheries of even the smallest infiltration of Missouri River biota (Loch et al., 1979), the judgment of what level of risk is acceptable or tolerable remains largely irreducible to scientific proof. Attitudes toward what constitutes an acceptable level of risk are subjective. They are influenced by considerations of voluntary consent as much as by probability of occurrence. This is also why canons of scientific inquiry, normally immune to nationalistic considerations, have thus far been unable to establish technical consensus over the problems posed by the Garrison diversion or over the means to resolve them. Political agendas drive the role of the scientists in the dispute. Scientific objectivity, to the extent such objectivity is even apparent, do not drive the political process.

Scientific opinion over acceptable levels of risk tends to divide along national lines. Canadian natural scientists who study the biota transfer problem consistently point to evidence that buttresses Canadian claims that the project would harm Manitoban fisheries. Canadian researchers, especially those employed by government, view the parameters of risk conservatively, an appropriate approach, since they have been hired to protect Canadian fisheries from catastrophic impacts.

Numerous U.S. studies, on the other hand, particularly by scientists from universities in North Dakota, contend that claims of harm from biota transfer are groundless (Oettig, 1977; *Fargo Forum*, 1983c). Understandably, U.S. scientists tend to have confidence in U.S. engineering schemes, which they have had the opportunity to observe, study, and use.

Nowhere is this conflict better exemplified than in the following. The Bureau of Reclamation, after performing laboratory tests on model fish screens at a research center in Denver, Colorado, and in North Dakota, concluded that the screen effectively eliminates all fish, fish eggs, and biota (GDCD, 1986: 12). However, scientists at Manitoba's Department of Natural Resources, after seeing this evidence, remain largely unconvinced. Their skepticism hinges on the effect of Lonetree Reservoir on biota transfer, with or without a fish screen on the McCluskey Canal. They argue that confidence should not be placed in an unproven technology, especially one whose effectiveness hinges upon American resolve to implement it correctly:

> The fact that the reservoir will be located within the Hudson Bay watershed increases the danger of accidental transfer. . . . We also question the ability of any government to enforce a non-fishing ban in a reservoir of this size. This will be particularly difficult when the recreational possibilities of the reservoir are . . . planned to be developed by the Bureau. (Clarkson, 1983)

These scientists further maintain that, while tests performed by the Bureau of Reclamation on mock-up fish screens may have been valid, no long-term testing has proven their efficiency or reliability. A reasonable, conservative estimate of the performance of an engineering solution should seek the best data available:

> Seals required around the screen panels have certainly been improved but problems still exist . . . and the durability of the inflatable seals have not been subjected to prolonged use testing. [In addition], the location of the fish screen structure on the McCluskey Canal will re-

sult in the need to filter water that has passed through a
number of small lakes and marshy areas, which receive
a good deal of surface runoff from adjacent agricultural
lands (Clarkson, 1983).

If Canadian and U.S. scientists are privy to the same evidence and
trained in similar canons of research, it would appear that they should
have been able to agree upon the same methodologies and findings.
However, what constitutes suitable evidence for adequate testing, for
assurance against risk, and for prudent precaution depends upon one's
role within the policy process. Information that emerged in the fall of
1983 that suggests that the Bureau of Reclamation may have doctored
its own reports about the environmental impacts of other aspects of the
project has buttressed Canadian concerns.

According to newspaper columnist Jack Anderson, Bureau of Reclamation biologists complained that bogus information was used to model
the wildlife impacts of the Garrison diversion project. He cited internal
bureau complaints about proposed mitigation measures for waterfowl
habitat (*Fargo Forum*, 1983c). Whether the claims are ever proven true,
a finding still unascertained, their implications are clear. Scientific information used for resolving a policy dispute must be absolutely beyond
reproach. If they are not, public trust in the ethics of scientists and
governments dissolves, compounding the difficulty in gaining political
consensus. Other accounts support the claim that the Bureau of Reclamation was torn by internal conflicts over the scientific evidence of the
impacts of the Garrison project. When the Council on Environmental
Quality ordered the bureau to prepare an environmental impact assessment on the Garrison project in 1971, the bureau was faced with two
choices it never successfully resolved: whether to justify a project that
Congress had already decided should be built and that the bureau itself
favored, or whether to be totally objective (Keys, 1984: 231).

INTERNATIONAL GOODWILL AND THE POSSIBILITY OF BINDING ARBITRA-
TION. The traditional lack of enmity between the United States and
Canada should provide a basis for amicably resolving the Garrison controversy. Unfortunately, the controversy is not, in the ordinary sense,
international. Unlike the issue of acid rain, for example, which has
prompted discussions between U.S. President Ronald Reagan and Canadian Prime Minister Brian Mulroney, most of the policy debate over
the Garrison project has been conducted at the subnational level. The
immediate environmental and economic impacts of the project are limited to the state of North Dakota and the province of Manitoba.

This is significant for two reasons. First, much of the foreign policy debate over the project has been conducted between Manitoban environmental agencies and interest groups, on the one hand, and, on the other, North Dakotan interests in conjunction with the Bureau of Reclamation. Canadian provinces, U.S. states, and interest groups in both countries indirectly affected by this project have continued to cooperate on other matters, which has served to weaken both Canadian opposition to the project and U.S. perception of the legitimacy of Canadian opposition.

Second, while environmental policymaking in Canada is somewhat more centralized than in the United States, the same propensity toward regional, institutional, and ideological cleavages and fragmentation characteristic of U.S. natural resources policy is found in Canada. In no area of natural resources policy is this more true than in water pollution control, traditionally shared by several agencies at the provincial and federal levels (Menzies, 1969). This fragmentation has placed Canada at a further disadvantage in exerting leverage against the Garrison project. Recall that political fragmentation is an important barrier to a coherent, rational policy. If this is true within a single society, then one can easily imagine how formidable an obstacle it can be in dealings between two nations.

Some illustration of this problem is offered by comparing the Garrison dispute with other U.S.-Canadian water resources issues. In the mid-1960s, while most Canadians were strongly opposed to the North American Water and Power Alliance, proposed by American engineers to divert Canadian rivers for irrigation, many residents of Alberta openly and wholeheartedly supported the project. A key component of the alliance, the so-called Rocky Mountain trench reservoir, would have been its largest single component and could have generated enormous revenues for the Albertan economy. Ironically, a federation of western Canadian and U.S. water users that supported the project referred the study of its feasibility to the International Joint Commission, the same body at the center of the Garrison controversy (Lloyd, 1969).

Closer in physical proximity to the Garrison project, the premier of Saskatchewan, Grant Devine, recently proposed the joint North Dakota–Saskatchewan construction of a dam on the portion of the Souris River flowing through his province. The dam would provide flood control, hydropower, and irrigation. This is the same Souris River whose possible contamination by Missouri River biota from the Garrison diversion might injure Manitoban fishery interests.

While Devine cautions that no construction should be undertaken until "we Canadians are convinced that the costs and benefits can be distributed fairly . . . between North Dakota and Saskatchewan" (*Fargo Forum*, 1982b), the implications of this case illustrate the complexity of U.S.–Canadian relations vis-à-vis boundary water resources. In essence, it suggests that neither side is immune to ignoring adverse impacts on others from a water project, if the project benefits one's regional interest. A Canadian political scientist, referring specifically to prospects for diversion of Great Lakes water but cognizant of such a scheme's more general implications, observes:

> There is no single Canadian position or no single Canadian perspective. Diversion issues like so many other issues in Canadian-American relations tend not to pit Canadians versus Americans in any sort of monolithic sense. They usually, much more often, pit some Canadians and some Americans versus some Canadians and some Americans (Munton, 1982: 170).

What compounds this problem is the fact that Canada's ability to stop controversial projects such as the Garrison is inherently weak. Assuming there was a national consensus to stop the project—which, as we have seen, there is not—it would take a concerted effort to place such an item on the agenda of both countries. As currently structured, the International Joint Commission has no mandate to enforce. It is an advisory body, comprising equal numbers of Canadians and Americans. Only after the United States and Canada jointly requested its assistance on the Garrison dispute was the commission able to come forth with a plan for study leading to recommendations.

The commission has never been used to review the environmental impacts of projects before they are formally proposed. This is problematic, because for an international solution reliant upon binding arbitration to work, an underlying consensus on policy values must exist. Thus, we are back to where we began, the need for an environmental ethic able to encompass the complexity of water resources and capable of transcending national boundaries.

Toward a More Permanent Solution: Some Modest Proposals

In chapter 3 it was suggested that, in order to optimize public preferences in the allocation and use of water, residents of a given area should agree to pool their resources in a coherent political-hydrological region governed by a common authority. Consumers would place natural resources under this authority for mutual benefit. This integrated system would attempt to optimize several values simultaneously and would not exclude any important value, meliorative or preemptory. Had such a comprehensive international natural resources management system been in place at the inception of the Pick-Sloan project, the dispute of the Garrison diversion might have been avoided.

The International Joint Commission, established to oversee the 1909 Boundary Waters Treaty, was envisaged as accomplishing part of what a more ambitious system would attempt. Article 4 of the Boundary Waters Treaty, while it does not "envisage any prior joint planning of a shared transboundary water resource" (IJC, 1977: 117), has encouraged joint planning and consultation on technical issues. Prior to the Garrison conflict, the United States and Canada worked together through the Joint Commission to manage water resources issues throughout the boundary waters region. During the late 1950s and early 1960s, for example, Bureau of Reclamation representatives served as members of the commission's study boards that gathered data on irrigation and water quality for the Pembina, Red, and Souris river basins. Much of this planning information was utilized by Bureau of Reclamation engineers in the development of the Garrison diversion project. Likewise, teams of Canadian scientists and technicians from both provincial and federal levels visited Bureau of Reclamation offices in Bismarck, North Dakota, to observe better American procedures for water resources planning (IJC, 1977: 2, 43, 246). In the early 1960s, both nations sought to develop a comprehensive plan for development of the Pembina River, which entailed a free exchange of data between governments. Even more ambitious was the joint development of a plan to manage migratory waterflow through cooperative studies conducted by U.S. and Canadian government scientists under Joint Commission auspices (IJC, 1977: 43).

It is obvious that both nations used the commission to avoid adverse impacts from water projects and to avert problems unmitigable by a single nation. This is further confirmed by the fact that the commission, early in its history, reached agreement on the priorities for the use of transboundary waters. Domestic and sanitary use were the first priority, followed by navigation. Power and irrigation were ranked last (Corps of Engineers, 1972: 9). What seems to have happened is that the Garrison project was conceived and partially executed in an environment that ignored these priorities and the reasons justifying them.

One modest suggestion, therefore, is that consultation with Canada during the formative stages of planning for the Garrison project might have uncovered potential problems before construction was under way. This courtesy might have avoided many of the problems and criticisms of the project. Moreover, there was abundant precedent for such action. Given these precedents, such cooperation might have led to development of a joint U.S.-Canadian scheme for Missouri River diversion able to encompass the economic and environmental concerns of both countries.

A second suggestion, less modest, is that residents of these two countries, facing each other across common waterways as well as common boundaries, have long seen themselves as part of a coherent political-hydrological region. Throughout the Garrison controversy, proponents of the project have suggested that its advantages should benefit Canada as well as the United States. It has been assumed that the benefits and costs of the project should be measured in transnational terms, even if benefit-cost assessments did not formally encompass this assumption. Moreover, many Canadians accepted these claims at face value. It is claimed, for example, that Canadian benefits from the Garrison project would include supplementing low flows on the Souris River, reducing total dissolved solids concentrations due to constant water movements, enhancing the head for generation of hydropower on the Nelson River, and potentially irrigating over 7,000 acres of farmlands in Manitoba (IJC, 1977: 60–61).

There are two problems with these claims, however, which point directly to the failure of U.S. policy makers to incorporate Joint Commission machinery in the implementation of the Pick-Sloan plan. First of all, there is little evidence that Canadians were either asked their opinion on, or expressed great interest in, these supposed benefits. While U.S. proponents of the Garrison diversion insist that these potential benefits would help Canada, Canadians were never formally consulted on whether they even wanted them. No attempt to weigh their preferences was undertaken. Second, the issues of costs outweighing benefits and of interregional equity were simply not addressed at all.

Considerably more Canadians live in the area affected by the Garrison project than do Americans: 800,000 Canadians to 500,000 Americans as of the late 1970s. The American states affected by the Garrison diversion has twice the cropland under development that the province of Manitoba has. Thus, flooding and water contamination from the project would conceivably impose a greater per acre burden upon Canada, especially considering the reliance of Manitoba's economy upon commercial and sport fisheries.

This is not to point blame or to take sides. It is merely a recommendation that all parties to such a dispute acknowledge the ecological principle that, if one claims transnational benefits as a reason for developing a commonly shared water resource, then one must similarly acknowledge that transnational costs require mitigation. To ignore this issue is hypocritical and violates both meliorative and preemptory value criteria, because it suggests that whichever party acts to develop a resource first need not regard the impacts upon another. Had both Canadians and Americans been incorporated into the decision-making framework from the inception of the Garrison diversion project—through the International Joint Commission, for example—then all parties would have been compelled to take a transnational perspective toward the project and would have recognized their obligations to each other as citizens of a common water resources region. The good of the entire region, not merely the particular good of one faction, might have been accommodated.

A remaining question pertaining to the settlement of this kind of problem is, What types of political structures encompass such values optimally, and can the Joint Commission, or some facsimile that reconciles the political and hydrological characteristics of natural resources, alleviate adverse environmental impacts through guidance by a coherent environmental ethic? Chapter 5 examines this issue.

5 The Pathology of Structural Reform in Water Policy: Ethics

and Bureaucracies

Jurisdictional problems which necessarily involve the Executive office of the President . . . need not arise if there were one water resource agency.
—PRESIDENT'S DEPARTMENTAL REORGANIZATION PLAN

If we do not reform the cost-sharing policies of the Corps of Engineers, then we face the growing possibility that [it] will become a mere caretaker agency.
—SENATOR JAMES ABDNOR

Components of a Rational Water Policy: The Organizational Context

A normatively defensible water policy would encompass the environmental and social costs of resource exploitation and depletion while simultaneously representing the interests of all affected members of the public. Previous chapters have defined such a policy by four parameters.

First, it must consider equity, promote noneconomic values, be feasible, and alleviate negative impacts to society and nature. Accommodating these values requires reconciling utilitarian and nonutilitarian (meliorative and preemptory) criteria, such as protecting the rights of the few as well as the interests of the majority. Second, such a policy would avoid gratuitousness and be responsive to needs on a planned, systematic basis. This means it would encompass broadly defined costs and benefits and oblige beneficiaries to compensate those affected by the risks and other impacts of resource development. Third, it would encourage multiple uses of water: power, recreation, irrigation, fish and wildlife protection, municipal, domestic, and industrial. Fourth, it would foster laws, regulations, and engineering practices that would assure that the disposition of the natural resource conforms with the region's political and economic institutions. Collectively, all four parameters form an environmental ethic.

Policy makers perennially reorganize or centralize natural resources agencies and restructure their missions in the hope of achieving at least some of these objectives. But no amount of reorganization of government agencies will help realize and promote an environmental ethic. First, reorganization does not address values. An environmental ethic must incorporate values amenable to diverse viewpoints, it must not consider economic efficiency the paramount value guiding government intervention, and it must take the long view of the benefits and costs of development. Changing the names, location, size, or relationship between natural resources agencies would not necessarily change the values of their engineers, planners, and other water resources professionals. Their values stem from long experience with solving problems in the manner expected by the agencies that employ them.

J. G. March and J. P. Olson contend that "Reorganization is a domain of rhetoric, trading, problematic attention, and symbolic action" (March and Olson, 1983: 291). While reorganization is often undertaken out of the noblest of political impulses, the fact remains that "in a society that emphasizes rationality, self-interest, and efficacy, politics honors administrative and realpolitik rhetoric. It provides symbolic and ritual confirmation of the possibility of meaningful individual and collective action" (March and Olson, 1983: 292). Symbols are important to politics, but they do not by themselves force changes in values.

Second, centralization only serves to heighten conflict between agencies. When personnel with different objectives are thrown together in a single agency, they tend to feel threatened. To some degree, the Garrison diversion controversy exemplifies this problem. In this conflictive environment, few people are free to address wrong-headed management techniques or the waste of natural resources.

Third, there is compelling evidence, exemplified by the discussion of groundwater management in chapter 3, that water policy should integrate quality and quantity issues into the same sets of decisions (Mosher, 1984a). Groundwater overdraft encourages the building of more surface water impoundments, which negatively affect the environment beyond depletion of aquifers. Nonpoint polluted runoff into surface waters may contaminate groundwater.

On the political level, however, the agencies that manage pollution issues, like the Environmental Protection Agency, differ from those charged with water resources development and project construction, like the Corps of Engineers and the Bureau of Reclamation. Public works agencies prefer structural methods to alleviate water problems and tend to treat even problems of water quality as problems of supply. The EPA and the Fish and Wildlife Service, on the other hand, tend to pursue regulatory and management strategies that emphasize such nonstructural methods as pretreatment of wastes and control of runoff. Thus, the integration of quality and quantity issues in the same water policy is heavily dependent upon interagency coordination.

A superficial interpretation of this problem might suggest that quality and quantity issues should be addressed by a coherent national department of natural resources. However, as was seen in the discussion of water law and water engineering in chapter 3, the integration of quality and quantity issues is contingent on reconciling divergent water use values and priorities.

Before one can propose specific administrative solutions to these problems, there must first be an agreement over policy goals and the responsibilities of participants in the water resources system. An environmental ethic can provide the basis for this agreement, and a comprehensive political-hydrological regional arrangement might make possible prior agreement upon rules for water allocation and quality. In the Garrison diversion controversy, however, the success of such an arrangement is contingent upon agreement over what constitutes acceptable risks, suitable benefits, and appropriate obligations by all major participants in the controversy.

The point is that resolution of these problems requires philosophical strategies, not structural ones. Members of a natural resources user system must agree upon goals and their priority as well as who will be allowed to participate in their formulation. The administrative organizations assigned to implement these goals can be decided upon later, through criteria of feasibility and efficiency. The need for such a bifurcation is illustrated by the Fish and Wildlife Service and the Bureau of Reclamation, two agencies with widely divergent philosophies and that are both part of the Department of the Interior. Significantly, they have both been charged with formulating philosophies for water use, which is why their mere presence in a single cabinet department has not encouraged coordination of water policy goals.

In this chapter, we discuss these issues by examining the components of a rational policy in the context of the administrative constraints of U.S. democracy. We then focus upon the political differences among water resources agencies as a source of irrational policy by focusing upon a case study: salinity in the Colorado River basin. Finally, consideration is given to alternatives to conventional reorganization, including improvement in planning.

Policy Structure and Policy Outcomes

All major actors in natural resources policy making are, in principle, committed to the ideal of a rational, normatively defensible policy. Few agencies set out to deliberately harm the environment, inflict unjust economic burdens on society, or ignore the obligations of beneficiaries to benefactors. Why, then, do natural resources policies so frequently fail? Generally, they are unable to overcome four obstacles: (1) defining the public interest, (2) defining equity, (3) encompassing the various dimensions of feasibility, and (4) controlling for transaction costs of policies or, in other words, costs entailed by the operation and maintenance of policies committed to by previous decisions.

The Elusive Public Interest in Natural Resources Policy

Contrary to popular misconceptions, even though water policy is fragmented and decentralized, there is no conspiracy to thwart the public will in environmental matters. All major actors in the policy process believe that the accomplishment of their goals leads to genuine achievement of a public interest. But what is the public interest in environmental policy? And why, if everyone wants to achieve it, is it so elusive?

One answer, put forth by Steven Kelman, contends that the basis for good public policy is the transcendence of self-interest. This goal is facilitated best when alternative points of view are expressed in the policy process. In essence, most policies fail to achieve what Kelman terms public spiritedness, because the policy process often discourages a genuine exchange of ideas. The role of government should be to "serve as a forum for public discussion of the value of different ways of life" (Kelman, 1987: 211).

However, the roots of U.S. governmental processes have become divorced from this original Madisonian approach. To many political scientists, public spiritedness is unnecessary and probably impossible, since the dominance of short-term self-interest is presumed to preclude general agreement upon ethical standards. Such an approach ignores ethical concerns (such as equity, noneconomic benefits, and participation by the public in decision making) unless they are also utilitarian. Moreover, such interest group interactions, with government viewed as a sort of impartial arbiter, often fail to protect small groups of unpopular persons from discrimination by the majority, a concern of Madison's (Kelman, 1987: 213–17; Madison, 1961).

Kelman is part of a long tradition of democratic theorists who advocate civic virtue. Achievement of that virtue and of a public interest needs to begin from the premise of a polity whose members accept that they are part of a coherent community in which each of their fates is tied to the fate of others inside their community and to nature. How can we accept such a premise, and why should we do so? We can do so through redefining relevant participants in the decision-making process and by explicitly raising justice to center stage in the allocation and distribution of resources. We need to do so to ensure that decisions will be equitable.

The making of resource decisions should not be reserved only for those with tangible, economic stakes they are likely to gain or lose. Instead, each and every citizen has a legitimate interest in the use of resources. In the Western democratic tradition, many political thinkers have passionately espoused this view, among them John Stuart Mill and Jean Jacques Rousseau. The former, a utilitarian and an advocate of pluralistic democratic decision making, conceded the need to consider minority rights in any concept of justice. The latter, on the other hand, sought to reconcile the classical liberal notion of a social contract stressing rights and liberties with a communitarian, non-self-interested framework for making decisions.

Mill was especially cognizant of the need to avoid radical, selfish individualism as a premise for justice. This is seen in the critique of his mentor, Jeremy Bentham, which reveals the apprehension of some early liberal thinkers in glorifying self-interest. In particular, Mill warns against accepting any principles of decision making that ignore "the impelling or restraining principles . . . or spiritual reflection [and] the existence of conscience" (Mill, 1962: 96, 99, 100). In his attempt to salvage utilitarianism from hedonism, Mill introduced the notion of a "unity of sentiment," which he borrowed from Aristotle, and which was designed to give shape to a larger public interest.

In "On Utilitarianism," Mill asserts that there is a natural sentiment binding all people together, stemming from our want of "happiness" and conditioned through our being taught that all interests "are to be considered equal" (Mill, 1962: 285). This sentiment leads us to identify our feeling with others, thus creating a natural sanction against selfishness. Unfortunately, however, Mill is not entirely clear as to whether this sentiment precedes the development of private interest or arises as a way to protect civic virtue in society. He hints that the latter is the case when he states: "if obedience to [these feelings] were not the rule . . . everyone would see in everyone else an enemy, against whom he must be perpetually guarding" (Mill, 1962: 316). Thus, this feeling appears hardly natural at all, but mechanistic and artificial and, thus, of limited force in arousing a feeling of communal fellowship.

Significantly, however, we owe to Mill a better understanding of the twentieth-century behavioral scientist's view of political interest, which takes its point of departure from utilitarianism inasmuch as it views political interests as aggregations of competing economic and social demands. Critics of this view, of whom there are many, contend that behavioral science has robbed utilitarianism of its passion and sense of community. Behavioralism atomizes and fragments the individual and assumes that he or she is a psychologically whole individual from birth, fully cognizant of his or her interests (Cropsey, 1977; Dewey, 1954, 1963; Maritain, 1951; Nisbet, 1962; Simon, 1960).

We need to base our inferences about the impulse for community within a larger framework for justice. Rousseau, among the many democratic theorists who have examined this problem, introduced a solution I believe is viable: the concept of the general will. While much maligned and misunderstood, Rousseau's premise is that obedience to a just community is, in reality, obedience to one's authentic self, which is over and above the physical impulses that shape our particular wills from time to time. We are capable of rising above avarice and self-interest through a moral commitment to the greater common interest of the polity. This is what Rousseau meant by *general will*. It is the opposite of *particular will*, or individual self-interest, and it is manifested whenever an individual examines the consequences of his or her actions upon the welfare of the larger community.

Taking a view quite different from other social contract theorists such as Thomas Hobbes or John Locke, Rousseau believed that self-preservation is not the driving force behind people's desire to form civil societies (Rousseau, 1967: 17). What they seek is "an association which may defend with the whole force of the community the person and property of each . . . yet may allow each to remain as free as before (Rousseau, 1967: 17).

What individuals gain from obedience to this general will is participation in a civic polity infused with regard for others and prepared to defend each citizen's rights and needs. This polity unleashes our potential for moral liberty, because each of us agrees to procedures for decision making that are not biased toward any individual's egoistic interest and do not enslave anyone to the interests of others.

What one gives up through the general will is the right of avarice, which Rousseau regarded as a source of slavery and a means of denying our capacity for good. Thus, by saying that obedience to the general will forces citizens to be free, what Rousseau really meant was that decisions made on behalf of self-interest reinforce our dependence upon childish impulse and materialism. Each of us sometimes has to be reminded that we are acting in our self-interest (Rousseau, 1967: 23, 33), just as an alcoholic might have to be forced to give up drink, however physically painful this may initially be, in order to regain moral freedom of choice and to reject slavery to physical impulse.

An example of this public interest approach in contemporary water policy is the opposition of radical environmental preservationists to the Blue Ridge project (discussed in chapter 6). In that case study, the values of these environmentalists, considered narrow and effete by the established actors in water policy, pointed up the deficiencies in the prevailing structural solutions to water problems. Thus, while these values, despite their unpopularity, should have been incorporated into the decision-making process at the outset, they were incorporated only through litigation and lobbying outside the normal channels of water resources policy making.

Proponents of the Blue Ridge project tried to exclude environmentalists from participation by asserting that they had no tangible stake in the outcome of the conflict. As it turned out, however, these environmentalists were supported by local residents who did have a tangible stake in the conflict: they were likely to lose their homes and jobs if this project was built. Although this fact in itself did not make the latter group competent to judge the merits of the Blue Ridge project, it did grant the group a special legitimacy to oppose it. Simply stated, the rules of the game in U.S. natural resources politics are based on the premise that natural resources are owned by the residents of the immediate region where they are found. Blue Ridge residents, as shall be seen, were able to exploit that sentiment.

These rules of the game are ethically ambivalent and, thus, inconsistent as a basis for defining the public interest. That is one lesson of Mill and Rousseau. Many people who lose jobs and homes without compensation are not particularly powerful and thus are not able to exert leverage upon policy. They can neither appeal to others to exercise a general will nor hope that the unity of sentiment Mill spoke of will be responsive to their needs and desires. Moreover, traditional benefit-cost analyses, by ignoring equity issues, assume that any net benefit to the economy of a particular region from a water project indirectly benefits everyone.

This is a problem exemplified by the Garrison diversion project. As will be recalled, local residents felt betrayed by the failure of the Bureau of Reclamation to undertake a large-scale irrigation project, which would have compensated them for the loss of bottomlands. In that case, however, the environmental appropriateness of such a compensation measure was open to question. Thus, the preferences of a minority who wanted compensation for their losses had to be balanced against the serious, extensive, and costly impacts to many more people.

In theory, the solution to this problem lies in expanding the boundaries of policy debate and thus increasing public participation. However, recent events illustrate the problem in accomplishing this relatively modest objective. For example, frustration over the effects of administrative fragmentation upon water quantity and quality, such as drought, groundwater depletion, and aging urban water supply infrastructure, has spawned a coalition called the National Water Alliance. Created in 1983 in reaction to the Reagan administration's cutting of federal funds for water planning and the dismantling of the Water Resources Council, the alliance sought to establish a national water resources research center and water information clearinghouse.

While the alliance is bipartisan and devoted to avoiding "any major water crises or emergency," its founder, Dennis De Concini, concedes that one of his major goals is to restore funding for the Central Arizona Project to be built in his state (Mosher, 1984a: 166). Rousseau would have called this an appeal to particular will.

Moreover, members of the alliance disagree over what constitutes a national water resources need. While De Concini views urban water problems, such as leaking aqueducts, as grave as the needs of western farmers and ranchers, other members of the alliance disagree, given budgetary constraints. Some alliance members even supported the dismantling of the Water Resources Council on grounds that too much control over water project spending was centered in the White House and too little influence over traditional water resources concerns (pork barrel projects) was centered in Congress (Mosher, 1984a).

An even more telling problem mars the prospects for success of such an alliance. While most reorganization discussions focus on the executive branch, few serious appraisals of the fragmentation of water policy consider how the fractured jurisdiction of congressional committees makes policy coordination and unification difficult. In the House, no fewer than eight committees comprising thirteen subcommittees oversee water policy, while in the Senate, four committees and ten subcommittees manage an array of water issues ranging from soil and water conservation to pollution, energy, public lands issues, and community development.

This is not the place to ponder why suggestions such as that of New Jersey Congressman Robert Roe, urging that one committee be invested with total jurisdiction over water resources, are not likely to be adopted (Mosher, 1984a: 167). Suffice it to say that, aside from the resistance of established committees to relinquish their present oversight control, there looms a larger question: Could such a supercommittee attain consensus over so broad an array of issues? More than likely, the answer would have to be in the negative, unless members of Congress could themselves agree on the priority to be accorded each of these issues.

When Is Equity Equitable?

Equity is a particularly difficult concept to defend in public policy because, as we have seen, what seems fair to one person or group often seems unfair to another. As regards water policy, competing perspectives on equity disagree on interbasin transfers as well as on the functions to be emphasized in the operation of particular water projects. As the Conservation Foundation (1984) suggests,

> people who have water offer the equity argument to oppose any action that might result in their receiving less, or paying more for what water they do receive. It is not equitable, the "haves" argue, to change the rules of the game. [Thus] several western states such as Montana restrict the transfer of water rights, especially out of irrigation . . . emphasizing the protection of existing cultures or lifestyles. (p. 368)

Those who have little water, on the other hand, are apt to posit a meliorative and somewhat rights-based definition of equity in water policy. In short, they often contend that the transference of water from those who have it to those who do not should be based on the criterion that everyone is entitled to a certain amount for various purposes. Particular laws written for the convenience of a region's original agricultural settlers, for example, may not be fair to newer, urban residents. By the same token, such laws may have excluded a region's original residents, such as native Americans. Oftentimes, water resources agencies adopt premises of equity suitable for the advancement of their particular missions.

The Corps of Engineers defines equity as the balancing of multipurpose water resources needs relative to the character and economic development of a region, defined not necessarily as a water resources region or river basin but sometimes as a highly localized subbasin. The corps tends to cling to this view even if a particular water project benefits only one area, fails to benefit others, or generates impacts harmful to a third. Likewise, the Bureau of Reclamation has historically defined equity as "western regional development," ignoring the fact that acreage placed under cultivation through federally subsidized irrigation in the Far West may necessitate taking acreage in other regions out of production because of overproduction of crops and the lowering of food prices.

Exemplifying these contending approaches are the competing roles of federal water resources agencies in the development of hydropower. This is a particularly vexing issue because hydropower is one of the few purposes of a water project that need not be incorporated in the project at its inception. In other words, it may be added later on if needs change or if some constituency demands it. As a general rule, when hydropower has been included in Corps of Engineers' projects, the decision has hinged upon four factors: (1) a guaranteed market for surplus power, (2) a large and diverse constituency of users, (3) a good fit between hydropower and the other missions of the corps, such as flood control and low-flow augmentation, and (4) local interests willing and able to support it.

The corps's hydropower projects are traditionally located in areas where regional development could be justified while, at the same time, economical energy alternatives have not been readily available. The project in the Columbia and in the Arkansas-White-Red river basins are two examples of this phenomenon. Conversely, there is a conspicuous absence of such hydropower projects in regions with large bituminous coalfields, such as the southern Appalachians. This is exemplified by the case of Summersville Dam on the Gauley River in West Virginia.

Summersville is the largest earth and rock-fill dam in the eastern United States. Despite having more than adequate head for hydropower generation when the dam was built in the early 1960s, the project did not include turbogenerators and penstocks on grounds that there were no markets for the power. After the 1973 oil embargo, however, low-cost hydropower became economically attractive, and the corps proposed the addition of turbogenerators at Summersville (Corps of Engineers, 1981).

Before the corps proceeded with the addition of hydropower facilities, however, it insisted that established purposes central to the project's and the corps's mission—flood control, water quality, and recreation—not be compromised by the addition of the hydropower facilities. It was also important to the corps that the Allegheny Power System, a consortium of private power companies serving the region, favored the project and would be allowed to purchase its power to resell to their customers. The corps did not want to compete with private utilities in the region by selling the power through publicly owned bodies such as Department of Energy power-marketing agencies.[1]

In other regions, similar patterns are revealed. While in theory the inclusion of hydropower is the result of rigorous feasibility studies and engineering and cost assessments, they in fact are often the product of a symbiotic relationship between local interests and the interests within a corps's district. This relationship makes the implementation of a single, nationwide standard for equity in water policy difficult, because local-district relations are inconsistent. The demands and needs of any two districts are not likely to be similar, nor is the political clout of local groups.

Local interests can express their water resources concerns at the corps's district level and place on the policy agenda issues that might otherwise lack an appropriate forum. The decentralized character of this process may provide a vehicle for weak interests to be nurtured, as the following case illustrates.

After World War II, in response to a burgeoning population in the region adjacent to the Brazos River in Texas, the corps formed the Fort Worth District by combining parts of other districts incorporating the Brazos drainage. According to corps historian, D. Clayton Brown, conflict between rural and urban residents of the district, coupled with the district's own search for a meaningful niche, led to the addition of hydropower to a project designed principally for flood control.

Residents of small communities and farms in and around the Brazos wanted the corps to include hydroelectric facilities in Whitney Dam, northwest of Waco, in order to supplement the meager amounts of power supplied by investor-owned utilities and rural electric cooperatives in the region. These residents found a naturally receptive forum in the corps's Fort Worth District, which was anxious to develop rapport with potential project supporters.

Urban residents of the district, residing in Waco and in small towns along the Trinity River, opposed inclusion of hydropower. They already had plentiful electricity and did not want any compromise in floodplain protection that might happen through the modifications in the dams for power production. They also believed that navigation was a higher economic priority than electricity and that it would also be compromised by power-generating facilities. In essence, they believed that the generation of electricity through the dam's penstocks could create excessive turbidity for navigation and lower flood storage capacity (D. Brown, 1980).

To compound matters, when the Fort Worth District included preliminary plans for hydropower facilities in the Brazos drainage project, the Federal Power Commission recommended against them because of negative benefit-cost ratios. The FPC argued that unregulated, plentiful natural gas, available throughout Texas, was a more efficient source of power (D. Brown, 1980).

The Fort Worth District did not back down from its original proposal, however. In order to establish its credibility as a servant of all residents, the district believed it had to try to achieve the goals of flood control, navigation, and power, simultaneously. In the end, the FPC could not stop the district from including hydropower at Whitney Dam. In order to appease all parties, however, the district offered assurances that hydropower would not compromise flood control (D. Brown, 1980). Nevertheless, the absence of an agreed upon formula for equity, exemplified by the Brazos basin, has lingering implications for both a national water policy and a national energy policy.

First, the corps could not afford to be politically neutral in this conflict. To do so might have been good public policy in the sense discussed earlier in this chapter (that an agency should view itself as implementing the public interest, not defining it), but neutrality would have jeopardized the corps's credibility among residents of the basin, particularly those most likely to promote its dam-building activities in the future. Second, while from one perspective, a single centralized process of decision making would probably have reached a decision regarding hydropower on broader, national criteria of efficiency, equity, and feasibility, the less powerful rural interests in this valley who sought a policy that would hasten economic development would have been thwarted. Not only would rural residents have felt slighted, but in a larger sense, their desires for a fairer distribution of the benefits of water resources development in their district might have been ignored at the expense of more powerful interests, giving them cause to feel unjustly treated.

Feasibility and Transaction Costs:
Economics Versus Technology

Natural resources policy decisions are, of necessity, projections about the future based on present-day demand patterns. By their very nature, such projections are subject to considerable error. In water policy, this error often leads to policy bias, exemplified by criticisms of the process of benefit-cost analysis itself. "Benefit-cost ratios are neither 'real' nor tangible. Rather, they are based on econometric models—theoretical projects of future economic behavior which are highly speculative in character and founded on assumptions which are open to question" (Wheeler, 1986: 90).

Ordinarily, because correct use of benefit-cost analysis requires a prediction of what will happen if certain decisions are not made, a bias in favor of development and exploitation of natural resources is by no means a foregone conclusion (Wheeler, 1986). In addition, those who use benefit-cost analysis do not ordinarily intend to thwart the public good by stressing monetary considerations over other policy considerations. It is simply that overreliance upon this tool may ignore the larger array of goals and interests that people have.

As exemplified by the attitude of the Tennessee Valley Authority toward water resources development in the mid-1960s, agencies often choose to assume that such projections are real, when in fact they are not. This is a particularly seductive trap for a large public works, mission-oriented bureaucracy whose planning orientations are based on projections extending over several decades. It was precisely such an orientation that led the TVA to dogmatically promote the Tellico Dam, even though few real economic or environmental justifications could be offered on its behalf (Wheeler, 1986: 90–110).

A broader problem is the disconformity between economic projections and technological change. Science often creates substitutes for resources not foreseen by most agencies because these advances do not fit their missions. The adequacy and utility of a resource is usually driven by pressures of price, determined by the supposed elasticity of supply and demand. If water is cheap enough to pollute without having to worry about the need to conserve it, then there will be little incentive not to pollute. Moreover, if it is supplied in abundance and at little direct cost, then it is likely to be overused despite the negative environmental consequences of overutilization.

On the other hand, if needed food supplies can be produced through cost-effective biotechnologies rather than by irrigating more acreage, then the cost of irrigation cannot be justified. In this instance, incentives to seek other solutions to the food crisis facing our globe become attractive. In other words, the economic feasibility and transaction costs of natural resources can be predicted only if economics and technology are understood to be interconnected (Crosson, 1982: 165–96). This interconnectedness between economics and technology is not understood by mission-oriented public works agencies, as demonstrated by the lack of congruence between their unchanging philosophies and the changing forces of supply and demand. These agencies (TVA, the Corps of Engineers, and the Bureau of Reclamation) came into existence animated by ideologies appropriate to the technological conditions of a bygone era.

In the case of the Corps of Engineers, these conditions were characterized by an expanding frontier and a lack of civilian competence in the field of natural resources management. The Bureau of Reclamation's approach to water resources development, on the other hand, reflects the view that land is valuable only if it is agriculturally productive and that the costs of irrigation are far outweighed by the benefits to a hungry, westward-expanding nation. This view was common in the early 1900s when the bureau was formed to provide irrigation water to southwestern settlers.

What this argument suggests about rational, normatively defensible natural resources policy is that, in assessing the benefits and costs of policy, it is necessary to determine the environmental costs of erosion, salinity, and pesticide runoff pollution resulting from irrigation. Since these costs are difficult to assess and are often indirect and take time to emerge, a prudent policy would be to examine the justifications for irrigation and other water intensive practices from a holistic standpoint, by looking at the entire spectrum of benefits and costs and the possible technologies that might increase the benefits or alleviate the costs. While information, too, has its costs, these costs rarely exceed the costs of forgone analyses, especially when considering the long-term, sometimes irreparable changes that might be wrought by decisions predicated upon incomplete information on environmental impacts.

If the negative environmental impacts of irrigation are far outweighed by agricultural yields that feed more people, then more irrigation projects may be justified. On the other hand, if other yield-increasing technologies are available that are cheaper and produce fewer and less-severe impacts than irrigation, then water policies should be changed to accommodate this fact.

As in the past, dramatic changes in natural resources technology were rarely anticipated by government planners (Crosson, 1982). Because of this fact, it is prudent not to become overly attached to the approaches of the agencies for which these planners work, since they are often the same ones that failed to anticipate these changes. Too often, these agencies are committed to fixed solutions to water problems, such as building more dams, diverting more water, and irrigating more deserts.

Over time, the environmental impacts of such "solutions" often prove to be irreversible or else expensive and difficult to reverse. Technology is most amenable to democracy when it is utilized to strengthen innovations in land and water resources management, not to heighten the power of vested institutions. This can be brought about by designing decision-making institutions in such a way that they encourage the viewpoints of nontechnologists as well as technologists. The Colorado River salinity problem exemplifies this argument.

The Colorado River Salinity Crisis: Technology, Values, and the Irrelevance of Reorganization

To Americans living east of the hundredth meridian (the so-called dividing line between the arid West and the wet East), the activities of the Bureau of Reclamation are simultaneously stupendous and enigmatic. The bureau has built this country's largest dams, yet its activities are relatively unfamiliar to easterners. Unlike the Corps of Engineers, whose mandate has evolved over time to incorporate many different water resources needs, the bureau's mission—the economic development and well-being of nineteen western states—has been unambiguous and clear-cut. This simple mission, however, while relatively free of political conflict in its region of operation, has nurtured single-purpose development and, in some instances, considerable environmental risk.

Beginning in the 1930s, the waters of the Colorado River, a bastion

Figure 5.1   Colorado River, Upper Basin

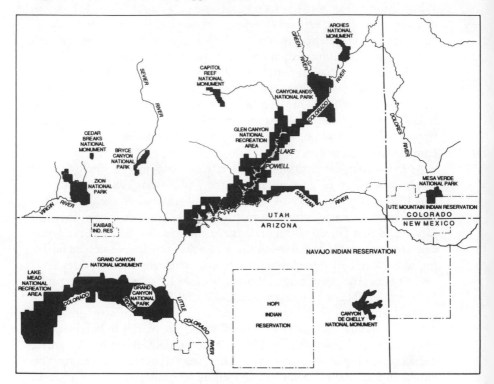

Source: Glen Canyon Dam (Washington, D.C.: Government Printing Office, 1965).

of bureau water resources development, began to increase in salinity. (Figures 5.1 and 5.2 depict the upper and lower basins of the Colorado River.) The principal dissolved cations in the Colorado are calcium, magnesium, and sodium, while the constituent anions are sulfate, chloride, and bicarbonate. When chemically combined, these dissolved solids produce heavy loadings of salts in the Colorado basin, which are harmful to agriculture, industry, and municipal use (Kleinman and Brown, 1980: 1).

About half of this salt comes from natural saline deposits in the upstream portion of the basin. It is the other half, produced from irrigation return flow over croplands, that is the greater source of concern. While these return flows increase the rate of salinity by dissolving constituents in the soil, a process known as *salt loading*, consumption of the river's fresh water by agriculture and burgeoning urban growth has increased at an alarming rate, preventing normal dilution of these

Figure 5.2 Colorado River, Lower Basin

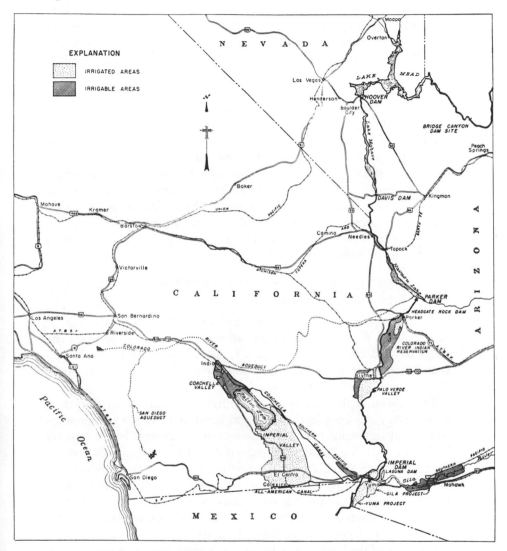

Source: Hoover Dam (Washington, D.C.: Government Printing Office, n.d.).

salts, which would keep their concentration low. This latter phenomenon is referred to as *salt concentrating.*

Of the 13.5 million acre-feet of average annual flow in the Colorado main stem, some 2.25 million acre-feet evaporate from large reservoirs such as lakes Mead, Powell, and Havasu. Another 2.1 million acre-feet are consumed by upper-basin irrigation, while about 1.7 are diverted to large cities such as Denver, Los Angeles, and Las Vegas. There are, of course, major diversions for intensive agricultural development in the Imperial and Coachella valleys, as well (Conservation Foundation, 1984: 374).

The Colorado is a major water resource in the intermountain West. Thus its degradation has an almost immeasurable effect on the quality of life in this region. Increased salt concentrations decrease crop yields and increase production costs for both agricultural and industrial users. To the average household consumer, the effects may be no less detrimental. Problems caused by salinity include reduced life of water-utilizing equipment, lowered palatability of drinking water, and, at higher salt concentrations, negative health effects. Moreover, in the absence of deliberate efforts to control salinity, this phenomenon is expected to increase as development of the Colorado basin advances (Kleinman and Brown, 1980: 1).

From Structural to Nonstructural Solutions:
Desalination Policies

Like the recipe for rabbit stew that begins with "first, catch a rabbit," early policies toward the Colorado salinity problem focused upon the single-minded goal of catching the Colorado basin's salt. What prevented planners from tackling the problem on a multidimensional basis? The answer is jurisdictional control.

The Bureau of Reclamation is essentially the only water resources agency with influence in the Colorado basin. All major water projects on the main stem and tributaries have been constructed by the bureau, beginning with the Boulder Canyon project in the early 1930s and extending through the Colorado River storage project (Glen Canyon and Flaming Gorge dams) of the 1960s. Moreover, all multipurpose plans for the use and development of the resources of the Colorado River have been designed and built by the bureau and have been defended, largely, by reference to regional agricultural benefits.

Residents of the lower basin, below Lee's Ferry, have long favored this approach because, even though it eliminates input from other agencies and minimizes discussion of alternative approaches to the management of the Southwest's water resources, it encourages structural solutions that produce the benefits traditionally favored by most residents: irrigation, cheap hydropower, and in some instances, flood control and recreation. In essence, because the costs of such projects are diffused throughout society, residents of the lower basin have sacrificed a meaningful voice in their design in exchange for not having to bear the financial burden of their construction (Ingram, 1978).

Proposals to mitigate the salinity problem reveal this phenomenon in operation. In 1974, Congress approved a scheme to construct a multi-million dollar desalting plant in Yuma, Arizona, in order to meet treaty obligations with Mexico to deliver some 1.5 million acre-feet per year of Colorado River water (Conservation Foundation, 1984: 374). The plan relied upon an expensive, technologically complex structural measure (which would also consume a great deal of energy) to solve a problem created by other technologically complex structural measures—large impoundments along the main stem of the Colorado River. This plan has come under criticism from many quarters, including a former Bureau of Reclamation director, who admitted that such a project cannot stand up to rigorous benefit-cost analysis. It would be more costly to taxpayers than simpler management measures undertaken by individual farmers (Conservation Foundation, 1984: 374).

As a result of such criticisms, and in response to worsening salinity, the bureau and water user interests in the basin are looking closely at another alternative: curtailing activities likely to cause salinity. In cooperation with the Department of Agriculture, an on-farm program is attempting to reduce saline return flows and to conserve irrigation water. The latter is a practice long sought by critics of intensive water use in this region. The problem is that the Bureau of Reclamation, assigned lead responsibility for assessing various measures to reduce salinity, continues to insist that comparisons between various reduction methods should be assessed largely on the basis of efficiency. Also, the bureau still holds fast to its structural alternative to resolve salinity problems. Agriculture thus remains the dominant policy consideration, despite changes in the economic character of the region and despite potential technological changes affecting agricultural productivity.

Conceding that more water is unlikely to be made available and that salinity imposes negative environmental and economic impacts upon all water users in the Colorado basin, the bureau has recently attempted to determine the comparative economic impacts of less structurally based mitigation measures. It is examining several management techniques: augmenting water in the basin through diversion from outside the basin; curtailing future water resources development; and imposing certain demands on water users.

These demands include irrigating less acreage in order to increase the leaching of salts by applying the same amount of water to a smaller area; installing special drains, ditch linings, sprinkler and drip irrigation systems; increasing the frequency of irrigation; planting salt-tolerant or salt-resistant crops; installing pumps to lower groundwater tables and thus provide more efficient drainage of cropland; and leveling farms to achieve more uniform water application (Kleinman and Brown, 1980: 4). The bureau has concluded that these techniques will require individual investments ranging from $50 an acre for leveling to upwards of $600 an acre for sprinkler irrigation.

A bureau-sponsored report detailing salinity damage to industrial and municipal users as well as to agriculture chronicles the monetary impacts of damage to water heaters, dishwashers, toilet flushing mechanisms, garbage disposals, and washing machines and estimates the costs of substitute water sources (Kleinman and Brown, 1980: 4). "Salinity is not believed to be a major problem [to industry] when compared to the associated damages of municipal and agricultural users" (Kleinman and Brown, 1980: 16).

While the effects of salinity on human health have proven more elusive, researchers agree that they are potentially serious. For example, water supply systems may deteriorate, adversely affecting the quality of drinking water. Even more problematic, higher salinity levels increase the hardness of water, necessitating the use of more soaps and detergents for bathing and washing clothes, burdening water with phosphates and other pollutants that require removal.

The most serious and uncontrollable problem in this matrix, however, is the rapid and incessant growth in demand for Colorado River water caused by the influx of new residents. The completion of the Central Arizona Project, designed to divert significant amounts of water for municipal, industrial, and agricultural use, extends the effects of salinity to an additional 245,000 households. An option being explored is mixing this water with water from aquifers in order to dilute salinity (Kleinman and Brown, 1980: 14). The report on these options displays less concern over the costs to consumers than the direct and indirect costs to farmers (Kleinman and Brown, 1980).

What is likely to come of these and other studies? On the one hand, a better understanding of the causes, consequences, and mitigation measures necessary to deal with salinity is emerging throughout the basin. This is leading to slow, yet methodical adoption of techniques that, over time, can reduce the level of human-induced salinity throughout the basin. However, Colorado River salinity problems will remain serious. For one thing, it is not clear that the Bureau of Reclamation alone has the ability to resolve this problem in a manner that can accommodate efficiency, equity, feasibility, and noneconomic concerns. Second, current solutions to this problem constitute an example of how society pays twice for mistakes in water policy—the first time to augment the supply of water for agriculture in the Colorado River basin, and the second time to alleviate problems created by the first solution.

Avoiding Gratuitousness: What Also Could Be Done?

What is most frustrating about the Colorado River's salinity plight is that better planning could have avoided much of the problem at the outset. The tendency of the river to become saline was recognized by settlers at least as far back as the great lower-basin floods of 1905–7, which transformed the Salton Sink into an inland sea when makeshift banks in the Imperial Valley failed to hold back the raging waters of the Colorado (Bureau of Reclamation, 1948). In some respects, the Colorado River salinity problem exemplifies the resistance of nature to human control and the limits of a natural resources governance predicated upon a rationalistic, engineering view (Bennett, 1987).

After this disaster, large water storage units were built to even out the cycles of stream depletion and flooding. Accounts of the formation of the Colorado River Compact of 1922, the legal agreement between Arizona, California, Colorado, Nevada, New Mexico, Utah, and Wyoming that led to construction of the first large impoundment on the main stem (Hoover Dam), compel the conclusion that the complexities of western water law made any other solution untenable at the time.

Under the law of prior appropriation, practiced in one form or another by all of the basin states except California (which practices a combination of riparian and prior appropriation doctrine), claims to water are based on timing. The first settlers in a region can rightfully claim first use for beneficial purposes. Unfortunately, residents of each basin state believed they equally could claim such rights, since there was no single basinwide appropriation policy but only a separate appropriation law for each state.

By the early 1920s, it began to occur to many basin interests that the stream flow of the Colorado simply could not support all anticipated plans for diversion and irrigation proposed by residents of the several states and defended by reference to prior appropriation doctrine. Compounding this problem was the desire of established interests in states in the upper basin for protection against water loss. Although residents of these states had not yet formulated plans for intensive agricultural use of the Colorado's headwaters, they wanted to reserve that option for the future (Bureau of Reclamation, 1948: 46).

A 1922 U.S. Supreme Court decision, in *Colorado v. Wyoming,* only made matters more difficult by ruling that the only equitable means of apportioning the flow of the Colorado between upper and lower basin states would be to grant first priority to the oldest individual rights, regardless of state boundaries. One result of this ruling was an anarchic rush into water resources development, with states furiously scrambling to develop the Colorado River in a way advantageous to their apportioned lot of the river, fearing that other states would try to do the same thing if they did not act first.

The culmination of these events was construction of the Hoover Dam and the attitude throughout the basin that their problems could be addressed only by the federal government and only by massive structural solutions. Thus, regardless of which water resources agency was assigned the task of resolving these conflicts—the Corps of Engineers, the Bureau of Reclamation, or another agency—it is unlikely that solutions would have been very different.

Conclusions: Planning as an Ethic

Had the potential for technological change in agriculture been anticipated, or at least thought to be possible, many salinity problems in the Colorado basin could have been averted. First, drip irrigation as well as water reuse, where its application is appropriate, could result in less salt dilution and more water conservation, while still producing food. Not only would this be equitable and environmentally sound, since more clean water would be available for other users in the seven basin states and Mexico, it is economically more efficient, as well. Food yields could be improved at less cost. Nationwide, agricultural irrigation accounts for approximately 80 percent of all consumptive uses of water (Corps of Engineers, 1978: 78; Bergsrud, 1978: 60).

Second, alternatives to impoundments could have been entertained. If the fundamental issue relating to the overuse and development of the Colorado's resources was the failure to find an equitable means of dividing the upper and lower basins, better and less expensive ways to do so were available than reliance upon massive dams. An effective river basin commission system could have managed the division of water and guaranteed deliveries of prearranged amounts. Price-driven incentives to conserve water during periods of low flow could have been imposed, and long-range regional planning to anticipate changing patterns of water use could have been undertaken. Moreover, when it is considered that evaporation and water seepage from large reservoirs cost millions of gallons of water per year, it is apparent that the appropriateness of large impoundments for the hot, arid climate of the Southwest was not weighed sufficiently.

Third, the secondary costs of salinity, costs expended to clean the river, could have been averted. This would leave more resources for water management, while lessening expenditures for resolving water hardness problems, replacing household and industrial water-using devices, and treating water-related health problems.

Finally, developments that encouraged population growth in the

Figure 5.3. The Water Policy Planning Process of the 1970s

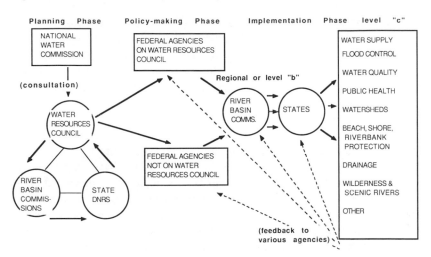

Southwest—air conditioning; the growth of the military-industrial complex attracted to the Southwest for its climate, isolation, and security; and improvements in transportation systems—could have been incorporated into economic development plans undertaken by engineers and others who were predicting robust economic growth. This might have made for a more equitable water policy. It makes no sense to encourage water use for intensive agriculture when the region is becoming predominantly urban.

The concept of water resources planning, as it germinated in the 1930s and became more sophisticated and refined by the 1970s, provides some models to accommodate change and to avoid gratuitous policy. Had such planning models been given the opportunity to work, and had they been established and funded within all river basins, countervailing values in water policy, values different from those held by any single agency, might have flourished.

One model is depicted in figure 5.3, which illustrates the basic components of the water policy planning system of the 1970s. Ironically, this planning system was itself quite unplanned. It evolved as an attempt to integrate public participation in all levels of policy formulation with the coordination of government agency activities across layers of government. The most important single element of this planning system was its emphasis upon fiscal responsibility. It was guided by the premise that alternatives to conventional dam building should be explored, costs should be shared across governments, and the search for more efficient means of providing water services should be encouraged (U.S. Senate, 1978a).

If it was so promising, why did it not continue? A somewhat simplistic answer is that powerful, traditional interests in water policy opposed reforms that might lead to the centralization of planning, to a shift of water policy authority to the executive branch of government and away from Congress, and to federal cost controls that would have discouraged more water projects. While this answer is largely valid, there is a better explanation; policy uncertainty. There were, and continue to be, widespread fears over what a comprehensive planning system would look like and what obligations it would entail.

An example of this fear, relevant for the Colorado basin, was the experience of the National Water Commission, depicted in figure 5.3. The commission was charged with solving water problems through government reorganization, policy redirection, and assessing the interface between the natural and social characteristics of water. While the commission had few constraints placed upon it, some of these constraints, on reflection, may have proved fatal for its long-term credibility. In particular, it was expressly forbidden to consider interbasin transfers. The great fear was that merely studying this issue would give rise to political movements to nationalize river basins and move water from region to region. This prohibition likely prevented the formation of river basin commissions across the southern United States and, in particular, along the Colorado basin (Howe, 1979: 33).

A final and more compelling uncertainty is the notion of policy trade-offs, a term bandied about among planners and politicians but rarely explained. Various uses of water often prove contradictory and self-defeating if pursued in the same place at the same time. For example, if one wants to maximize flood control, it may make no sense to build a dam to generate large amounts of hydropower. Likewise, if replenishment of water resources in a particular region through adequate rainfall is unlikely, then encouraging two different consumptive uses—agriculture and steam power plants, for example—may make no sense.

To actually make these trade-offs, however, is to commit to difficult choices based usually on assumptions of austerity or of limits on money, water, or time. Since political officials must be responsive to a variety of interests, it is difficult to make these choices and risk angering any set of water users. In principle, this should be the advantage of comprehensive planning. Such planning, by compelling interstate cooperation, compacts, and agreements, commits everyone in a basin to rules for managing resources. Each state is responsible for decisions, because, in theory, all river basin commission members agree to abide by the rules for the greater good of the basin.

Unfortunately, even planning involves making trade-offs. Comprehensive planning requires the active involvement in decisions by citizens and government officials. In the Four Corners states of the Colorado basin—Arizona, Colorado, New Mexico, and Utah—this is precisely what state officials least want to do regarding water resources management. Because increases in supply are unlikely to occur, the only option open to state legislators is to encourage cutbacks in water use among their voters, which can be politically suicidal. Thus, state legislators continue to forgo active involvement in water resources policy, and few residents of these states want enforced cutbacks on water use (Ingram, Laney, and McCain, 1979: 299–302).

The only remaining alternative is a federal solution, whose failure can be blamed on outside interests, and whose success, if any, will impose few direct monetary costs on the region. This is not a problem unique to the Colorado basin or to the West. As shall be seen in chapter 6, while water problems may vary from region to region, the failure to accommodate public participation in meaningful ways may cause concerted opposition to policies undertaken in response to social changes. If benefits to a region from an agency's actions are not seen as valuable, then even deferral to an outside solution may be unacceptable.

6　The Blue Ridge Pump Storage Project:

Conservation, Preservation, and the

Search for an Environmental Ethic

The [Blue Ridge] project will make a shell out of Grayson County. . . . We've been sold out by our politicians. . . . We are asked to produce electricity here to keep people half way across the country warm in winter, then cool in summer. It hardly seems fair to destroy our river and way of life to do it.
—D. T. PAINTER

Construction of the [Blue Ridge] dams would create a new and better river environment for many people in the region.
—WILLIAM LEVY

The Defeat of the Blue Ridge Project as a Microcosm of Environmental Policy Change

On 11 September 1976, a decade-long struggle to protect one of the last white-water tracts in the eastern United States reached its culmination. On that date, President Gerald Ford Signed Senate Bill 158 (An Act to Amend the Wild and Scenic Rivers Act), which designated a 26.5-mile stretch of the New River in North Carolina as a National Scenic River (Schoenbaum, 1979; U.S. Senate, 1976). This act remanded a license to construct a pump storage hydropower plant on the New River in North Carolina and Virginia, which had been granted to the American Electric Power Company. While President Ford's signature signified the victory of a coalition of environmentalists, white-water enthusiasts, and local residents, preservationist goals triumphed not because of widespread agreement on their preeminence but because of a unique collaboration of political forces.

The theme of this chapter is that the coalition opposed to the Blue Ridge project concurred upon one vital point, that a relatively undeveloped water resource serving local residents is preferable to a project whose benefits would serve, and be controlled by, groups residing outside the affected region. This case study exemplifies two recent, interconnected trends affecting water and other environmental policy in the United States: (1) an increasing public resistance toward government-endorsed but privately owned projects that are not economically viable without heavy public subsidy (one measure of a gratuitous policy), and (2) an increasing government resistance to such projects if they are so complex and esoteric as to be unable to marshal significant public support.

The Blue Ridge project most of all exemplifies the ongoing debate between preservationist and conservationist values. Project proponents, who defended the project on conservationist grounds, were unable to meet their own criteria of good policy. They were unable to show how the public would benefit from a hydropower project that consumed more energy than it produced. As a result, the public ended up choosing preservationism, not because it was valued as intrinsically preferable, but because it offered the least change in the status quo.

Other recent environmental policies exemplify many of the same issues. The Clinch River breeder reactor, initially canceled by the Carter administration and then revived by President Reagan, was finally canceled in 1983 largely due to the concerted efforts of the National Taxpayers Union, the Heritage Foundation, and several antinuclear groups (*Energy and the Environment*, 1985: 76–81).

The so-called Storm King pump storage project on the Hudson River, proposed by the Consolidated Edison Company of New York, encountered both strong bureaucratic support and popular opposition. After satisfying the economic and technical requirements of the Corps of Engineers and the Federal Power Commission, the project was untracked by environmental groups concerned with the project's impacts upon fisheries, stream flow, and regional aesthetics. A coalition comprising the Sierra Club, the National Audubon Society, and the Natural Resources Defense Council joined forces with the City of New York, which was concerned with the economic impact of the project on Con Ed's customers (Sheinbaum, 1983; Talbot, 1972).

The Blue Ridge project, while not as well known as, for example, the Garrison diversion or the Clinch River breeder reactor, aptly reveals the need for reform in the way environmental policy is formulated. The reason for this is twofold. First, the Blue Ridge project was dominated by the so-called iron triangle of interest groups, congressional public works committees, and water resources management agencies. In this particular instance, the water resources agencies were the Corps of Engineers, the Federal Power Commission, and the Environmental Protection Agency (Mann, 1985; Miller, 1985). Demands for local control of natural resources, for the preservation of scenic wonders, for the termination of interest group subsidies, and for more rigorous clarification of the benefits, costs, and objectives of resource policies are all exemplified by this case. These demands led to a breakdown of the iron triangle.

Second, the project's defeat tells us a great deal about the consequences of not having an environmental ethic in natural resources policy. In essence, opponents of the project successfully labeled proponents *exploiters*, even though these proponents had good reasons for thinking the project would support balanced, sustained growth. Regardless of which side was correct, and there is sufficient criticism of both extremes to go around, one lesson of the Blue Ridge project is that technically respectable arguments failed to win political support for the project because of their perceived complexity and social inequity and because of the lack of public trust in the engineers and planners who worked for the government agencies and private enterprises promoting the project.

Evolution of Blue Ridge: Proponents, Opponents, and the Problem of a Conservationist Ethic

When the Appalachian Power Company (APCO), a subsidiary of the American Electric Power Company of New York, applied for a license to build a pump storage hydroelectric project in the New River valley in February 1965, few of the residents of Grayson County in Virginia or Ashe and Alleghany counties in North Carolina expressed much concern. What made the absence of criticism especially curious was the APCO's proposal was the culmination of years of effort (Schoenbaum, 1979: 47; *New York Times*, 1965) and was thus by no means unexpected.

Under the Federal Power Act of 1920, all proposals for hydroelectric projects must receive prior approval from the Federal Power Commission.[1] The FPC's mandate is to ensure that multipurpose planning objectives such as flood control, water quality, and the potential for power markets are adequately assessed in plans by public or private bodies to impound navigable streams (Seidman, 1970: 44; White, 1969: 34). These relatively limited powers are a concession to the federal government's own water resources agencies, the Corps of Engineers and the Bureau of Reclamation in particular. These agencies are concerned that other water policy actors enhance, or at least do not detract from, their own watershed programs.

In reconciling itself to this balance of power, the FPC has often been accused of serving as a patron for the nation's investor-owned electric utilities. While independent regulatory commissions such as the FPC do become tied to regulated interests due to lack of independent expertise, reliance upon congressional support, and a wish to promote the regulated industry's goals, it is inaccurate to charge the FPC with not being able to make independent policy judgments.[2] In fact, the FPC frequently embraces policies that discourage hydropower projects.

For example, the FPC often assesses project viability by examining the potential spillover effects from power projects, which serves to discourage projects lacking broad economic justification. In addition, although critics charge that the FPC rarely authorizes higher rates during peak usage periods—an incentive to conserve electricity—for fear this might lessen the need for new projects, such a criticism is outdated and simplistic. The FPC has made efforts to bring the charges for electricity from licensed projects in line with the marginal costs of its production. Subsequent to passage of the Public Utilities Regulatory Policy Act of 1978, state public utility commissions, as well as the FPC, have adjusted their rate structures to reflect peak use by authorizing time of use, seasonal rates, and demand charges (Schoenbaum, 1979: 84; Webster, 1969; *Nation*, 1976; P. Davis, 1983).

As a result, the FPC's outlook is shaped as much by economic perceptions as by so-called territorial imperatives. During the 1960s, when it appeared that nationwide demand for electricity would inexorably increase, the FPC encouraged rapid electric utility growth. When this high-demand climate shifted to one characterized by austerity and conservation in the mid-1970s, as a result of the Arab's oil embargo, so did the attitudes of the FPC. It is against this setting that the Blue Ridge project must be assessed.

Controversies over Benefit-Cost Analysis

At the outset, APCO requested a twin-reservoir project, costing around $140 million and consisting of an upper reservoir of 16,600 acres at full pool and a lower reservoir of 2,850 acres, from which water would be repumped into the upstream lake during periods of slack demand. This project would have a total installed capacity of 980 megawatts. At the time of this proposal, APCO also applied for an FPC license to construct a 60,000-kilowatt plant at the Corps of Engineers' Bluestone Dam on the New River 140 miles downstream in West Virginia (Laycock, 1975; *New York Times*, 1965). The setting of the Blue Ridge project is depicted in figure 6.1.

A critical juncture in the project's history was reached in June 1966. Prior to FPC licensing, the Department of the Interior asked the commission to delay approval, pending modification of the project for purposes of downstream pollution mitigation. At this time, Interior was

Figure 6.1   The Setting of the Proposed Blue Ridge Project as Envisioned by the American Electric Power Company

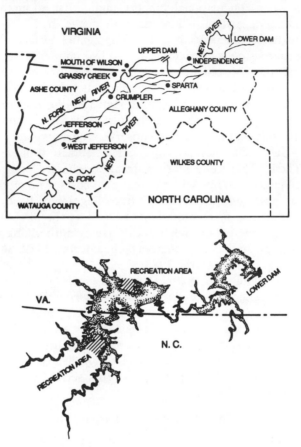

Source: Schoenbaum, 1979.

responsible for enforcing federal clean water laws, then in their infancy but gradually becoming strengthened—a fact of consequence for the fate of Blue Ridge, as shall be seen. Interior wanted enough storage capacity included in the reservoirs to dilute pollution from the large chemical complexes centered around Charleston, West Virginia, during periods of low flow in the Kanawha River. (The New becomes the Kanawha about thirty-five miles downstream of Charleston at a point called Gauley Bridge.)

The FPC, responding to this mandate, ordered APCO to modify its plans accordingly, and in June 1968 the company submitted a design for

Table 6.1 Original and Modified Proposals for the Blue Ridge Project

Item	Original Project	Modified Project	Percentage Change
Upper reservoir area	16,600 acres	26,000 acres	61
Lower reservoir area	2,850 acres	12,390 acres	435
Estimated project cost	$140 million	$430–$850 million[a]	325–607
Upper dam		300 ft. high, 1,500 ft. long	
Lower dam		236 ft. high, 2,000 ft. long	
Anticipated relocations	500 people	3,000–5,000 people (200–900 families)	600–1,000

Sources: Schoenbaum, 1979, p. 49; Laycock, 1975; *Time*, 1976, p. 68; Kenworthy, 1971; 1974a.
[a] 1965–76.

a project roughly twice the size of the original (Webster, 1969). The size and scope of the modified and original APCO proposals for Blue Ridge are compared in table 6.1.

The modified project would almost double the generating capacity of the original design, raising it to 1,800 megawatts. The plan caused an immediate outcry from valley residents. First, as revealed by table 6.1, the increase in the project's size multiplied the number of family relocations in the valley. Second, there were strong objections to the destruction of prime farmland to provide peak power for persons living hundreds of miles from the valley. Both of these anticipated impacts were thought to derive from a callousness toward the folkways and values of the New River valley's residents (Mizell, 1972).

Most compelling of all, however, was that these criticisms focused upon specific economic costs of the project not explicitly addressed by APCO's plans. These costs included

- the loss of ancestral homes and farms owned by some families for over 200 years;
- the erosion of the property tax base of three counties in two states;
- the busing of schoolchildren many additional miles due to the inundation of several roads;
- the destruction of prime farmland with an annual yield conservatively estimated at $13.5 million,[3] a cost that APCO conceded was not outweighed by anticipated tax and other benefits of the project;
- the establishment of a recreation industry of dubious value, since drawdowns from the upper reservoir would create large mudflats along the New River (Schoenbaum, 1979: 52; Webster, 1969);

- harmful impacts upon downstream fisheries and riparian habitat due to excessive fluctuations of the river and cold-water releases into warm-water streams (Laycock, 1975; Mizell, 1972; *New York Times*, 1971a); and
- skepticism over the efficacy of using stored water behind the dams for flushing out downstream pollution (Kenworthy, 1971; *New York Times*, 1971a, 1971b).

What made all of these objections credible was the Department of the Interior's intervention in enlarging the project's original design. There is a long and venerable tradition in American environmental thought that constitutes the intellectual foundation for many water, energy, and environmental policies. This tradition, usually labeled *conservationism*, has roots in nineteenth-century utilitarianism.

Conservationism posits that natural resources are utilized most efficiently, and on behalf of the greatest number of citizens, when they produce sustained yields for present and future generations through the application of technology. This approach may be more accurately labeled a benefit-cost optimizing view of development that tries to balance use and preservation of natural resources.

Benefit-Cost Optimization as a Conservationist Approach: Implications for the Blue Ridge Project

In chapters 1 and 2, it was suggested that one barrier to the articulation of an environmental ethic in American public policy is the fact that conservation encompasses a number of different strategies for natural resources management, which are neither synonymous nor compatible. Moreover, the conservation tradition as it has evolved in American politics had proven amenable to the development of natural resources, so long as that development is restrained by prudent limitations upon exploitation. These limitations are supposed to be based on a resource's natural processes of recuperation.

As espoused by such environmental luminaries as Gifford Pinchot (1865–1946), father of the U.S. Forest Service, conservation meant the use of science and technology to guide "an intensely felt hope for social betterment" (Hays, 1958: 41). It was an optimistic, liberal, and development-oriented doctrine, which exhibited profound faith in the ability of the human race to overcome virtually all natural obstacles. This doctrine has generally been favored by planners, engineers, and natural resources economists, while natural scientists have usually subscribed to more preservationist approaches to natural resources, which see narrower limits to growth, development, and modification of the environment (Luten, 1980: 129). How are these two doctrines related to the Blue Ridge project?

Although it has come under attack in recent years for its allegedly materialistic bias and naive confidence in the reversibility of negative environmental impacts, the benefit-cost optimizing approach to conservation, sometimes relying on benefit-cost studies of proposed water projects, is highly regarded in most quarters. The reason for this is that the benefit-cost optimization approach is seen as a philosophically well-grounded alternative to a purely exploitive view of the environment, in which short-run economic returns are the only bases for policy.

Prior to the advent of the benefit-cost approach, it was rarely emphasized that natural resources are finite, require careful management to be sustained, and can be irreparably harmed by overutilization. Moreover, although Pinchot's own Forest Service has recently been accused of adopting a purely exploitive view of forest resources (through clear-cutting of trees in Alaska and other parts of the United States, for example), Pinchot would not have approved of these practices. He opposed practices that would liquidate natural resources under appropriate price conditions, reasoning that the multipurpose character of national forests as wildlife preserves and watersheds made them irreplaceable and dictated a balanced approach to their management (Pinkett, 1978).

Three characteristics of the benefit-cost optimization approach help to promote prevailing government water policies. First, the approach favors policies that promote efficient and equitable utilization of resources through public expenditure. Thus, a water project in a particular region could be justified as compensation for losses due to other policies affecting that region (Ingram, 1978). This implies that local control of resources, a cherished tradition in the United States, is appropriate, and that it is the job of the national government to promote prosperity in particular regions, even at the expense of nature.

Second, proponents of this approach are optimists. If wisely used, they reason, water and other natural resources can last indefinitely. In all cases, wise use means developing and augmenting resource yields, not preserving them in a pristine state, as preservationists advocate.

Finally, benefit-cost optimizers are guided by a human-centered and practical outlook toward nature. Resources are viewed as economic commodities to be exchanged and utilized. Thus, in weighing the economic value of a particular policy alternative in water resources development, a conservationist will pose two types of questions: for example, What are people willing to pay to keep a white-water stream like the New River undeveloped? (economic benefits from tourism could stem from such a policy); and Will preservation of the New River or other water resources have other human uses, such as continued access to the shoreline and to riparian habitat? As shall be seen, these were the very types of questions posed by opponents of the Blue Ridge project. It was largely the failure of proponents to provide convincing answers to these questions that contributed to the defeat of the project.

Applying Benefit-Cost Optimization to Blue Ridge: The Failure of Conservationism

In the incipient stages of the Blue Ridge Project, APCO spokesmen argued that the project's benefits would be widely distributed through-out the region. Consistent with this optimizing approach, project ad-vocates further attempted to convince community leaders throughout the New River valley that construction of a hydroelectric plant, and resulting flat-water recreational benefits, constituted progress, by any reasonable standard. The major selling point was that opposition to such a project was extremely provincial (Schoenbaum, 1979: 49).

The Interior Department's intervention to force enlargement of the project ultimately delayed the licensing of Blue Ridge and led to its defeat. Initially, however, proponents viewed these changes as additional evidence of the project's multipurpose objectives. Thus, APCO and the FPC argued, the project would spur economic growth in a long-depressed region; would substantially increase one utility's ability to respond to peak electrical demand, an issue that took on special im-portance after the Arab oil embargo of 1973–74 (*Time*, 1976); and would enhance downstream water quality while possibly reducing air pollu-tion.

Each of these justifications falls squarely within the traditional ben-efit-cost optimization approach to conservation. By stressing the im-portance of water projects to the enhancement of social welfare, these justifications further converged with Gifford Pinchot's view of conser-vation as "the development and wise use of resources [which] aligned itself with the developmental thrust of American politics . . . with the constraint that renewable resources should be used only on the basis of 'sustained yield'" (Caulfield, 1978: 115). The FPC frequently embraced such arguments in its licensing proceedings for Blue Ridge. The FPC staff argued that the project would not injure renewable resources, since releases from the proposed lower impoundment would be limited to 3,000 cubic feet per second, an amount biologists deemed safe for aquatic life downstream of the project (Kenworthy, 1971).

Opponents of the project exploited three characteristics of these ar-guments in an attempt to disparage it. First, neither APCO nor the FPC demonstrated that the project would fill a gap in the extensive power generation network of the American Electric Power Company or that the power would directly benefit the New River region. This is one of the implicit parameters of the benefit-cost optimizing approach to conservation.

The Blue Ridge project was not designed to produce new power for APCO at all. Its purpose was to augment the firm generating capacity of the utility. Blue Ridge would actually use power from other APCO plants during slack demand periods to pump water back into the upper reservoir. Like most pump storage hydropower projects, Blue Ridge would consume more energy than it would produce; three kilowatts for every 2 kilowatts generated (Kenworthy, 1973d). While justification for such a project might appear incongruous, since the off-peak power used to refill the upper lake would be cheaper per kilowatt hour than would the substitute peak power APCO would otherwise have to purchase, the project was based on sound economic grounds. Thus, it was fully justifiable from the standpoint of a benefit-cost optimizing approach, which emphasizes efficiency.

Politically, however, the strategy proved awkward for proponents to explain to valley residents. The economic reasoning behind the project was so complex and esoteric that it was difficult to sell to the average person, a significant fact for democratic theory. Project opponents wisely focused on overall net increases in power, not on the internal economics of operating a large public utility. Had APCO anticipated this objection, it might have sought to defuse this controversy at the incipient stages of the project.

Second, the logic of a pump storage project did not fit well with APCO and FPC's other major economic justification for the project, that Blue Ridge would lessen U.S. dependence upon imported oil. The project could conceivably have produced fuel savings for APCO, since the stored energy repumped into the upper impoundment would be produced with less initial power. However, little imported oil was used for generating electricity in the New River area or even the greater Ohio Valley. Most fossil fuel plants in this region were coal fired, not oil fired. In short, this argument was also esoteric and compounded the difficulty in defending the project on grounds that it would constitute a partial panacea to energy shortages. Because the project would neither reduce dependence upon foreign energy supplies nor produce new power, it did not represent a viable economic base for sustained growth, an expectation of the benefit-cost optimization approach to resource conservation.

The third characteristic of the proponents' argument hinged upon the so-called environmental benefits of the Blue Ridge project. Recall that under this older, conservationist approach, a policy that exploits nature in order to augment or improve a natural resource is viewed as good public policy. In 1970, after the EPA was formed, a study was undertaken on the environmental impacts of the Blue Ridge project. The EPA publicly indicated, after this study was completed, that the project might indirectly *increase* air pollution in the region. The coal-fueled power plants from which Blue Ridge's pump storage power would be derived were older facilities located in the Ohio River valley—facilities designed prior to the stringent air quality regulations of the late 1960s and early 1970s (Kenworthy, 1973d).

This public revelation had the unintended consequence of making it appear as if the project's advocates had failed to consider more ecologically palatable alternatives. Over time, many of these older plants would have been retired and replaced with less polluting boilers equipped with electrostatic precipitators. Nevertheless, as a result of such criticisms, Blue Ridge proponents found it increasingly difficult to defend the project on ecological grounds. The usual criterion favoring hydropower, that falling water produces no pollution, simply could not be met by Blue Ridge.

Another environmental obstacle exploited by opponents of the project was encountered when the FPC adopted Interior's modified plan for mitigating water pollution through low-flow augmentation. Stored water would be released during periods of low flow to literally dilute concentrated areas of pollution downstream of an impoundment. This was an unpopular plan and difficult to defend under traditional conservationist grounds. Pollution dilution raised two ancillary issues: whether outside interests should become beneficiaries of the New River's resources at the expense of valley residents, since none of Blue Ridge's power would be sold in North Carolina or Virginia (Webster, 1969); and whether this method of pollution abatement was, in fact, a public subsidy of the chemical industry of West Virginia's Kanawha valley.

The acceptance of Interior's modifications resulted in APCO and the FPC tacitly divorcing themselves from a conservationist strategy justifiable on grounds of environmental enhancement. This is exemplified by the testimony of Lorne R. Campbell, general counsel for Grayson County, Virginia, and project critic: "Any industrial complex, by similar strategy, might continue to . . . inundate land under guise of emergency power needs or pollution control" (Kenworthy, 1971). Interior's adamant insistence upon sticking with the legal precedent of using stored water for pollution abatement became increasingly indefensible over time. This is ironic because pollution dilution had been seen as a workable and acceptable strategy in other parts of the United States, even though the strategy came in for environmental criticism in the 1970s. When applied to the Blue Ridge project, however, it alienated local residents, killed what little local acquiescence there was for the project, and isolated proponents in the newly formed EPA, further compromising the project's credibility.

Proponents and Opponents of Blue Ridge: Differences in Philosophies

Blue Ridge was supposed to epitomize the long-standing tradition in federal water policy of gratuitous politics of providing public works projects to local constituencies at a cost diffused throughout society. This approach is characterized by active political advocacy of projects by government agencies. Critics of Blue Ridge, however, argued that the project's costs were going to be borne by the locals while the benefits would be diffused throughout society. The conflict between national, state, and local proponents and opponents of the Blue Ridge project and among affected states in the New River region can be seen in the following lists (see Schoenbaum, 1979: ix, 105ff; Laycock, 1975; *New York Times*, 1971b; Kenworthy, 1974d). Those in favor of the Blue Ridge project were

- Interior Secretary Stewart Udall (1965–69)
- Interior Undersecretary James Watt (1969–75)
- American Electric Power Company
- Federal Power Commission
- Army Corps of Engineers
- Senator Harry F. Byrd, Virginia
- Senator William L. Scott, Virginia
- Virginia congressional delegation
- National AFL-CIO
- Governor Goodwin, Virginia
- Attorney-General Miller, Virginia
- Governor Moore, West Virginia
- Water Resources Chief Henry, West Virginia

Those against the Blue Ridge project were

- Interior Secretary Rogers Morton (1969–74)
- Bureau of Outdoor Recreation
- Fish and Wildlife Service
- President Gerald Ford
- Presidential candidate Ronald Reagan
- Presidential candidate Jimmy Carter
- Senator Jesse Helms, North Carolina
- Senator Sam Ervin, North Carolina
- Representative Stephen Neal, North Carolina
- Representative Wilmer Mizell, North Carolina
- Representative Ken Hechler, West Virginia
- United Mine Workers of America

- American Rivers Conservation Council
- National Committee for the New River (Winston-Salem)
- Environmental Protection Agency
- Governor Holshouser, North Carolina
- Attorney-General Gambill, North Carolina
- Attorney-General Browning, West Virginia
- Ashe County, North Carolina
- Alleghany County, North Carolina
- Grayson County, Virginia
- North Carolina AFL-CIO
- Farm Bureau Federation of North Carolina
- Conservation Council of North Carolina
- Upper New River Valley Association
- Izaak Walton League—New River chapter
- Highlands Conservancy of West Virginia
- Natural Resources Council of West Virginia
- Alleghany Farm Bureau
- Conservation Council of Virginia

The point highlighted by the lists is that the most significant factor dividing proponents and opponents was proximity to, and perceived benefits from, the project, as well as a traditional stake in water projects. Thus, the Corps of Engineers supported the project because it conformed to its own developmental approach to river basin planning. The corps was favorably impressed by the fact that the project would provide 160,000 acre-feet of flood storage for the New River valley, long a corps priority, both generally and for this region in particular. In addition, the corps had long favored the principle of pollution dilution (Morgan, 1971; Mazmanian and Neinaber, 1979: 10).

On the state level, North Carolina officials almost wholly opposed Blue Ridge. Senator Sam Ervin, while sensitive to the concerns of valley residents, was most strongly motivated in his opposition to the project by a strict constructionist view of congressional power. He accused the FPC of usurping congressional prerogatives by granting initial approval to APCO to build the modified Blue Ridge project before both houses of Congress completed a review of the feasibility of including the New River in the National Scenic River system. Adding insult to injury, the FPC made the effective date of this license January 1975, instead of July, as the Senate had requested, in order to give the Department of the Interior time to complete all necessary studies associated with the scenic river decision. In Ervin's opinion, "this arrogant act ultimately won many more votes in Congress for preservation of the New River than might otherwise have been the case" (Schoenbaum, 1979: viii; Kenworthy, 1974c). In reality, the FPC's attempt to expedite matters was hardly surprising nor unprecedented. However, given the concerted opposition to Blue Ridge, this action constituted but another source of friction, which aided project opponents.

Representative Wilmer Mizell, representing North Carolina's Fifth Congressional District (the New River region), introduced legislation in 1972 and 1973 to the House Public Works Committee to authorize the Corps of Engineers to investigate the "recreational, conservation, and preservation uses" of the New River (Kenworthy, 1973b). Mizell's actions were prompted by his own opposition to pollution dilution as an effective means of pollution abatement; the EPA's reluctance to criticize pollution dilution, even though it seemed contrary to the recently passed Clean Water Act of 1972; and the absence of any direct benefits accruing from the Blue Ridge project to residents of the Fifth District, a basic requirement for public works projects supported by an iron triangle. Stephen Neal, Mizell's successor elected in 1974, continued to oppose the Blue Ridge project and voted for the Scenic River Bill in 1976.

The Role of the States in the Blue Ridge Controversy

Pivotal to the defeat of Blue Ridge was North Carolina's governor, James Holshouser. Historically, gubernatorial opposition to federal water projects has usually been fatal to their construction. What made the Blue Ridge case more complicated, however, was the fact that it was a private project supported by a federal agency. In July 1973, Holshouser approached the Department of the Interior's Bureau of Outdoor Recreation and Fish and Wildlife Service. He found both agencies to be favorably disposed toward scenic river status for the New, an action that would have remanded APCO's license for constructing Blue Ridge. Moreover, Holshouser persuaded Interior Secretary Rogers Morton, a close friend, to favor scenic river status. Morton believed the Blue Ridge project would provide only a short-term energy solution.

The mutual interest of Morton and Holshouser were also linked to the 1976 presidential campaign. Holshouser was the southern regional coordinator for Gerald Ford's presidential campaign, while Morton was its national chairman. Ironically, Ford's loss to Ronald Reagan in the North Carolina presidential primary was partly due to Reagan's early, and vociferous, stance against Blue Ridge, a position urged on him by Jesse Helms. After Ford was apprised of the intensity of the issue in North Carolina, acting Interior Secretary Owen Kleppe approved Holshouser's request for scenic river status. Although final disposition would still rest with Congress, the significance of the decision, coming a week before the North Carolina primary, was not lost on the state's voters (Schoenbaum, 1979: 67; Kenworthy, 1974b, 1976a, 1976b).

In West Virginia, an alleged beneficiary of low-flow augmentation, divided opinion worked to the advantage of Blue Ridge opponents. While the sprawling chemical industry of the Kanawha valley stood to benefit from the modified project's pollution dilution plan, the risks entailed in that plan aroused significant opposition to the project. Governor Arch Moore of West Virginia was a staunch supporter of Blue Ridge and cited the project as an effective example of low-flow augmentation to mitigate water pollution. A strong advocate of state cooperation on environmental problems, Moore was also a strong advocate of the benefit-cost optimization paradigm and a critic of preservationists.

As far back as 1971, Moore cited the "mutual interest [of Virginia and West Virginia] in controlling the pollution that flows from the New . . . into West Virginia." He also stated that water pollution "is by far the most vexing environmental problem . . . simply because of the difficulty in tracing pollutants" (Frasure and Davis, 1977: 355). Concluding an address to southern governors on the subject, Moore left no doubt as to where his sympathies in the Blue Ridge controversy lay: "unending questioning of the justification for new dams [by environmentalists] constitutes an overreaction of panic and a growing sentiment of no-growth" (Frasure and Davis, 1977: 357).

However, other state officials contended that the project would have negative impacts. Biologists from the West Virginia Department of Natural Resources joined those in North Carolina in criticizing the project on grounds that excessive fluctuation, turbidity, and temperature changes downstream of the project could adversely affect riparian habitat, fishing, and white-water canoeing (Laycock, 1975; Webster, 1969). State Attorney General Chauncey Browning also opposed the project on grounds that pollution dilution allowed chemical plants in the Kanawha valley a means of avoiding responsibility for mitigating their own wastes.

In essence, Browning charged, the use of stored water to mitigate pollution placed the burden of waste treatment on the state, not the chemical industry. This was especially galling since the chemical industry had steadfastly resisted compliance with the standards already in effect. It should be noted, however, that this viewpoint was not universally shared. West Virginia Water Resources Board Chief Edgar Henry, responsible for enforcing federal water quality standards, saw the Blue Ridge project as a means of making his job easier. He and Browning clashed over Blue Ridge until the project was finally canceled in 1976 (Laycock, 1975; Webster, 1969; *New York Times*, 1971a).

The EPA, the National Environmental Policy Act of 1969,

and the Blue Ridge Controversy: Limits to Gratuitous Politics

When the Department of the Interior endorsed pollution dilution, it ignored the controversy surrounding the technique. Although pollution dilution was long practiced by the Corps of Engineers in a variety of watershed projects, it was rarely promoted as a principle project benefit. The newly formed EPA, groping for test cases to assess its authority over federal environmental policy in competition with other, longer established agencies, saw the planned use of the technique as a test case and as a means to disprove the technique's efficacy. Fortuitously, Blue Ridge became a target for attacking a controversial means of abating water pollution long practiced by the federal government. The EPA's influence grew considerably as a result of growing preservationist sentiments.

The 1972 Federal Water Pollution Control Act required EPA consent for low-flow augmentation as a means of pollution abatement. The technique is implicitly discouraged by the act's requirements that polluters pretreat effluents and that the federal government promote the best practical and eventually best available technology to eliminate discharges into the nation's navigable streams. It is up to EPA discretion to determine the technique's usefulness.

Although the EPA formally prohibited water storage for pollution dilution in April 1973, the decision did not have the effect upon Blue Ridge some project opponents had hoped. As if anticipating EPA's decision, A. Joseph Dowd, general counsel for the American Electric Power Company, the holding company for APCO, announced in November 1972 that his company now embraced the idea of larger reservoirs for more power generation. Moreover, EPA's authority to prevent water storage for pollution dilution was open to contention.[4]

Before passage of the Water Pollution Control Act, the EPA was reluctant to challenge the Department of the Interior's preference for pollution dilution for fear of engendering interagency conflict. This reticence was exemplified by a 1971 incident involving the EPA, the FPC, and the Department of the Interior. In May 1971, prior to an initial licensing decision for the modified Blue Ridge project, the FPC requested an advisory assessment of pollution dilution from the EPA. The EPA designated a spokesperson from the Department of the Interior, more knowledgeable on the issue, to represent the EPA at public hearings (Mizell, 1972; Kenworthy, 1972)

Without a legal mandate and support from other agencies, the EPA was fearful of exerting too much authority in the conflict. Support for the EPA did not materialize until environmental groups were able to

stall the FPC's licensing efforts in the courts. This was a lengthy, te-
dious, and confusing process, which eventually bought time for scenic
river advocates to persuade Congress to remand the Blue Ridge license.

Other ammunition for environmental groups opposed to the project
was indirectly provided by the National Environmental Policy Act of
1969, which required an environmental impact analysis (now known
as environmental impact statements) to be filed for all federally sponsored projects. When applied retroactively to Blue Ridge, in 1974, project
opponents found that weaknesses in the FPC's initial statement for the
project could be turned to their advantage.

Environmentalists discredited the project by demonstrating that its
planners had inadequately assessed the value of archaeological sites destined for inundation, as required by the National Environmental Policy
Act and by a 1974 amendment to the Historic Preservation Act of 1960.
They also argued that project planners had entertained no serious alternatives to the original site for Blue Ridge that would not have threatened a unique stretch of white water, and that they had provided
inadequate plans for the relocation of families and compensation for
those whose property would be lost.[5]

These inadequacies helped isolate proponents from other federal agencies and from influential groups close to the project. The opposition of
organized labor is typical. The North Carolina Labor Federation opposed the project because little local labor would be used, while the
national AFL-CIO supported it. The local United Mine Workers affiliate
broke with national leadership and spoke out against Blue Ridge, arguing
that hydropower might hurt an already depressed coal industry (Kenworthy, 1974d; *New York Times*, 1976b).

In short, benefit-cost optimization or conservation as a principle of
resource development were simply not sufficient to gain political support for the project. The decisive consideration, consistent with the
gratuitous character of environmental politics and the lack of an environmental ethic, was whether groups in close proximity to the project
would receive benefits from it. Blue Ridge project critics were able to
demonstrate that greater benefits to local constituents would likely accrue by leaving the New River undeveloped.

Environmentalists and the Scenic River Controversy: Preservationism on the Offensive

The environmental groups that joined with local residents to oppose
the Blue Ridge project were composed largely of nondevelopment advocates. They held a pristine, preservationist view of natural resources
and were committed to limiting economic growth. They were also skep-

tical of technological change. Most of them believed that limiting the size of the project and narrowing the scope of activities permitted along the New River were realistic goals. Unlike the practitioners of the benefit-cost optimization approach to conservation, which advocates the efficient exploitation of natural resources, preservationists hold to a nonexploitive, nondevelopment view.

This view is predicated on the assumption that human beings are intellectually finite creatures and that nature is infinitely complex. Such a view, held by many scenic river advocates, is similar to that espoused by classic environmental philosophers such as John Muir and Aldo Leopold, who ascribed psychologically and spiritually rejuvenating qualities to rivers and spoke of natural objects as having rights (Leopold, 1966: 176).

Initially, these environmental groups, who represented nonresidents of the valley, were perceived by residents as contemptuous of Appalachian culture, narrowly committed to aesthetic preservation, and opposed to the most cherished of all land use values in the United States— local control of natural resources (Lepawsky, 1950). This latter value is often at odds with federal mandates for preservation, which are typically favored by ecologists.

Initially too, these environmental groups were regarded by residents as outsiders, as was APCO, and thus without right to interfere in the affairs of the valley. This is precisely why the scenic river concept, as a strategy for defeating the Blue Ridge project, angered many valley residents. Fears of federal intrusion and socialism as a result of the intervention of environmentalists aided dam proponents. Residents had no real idea what a scenic river would be like. Moreover, as is to be expected, environmentalists were often unable to articulate, in practical, tangible terms, the types of activities that would be allowed or prohibited on a scenic river. The ethical vision held by many environmentalists was more amenable to long-winded discussions of the sublime qualities of a preserved river and less amenable to explanations of the economic characteristics of its management. That environmental groups were viewed with some trepidation is exemplified by the following observation by Thomas Schoenbaum, a North Carolina litigant involved in the scenic river controversy:

> Most people did not have a clear idea what a "National
> Scenic River" would mean for them or the valley. They
> thought of it as a large national park [which] represented
> the intrusion of the federal government. . . . They also
> feared . . . outside environmental groups and thought
> they would be restricted in the use of their lands to ac-

commodate hordes of backpackers. (Schoenbaum, 1979: 101–2)

How then, did the scenic river advocates achieve their goal, the inclusion of the New River in the National Scenic River system, and the cancellation of the Blue Ridge project? The victory can best be explained as a convergence of their interests and those of most valley residents. The former wanted to halt a project they saw as benefiting corporate interests and imposing irreparable harm to the environment. The latter, for the most part, merely wanted to be left alone to manage their own resources as they had always done.

Blue Ridge proponents were unable to counter local residents' belief that, after the valley was inundated for power production, the region would receive no benefits to offset loss of jobs, farms, and homes. The proposed enlargement of the project, whether for pollution dilution or for increased power, only served to strengthen this belief, converging it with the fears of environmentalists. The following comments exemplify local sentiments. From a spokesman for the Izaak Walton League of Virginia: "If they [APCO, AEP, and FPC] had stuck to their original proposal, they probably would not have had any trouble" (Laycock, 1975). From a retired agricultural specialist near Independence, Virginia: "These residents are the finest folks in the world. . . . They simply do not comprehend the extent of the changes this project would bring to their lifestyles. . . . The modified plan [is] two and a half times as big as it was. . . . The project will make a shell out of Grayson County" (Laycock, 1975).

The theme of "our way of life" versus "the selfish interests of outsiders" was a constant refrain of property owners in the valley, whose homes represented heritage as well as brick and wood. As one Piney Creek, North Carolina, resident put it: "My ancestors got title to this land by fighting in the battle of Kings Mountain [in the Revolutionary War]. My people have been in this valley for more than 200 years. . . . I don't need a new job [from the dam], my job started here 200 years ago" (Time, 1976: 71). Repeatedly, valley residents and public officials expressed dismay, anger, and frustration over what they perceived to be the incongruous justifications for the project. They wanted to be left alone, and they made it clear that, if another region had natural resources problems that required the construction of a massive water project to solve, it could build such a project itself.

Two residents of Independence, Virginia, were interviewed by the New York Times (Kenworthy, 1971). Guy Halsey said, "This is the best land that lays out of doors. We are taking out of production the most efficient land in the country." Page Evans remarked, "it's the ruination of the beauty of our country. Let West Virginia industry build their own flush-pot, we shouldn't be punished 200 miles upriver."

By the mid-1970s, when it became apparent that such grass-roots criticisms of the project would almost certainly pressure Congress into remanding the Blue Ridge license, APCO modified its strategy for selling the project. The utility conceded that, to some extent, disruptions from the project might create irreversible hardships. However, the scenic river alternative might pose even greater economic hardships upon residents of the valley than the dams would.

In a full-page advertisement appearing in several newspapers, including the New York Times, (1976a), the company reiterated its claims for the project's benefits and argued that environmental opponents of the project were an affluent elite, contemptuous of the residents of the New River region. It offered to pay residents more than market value for their homes, to provide free relocation services, and to cover all moving costs and personal property losses from the project's construction.

To New River valley residents, however, these efforts were too little, too late. Environmental groups countered on several fronts. In congressional hearings and in grass-roots discussions at antidam rallies in the valley, they addressed fears of a nationalization of the New River by moving their position closer to that of the traditional conservationist approach. Recognizing that preservationist values alone are "too elitist to appeal to a broad segment of society" (Schoenbaum, 1979: 183), they accepted the establishment of a scenic river with few changes in land use. This included conventional floodplain zoning, rather than unique scenic river restrictions. Public access to the river itself would remain basically unrestricted (Schoenbaum, 1979: 160).

Conclusions: The Ambiguous Status of Environmental Values in American Politics— Policy Implications

Environmental values have an ambiguous status in American politics. The conservationist point of view, which advocates the development and exploitation of natural resources, tends to be favored by most members of society. On the other hand, the preservationist point of view, which advocates controls on exploitation and use, is favored by a relative minority of citizens. The Blue Ridge controversy shows how this ambiguity, while working to the disadvantage of the preservationist approach that promotes locking away resources, can work to the advantage of conservationist values, which can be linked with the powerful traditional values of local control.

The dominance of natural resources use through local alliances with national agencies is, as we have seen, commonly labeled distributive politics. However, unchecked by considerations other than local economic gain, such an approach is politically gratuitous: harmful to the environment, inconsiderate of policy benefactors, and economically inequitable.

How can gratuitous policy be avoided? Does Blue Ridge demonstrate that there are viable alternatives? One major lesson of this controversy is that the structure of natural resources conflicts in the United States makes it difficult to articulate policies based upon the philosophy that mankind should work with, rather than against, nature—what we have termed an environmental ethic. That goal, if it can be attained at all, requires major changes in the manner in which environmental policy is made and, just as important, major changes in the way we think about environmental problems (Caldwell, 1981: 43). What Blue Ridge suggests is a middle-range possibility: policy change resulting from unpopular, environmentally unacceptable projects. It may also portend a positive trend in policy making.

Blue Ridge shows us that traditional water policy, by resting upon an iron triangle of special interests, agency largesse, and congressional committee promotion, reflects the fragmented, decentralized character of representation and group access in U.S. political culture. As a consequence, policy implementation tends to be placed in the hands of engineers and technocrats interested in structural solutions to water problems that will maximize economic growth. These values are elitist and inhibit broad-based participation. Public apprehensions about such elitist values underlie the decline of public confidence in nuclear power and the concerted opposition to projects at the cutting edge of that technology, such as the Clinch River breeder reactor.

This combination of shielded, insulated policy making and elitist policy implementation produces a political environment that minimizes public trust in natural resources agencies. It may also promote an adversarial relationship between policy actors and produce value dissensus over long-term goals for the prudent management of natural resources. This adversarial relationship, in turn, may delay the implementation of urgently needed solutions to energy and environmental problems. Con Ed's cancellation of the Storm King hydroelectric power project on the Hudson River is perhaps the best additional example in recent water policy (Sheinbaum, 1983; Talbot, 1972).

The Blue Ridge experience suggests that policy makers need to formulate policy that is not only environmentally acceptable but socially acceptable. This is going to be difficult—there is a long-standing tradition of antistatism in American environmental policy, which reflects our regional and ethnic diversity and our enthusiasm for private enterprise.

In addition, while Americans generally favor conservationist, benefit-cost optimization strategies, which create environmental disruptions on behalf of economic progress, they generally oppose strategies that disrupt local access to, or control over, natural resources. The Blue Ridge project exemplifies this problem inasmuch as the announced benefits of the project were diffused over a broad region while the costs were going to be paid by local communities in their loss of traditional ways of life and work. Value consensus hinges upon transcending the narrow benefit-cost optimization approach. From their inception, such projects must demonstrate that they are well reasoned from the standpoint of public safety, energy security, and environmental quality; that they are fair to all regions; and that they provide members of the community new opportunities for self-development.

The difficulties in achieving consensus are illustrated by hazardous waste policy, where antistatism and opposition to disruption of local land use are exemplified by the not-in-my-backyard phenomenon, in its way as direct an assault upon federal environmental policies as resistance to dams or nuclear power plants. The significance of this phenomenon is that the standard benefit-cost approach to environmental policy may be unacceptable on equity or noneconomic grounds. This sort of opposition is extremely difficult to defuse.

Finally, civil servants and public agencies invested with making natural resources decisions are generally held in low esteem unless they are perceived as generators of wealth. In certain regions of the United States where government-sponsored environmental disruptions occur, such as Appalachia, this perception is often compounded by an anti-outsider complex (Rothblatt, 1971). Efforts to promote a pump storage hydroelectric project on the New River stirred powerful resentments in the valley because the plan was viewed as an assault upon the values and practices of a region that reveres local initiative. While the attempt to build Blue Ridge was neither underhanded nor surreptitious, the hostility stemming from the failure to integrate project objectives with residents' values proved insurmountable.

To some extent, the same opposition is seen, only in partial reversal, in the case of the Garrison diversion project. Potential beneficiaries in the northern Great Plains at first resented federal intrusion in the upper Missouri basin due to their loss of land. Later, these residents were willing to cooperate in exchange for perceived benefits from the project for later generations. When those commitments failed to materialize, any federal intervention was resented, especially since the federal gov-

ernment seemed to side with outsiders who were overwhelmingly preservationist.

In the Blue Ridge project, the power companies and the Federal Power
Commission failed to convince New River valley residents that the
promised construction jobs, flat-water recreation, and new industry
would fill an economic void. In terms of the economic values that residents themselves defined as important—preservation of small farms,
access to shoreline, and protection of ancestral homes—construction of
the Blue Ridge dams would have imposed changes outside the control
of local residents. In essence, the residents of the valley did not want
the dams in their backyard unless the benefits to the local community
outweighed the costs imposed upon it. If they bore the major costs of
the project, in other words, they expected to receive the principal benefits of it. Project proponents failed to show how this would come about;
they failed to define developmental objectives in ways salient to this
community.

Put another way, New River valley residents did not view themselves
as living in economic scarcity. Economically, they had an abundance of
those things they defined as valuable. It is not that the economic arguments used by the government or the utility were invalid. In other
regions they might have been convincing. It is merely that, in this instance, they were unsellable. A technically valid argument, which would
have made political sense, would have stressed regional development,
equity between regions, and local participation in shaping the parameters of the project.

What complicated matters further is that the usual pattern of subsystem politics backfired; that is, the typically decentralized and fragmented process by which environmental decisions are made simply did
not function in its usual fashion. Two disparate groups came together
to express profound dissatisfaction with a federally sponsored and, as
they saw it, federally subsidized project. Ordinarily, one would expect
these groups to be on opposite sides of an issue. While neither group
alone might have been able to defeat the Blue Ridge project, together
they were invincible. Environmentalists focused upon pollution dilution
and other preservationist, ecologically oriented issues. Local residents
and politicians seized the economic, benefit-cost high ground by criticizing the energy idiosyncrasies of pump storage power plants.

A similar coalition with similar concerns overcame and defeated the
Clinch River breeder reactor, another technically complex and somewhat esoteric venture. Environmentalists focused upon the dangers
from the plant's production and use of plutonium, while the National
Taxpayers Union asserted that the project would not repay its own costs
for a very long time, if ever, due to the relatively small amounts of power

it would generate, its outdated design, its high construction costs, and the relative stability of world uranium prices.

Finally, in the case of the Storm King pump storage project in upstate New York, a project similar to Blue Ridge, a coalition of environmentalists and New York City officials delayed the project. While New Yorkers were concerned with rate hikes to pay for the project, environmentalists concentrated upon the project's anticipated negative impacts upon fisheries, recreation, and aesthetic preservation. In this instance, as in Blue Ridge, subsystem fragmentation made it possible for each coalition member to attack the project from different points. Economically oriented groups addressed public utility commissions, while environmentalists lobbied Congress, the EPA, and the Department of the Interior and submitted briefs to courts. In each case, the projects were delayed long enough to make project proponents look impetuous and project opponents methodical and patient, even though both projects had been planned for a long time.

What are the lessons here for an environmental ethic? One lesson is that all changes in water policy from this point onward are likely to come about through the efforts of such disparate coalitions. What remains to be seen is whether or not these changes portend a genuinely new and qualitatively different policy climate. Recent case studies suggest that the verdict is still out on this matter (Palmer, 1982). These coalitions function most effectively when a proposal is seen as complex and, thus, vulnerable to criticisms of groups opposed on ideological grounds. Thus, the challenge for policy makers is to develop environmental policies that are not only relevant and comprehensible to the average person concerned with the various impacts of programs but that truly address the ethical issues. Moreover, it must be assumed that the average person is simply unwilling to accept a project whose benefits accrue only to others.

In the case of Blue Ridge, proponents chose the almost politically indefensible ground of benefit-cost optimization. Furthermore, the project was designed to generate power in an unconventional manner, through pump storage. Preservationists rejected both the benefit-cost approach and the technology and succeeded in equating proponents' views with those of pure exploiters.

The dilemma exemplified by this case is that the do-nothing alternative, while politically palatable, does not solve energy and water crises. We can take heart when projects that are purely exploitive are defeated by public opposition, but potentially beneficial developments are often lost merely because their benefits are difficult to quantify. For example, much of the merit in the pump-storage concept in Blue Ridge was lost in the debate over justifications for the project itself.

Arguments over the wise use of resources, a goal of conservationists and preservationists alike, often hinge upon the confidence these advocates have in human understanding of natural processes and of the long-term impacts of human activity on nature. I suggest that the weight of experience dictates limited confidence in that understanding and in our ability to balance human activity with natural processes. At the very least, Blue Ridge shows the need to combine conservationist and preservationist values.

If we adopt a preservation approach to the exclusion of conservation, we risk harming some groups. Preservation pursued without regard to the economic needs of people would heighten the inequities of some regions relative to others. For example, in the case of the New River, locking up the river by preventing any development or access would hurt local residents by denying them the right to use its resources to maintain their existence. So long as these people used the river in a manner that sustained its fisheries, forest resources, and wildlife for future generations, they would be following a conservation approach, which could well be beneficial to themselves, others, and to the resources.

By the same token, conservation approaches pursued without regard to preservation might also be inappropriate. For example, inundating the New River valley by building a dam for hydropower could benefit outsiders who want cheaper electricity. It could also provide a renewable, nonpolluting source of power. However, it would do so by permanently destroying some forest cover and might also place some species of fish and wildlife at risk.

Nuclear breeder reactors, pump storage projects, and hazardous waste facilities are but three examples of hard-to-sell projects. Because their logic is difficult to define, they generate several levels of resistance, which confound long-term solutions. The beginnings of a solution to this dilemma involves redefining benefits and costs in some normatively defensible manner. That is the subject of chapter 7.

7 Benefit-Cost Analysis as an Inadequate Substitute for an Environmental Ethic

Even an ideal benefit-cost analysis is normatively incomplete. . . .
Efficiency is best regarded as an instrumental value, a tool for
comparing policy options in terms of other values. Efficiency is
merely an economic criterion once other needs have been met.
—CHARLES ANDERSON

Benefit-Cost Analysis and Utilitarianism:
Getting to the Root of the Problem

The lack of an ethical basis for natural resources policy, a lack widely shared among citizens and policy makers, makes benefit-cost analysis an attractive means of justifying decisions. Despite criticisms by many political scientists and economists of the misuse, misapplication, or overreliance upon this methodology by government agencies, benefit-cost analysis remains secure because it is a relatively simple and lucid way to depict advantages and disadvantages of natural resources development.

Proponents of benefit-cost analysis believe it constitutes a valid tool for gauging the conformance of water policies to the public interest because it is designed to promote the greatest good for the greatest number of citizens. Benefit-cost analysis conforms to that particular brand of American democratic theory that contends that, in order to satisfy the material preferences of the many, government programs should be economically sound but minimally intrusive upon their lives. In practice, this goal of promoting the needs of the greatest number remains elusive and may not even be worth pursuing. This is due to the measurement criteria employed by its practitioners, the ethical limitations inherent in the concept of economic efficiency (which lies at the heart of benefit-cost analysis), and the fact that this methodology can identify economically sensible means to an end only after society has first decided what it wants. It cannot prescribe what the proper ends of policy ought to be, even though its proponents sometimes presume that it can. A normatively defensible policy should seek to conform to a higher plateau of democratic aspiration, a plateau on which the values of justice are animated by a participatory framework for making decisions, which broadens the perspectives of participants and deepens their understanding of issues encompassed by environmental decisions.

By examining the theory and practice of benefit-cost analysis in water policy, I show that it fails to encompass a social optimum, is inequitable, and fails to clarify alternative means to achieve desired ends. A normatively defensible policy cannot be merely efficient. It should also be equitable; be able to reduce risks to human health, welfare, and well-being; make ecologically sound use of resources; be formulated through broad participation by the affected public, not just policy "experts"; and, most of all, avoid gratuitousness by repaying society for programs directly benefiting a certain region or group. A case study of dam safety in the United States, an area that does not usually come to mind when discussions about benefits and costs are raised, is used to illustrate these points. It is concluded that the character of liberal society makes the emphasis upon efficiency in resources use inevitable.

A curious duality pervades concepts of justice in the liberal state. On the one hand, there are those, such as social welfare maximalists, who define justice as the satisfaction of the needs of atomistic individuals, each of whom is equipped to fully understand and satisfy his or her needs (Nozick, 1974). Critics of this notion, including John Dewey, Josiah Royce, and, more recently, C. B. Macpherson, join the larger debate between communitarian thought and radical concepts of individualism. These critics contend that the social welfare maximalist concept of justice is untenable.

First, people are not found in societies as isolated individuals but are found associated with one another as members of communities, which affect, shape, and nurture their needs and desires. Moreover, these communities reshape, temper, and clarify these needs and desires through common language, culture, and patterns of thinking (Dewey, 1954; Royce, 1936). Second, to act as if society were mutually a collection of atomistic individuals would be destructive of intuitive concepts of justice, because it would ignore the fact that every citizen is not equally equipped to obtain various goods and may therefore be either consciously or subconsciously excluded from decision making. It also ignores the fact that the pursuit of maximum individual advantage is destructive of nature and of the long-term interests of society (Macpherson, 1978).

While dialogue between these pure theorists and policy practitioners has rarely been engaged in, decades of criticism by the theorists have made some notable impact upon the way policy makers make decisions. The most important impact has been in the emphasis on direct decision making by affected members of the public in especially complex areas of policy. On the pure theory side are those who, like John Dewey, argue that a democratic society must invest responsibility and authority in individuals for the guidance of civic groups and other organizations (Dewey, 1954). From the environmental policy side have come, most notably, political scientists such as Lynton Caldwell, who contend that the predominance of experts in administrative decision making in government undermines democratic accountability. But in areas of policy especially critical to health, safety, and the quality of life, it is difficult to include viable alternatives important to all parties (Caldwell, 1975, 1988).

Theorists such as Dewey and political scientists like Caldwell advocate decision making that maximizes public participation, the representation of ecological values, and the consideration of noneconomic criteria. Such means of decision making are exemplified by relatively recent reforms in the field of natural resources policy, such as environmental impact analyses prescribed by the National Environmental Policy Act of 1969. One purpose of this act, sometimes lost in the shuffle of environmental impact statements, public hearings, injunctions against developers, lawsuits, and other newsworthy events, is the philosophical basis of this law and its relevance for water policy.

Lynton Caldwell, a consultant to the U.S. Senate Interior Committee during formulation of this act, argues that the real purpose of the act was to force serious consideration of alternatives to prevailing government actions in the field of natural resources. The act attempts nothing less than a fundamental reconstruction of national priorities in development, in accordance with a range of popular concerns, and a conscious rejection of the single-minded goal of maximizing economic benefits for the majority (Caldwell, 1975, 1988).

Caldwell contends that no act designed to limit the exploitation of nature through the consideration of environmental, noneconomic, and other public concerns could achieve its intention unless a mechanism for agency conformance was provided. This mechanism is the requirement that specific evaluations of the effects of a decision accompany proposals for construction or modification of the environment by public works agencies (Cahn, 1978: 25–26). This suggestion was directly incorporated into the act through the concept of environmental assessments. These assessments are supposed to utilize "a systematic, interdisciplinary approach," which weighs intended actions and their effects, alternatives to such actions, and irreversible or irretrievable impacts stemming from them (NEPA, sec. 102a).

For water policy, such an approach means that the Corps of Engineers, the Bureau of Reclamation, other public agencies, and private developers sponsored by public agencies (the Appalachian Power Company and its relation to the Federal Power Commission being an example) can no longer simply weigh the benefits and costs of building a dam. Alternatives to the dam and its impacts upon fisheries, shoreline development, erosion, riparian habitat, turbidity, and sedimentation, and a whole array of other concerns now have to be factored into the decision. Moreover, measures to mitigate such impacts have to be taken into account by the sponsoring agency.

The act attempts to foster an environmental ethic through encouraging groups normally excluded from decision making to participate in the formative stages of policy. However, this goal requires public acceptance of these alternative values and their consequences or, at the very least, public acceptance of procedures that would allow these values to be debated. This entails going beyond a conventional critique of benefit-cost analysis.

The Conventional Critique of Benefit-Cost Analysis: Benefits and Costs as Gratuitous Policy

Boiled down to their essence, most political science critiques of the use of benefit-cost analysis in water policy contend that the approach is used in an unwarranted manner. It is tacked on to reports to justify water projects that agencies have already decided to promote. As a result, it fails to illuminate why certain benefits are worth pursuing, despite their consequences upon nonbeneficiaries or the environment, and it obscures the obligations of beneficiaries to repay those who subsidize projects.

This was not always the case. In fact, benefit-cost analysis of water policy was a conscious attempt to establish economic standards that would avoid gratuitous policy and waste money. The history of benefit-cost analysis as a tool for government control over spending closely parallels the growth of the progressive movement in the field of natural resources policy.

Benefit-cost analysis was the economic component of the so-called benefit-cost optimization approach, or conservationist paradigm. It was closely linked to this paradigm's promotion of resource exploitation on behalf of the material well-being of present and future generations. By assuring that policies combine prudent development with preservation, benefit-cost analysis was to guide policy makers in making balanced investment decisions. This goal was explicitly stated in legislation requiring its use in water resources development.

The Flood Control Act of 1936 first enunciated the now familiar standard, that water resources agencies assure that "the benefits to whomsoever they may accrue [be] in excess of the estimated costs" and that the "lives and the social security of people [not be] otherwise adversely affected" (Gramlich, 1981: 7; Biniek, 1985: 137). Problematically, this act, and the many rivers and harbors authorization bills that followed, provides no specific guidance on how benefits or costs should be defined. The history of federal water policy in the United States since the mid-1930s is, in some respects, the story of attempts to define these concepts more clearly and to avoid gratuitous policy.

In May 1950, the Interagency Committee on Water Resources, composed of officials from the departments of Agriculture, Army, Interior, Commerce, and the Federal Power Commission, issued the so-called Green Book, which attempted to reconcile these agencies' different evaluation techniques. Guidelines proposed by this interagency agreement, which were later voluntarily adopted by water resources agencies, included defining primary and secondary (or direct and indirect), as well as tangible and intangible, benefits. Human life and health were assigned a value on the basis of commonly agreed upon estimates of acceptable expenditures (i.e., what must persons were thought to be willing to pay to alleviate certain forms of misery) (Biniek, 1985: 137).

In 1952, the Bureau of the Budget (forerunner of the Office of Management and Budget) introduced its own evaluation criteria for determining benefits and costs for water resources developments. This established a precedent later adopted and modified by the Water Resources Council. These criteria included executive office review of proposed expenditures before authorizing reports to Congress. In other words, they converted what was originally a voluntary procedure into a requirement. Nevertheless, these guidelines still had no "official standing in planning and assessing" until the issuance of Senate Document 97, in 1962 (Biniek, 1985).

Senate Document 97 made explicit three objectives: planning, development, and the well-being of people, each of which was explicitly defined by reference to utilitarian criteria:

> Care shall be taken to avoid use and development for the benefit of a few or the disadvantage of the many. In par-

ticular, policy requirements and guides established by
the Congress and aimed at assuring that the use of natural resources, including water resources, safeguard the
interests of all of our people shall be observed (U.S. Senate, 1962: 2).

This document was eventually supplanted by the so-called Principles
and Standards of September 1973, issued by the Water Resources Council (WRC, 1973). The major difference between the latter and Senate
Document 97 is that the Water Resources Council further defined human interests as benefits that promote, or prevent harm to, life, health,
and safety as measured by the reduction of hazard, the saving of lives,
and the alleviation of pollution (U.S. Senate, 1972; Biniek, 1985: 138).

On one level, all of these attempts at defining benefits and costs
succeeded admirably, even though no attempt was ever made to place a
direct economic value upon human life or to come to grips with the
ethical dilemmas posed by that issue. Agencies spent considerable time
and effort trying to prove that projects had economic merit that could
be quantified and compared with other proposals. Arguments were put
forth to show how prevention of floods, production of electricity, and
irrigation of cropland would improve the management of natural resources, which would repay taxpayers many times their original investment. Agencies also had to establish that the hardships being alleviated,
such as flooding, could be measured, chronicled, and depicted in detail.

On a deeper level, however, these benefit-cost analyses never really
addressed the fundamental issues upon which water policy turned.
Rarely did benefit-cost analyses draw comparisons among techniques
capable of alleviating water problems at a single site. A structural solution to resolve a water problem was almost invariably selected over a
nonstructural, yet less environmentally harmful, measure, such as
floodplain management or water conservation.

As a result, while a single water project might be shown to save lives
and produce economic benefits, it was rarely demonstrated how many
lives would be saved or economic benefits generated by alternative measures. Worse, different agencies had their own criteria for depicting benefits and costs, which tended to be biased by agency priorities to prevent
flooding, alleviate soil erosion, promote irrigation, or generate hydroelectricity. Sometimes, these priorities varied from project to project and
were further colored by the priorities of powerful interest groups residing
in a particular region.

The failure to address these issues is what I term the conventional
critique of benefit-cost analysis. It does not question the methodology,
its applicability to water policy, or its desired ends; it merely questions

the manner in which the methodology is employed by agencies and assumes that it can be refined to address these issues. The conventional critique suggests that water resources agencies have consistently failed to use this methodology correctly because they are biased toward development of water resources.

The Corps of Engineers and the Bureau of Reclamation are not neutral referees, impartially applying benefit-cost analysis to projects over which competing interests are contending. They are advocates for the projects they sponsor and are, thus, highly interested in the outcomes of policy debates. Under such conditions, it is unavoidable that benefit-cost analysis will be used to the advantage of the agencies doing the analyses. It may be employed, in other words, to encourage the building of more water projects and to avoid too careful scrutiny of a project's shortcomings. This conventional critique has three components: social optimum criticisms, equity criticisms, and project and program quality criticisms. The social optimum criticism is the failure of water resources agencies to illuminate issues over which value judgments should be made.

Oftentimes, benefit-cost analyses are assumed to be substitutes for common sense. If it can be shown that water projects create net improvements over the status quo, then these improvements are treated as a panacea for all water problems. There is no way anyone can lose, and every water project would represent a real gain to society. Common sense dictates that this simply cannot be the case, yet advocates of water projects often commit this error. The Blue Ridge dam controversy exemplifies this problem.

During licensing proceedings for this project, the administrative law judge presiding over the decision to grant approval was enamored by the prospects for economic gains to the New River region. Judge William Levy pointed to growth in construction jobs, recreational activities, the retail economy, and the tax base. Ignoring for the moment the criticisms of valley residents of these gains, their satisfaction with an agriculturally based economy, and their dismay over mud flats and reservoir drawdowns, which would seriously impair the project's recreational attractiveness, there were other concerns largely ignored by the Federal Power Commission.

These problems represent the limitations of benefit-cost analysis for generating prudent resource decisions. First, recreational activities are not always seen as benefits by the intended beneficiaries. Tourism may generate new employment, but this employment is likely to be in seasonal, low-paying jobs unlikely to enhance the quality of life of a region. While a tax base may seasonally expand, it may also seasonally contract, even though the commercial infrastructure—the area's recreational industry, roads, utilities, and the like—still require constant attention and maintenance.

Second, even if it is assumed that recreation is a benefit, its costs and environmental risks need to be acknowledged. Camping, fishing, water skiing, swimming, and other water-based activities impose population density and associated land use pressures upon adjacent parks, water treatment facilities, public utilities, and other community infrastructure. Yet few analyses of recreation factor these costs into benefit-cost formulas. This was true for Blue Ridge as for other water resources projects. Finally, as shall be seen in the discussion of dam safety later in this chapter, a water project entails permanent bureaucratic commitments. It should not be managed singly, but as a part of a larger river basin program. If it is built primarily for one purpose, then other purposes may be ignored or may require additional projects to satisfy.

Such was the case in projects built in the Colorado River basin, which failed to address the hydrological and geological character of the basin. While the Hoover Dam does alleviate seasonal flooding and provide adequate water supply for the lower basin, it has generated few direct benefits for residents of the upper Colorado basin. Glen Canyon Dam was built to provide water storage upstream of the Grand Canyon. Unfortunately, use of this water for irrigation, coupled with inadequate dilution of downstream supplies, has generated salt loading and salt concentration in the river, harming agricultural and municipal use.

Despite the fact that these costs were imposed upon an entire region, one will search in vain to find an assessment of these possible impacts in benefit-cost studies proposing construction of Hoover and Glen Canyon dams. While better knowledge of the hydrology and geography of the region could have prevented these problems by a factoring of these variables into benefit-cost analyses, avoiding the problems would have required anticipating them. An environmental assessment, such as that required by the National Environmental Policy Act (had such a requirement existed when these projects were built), might have served this purpose. Clearly, however, benefit-cost analysis alone wold not have accomplished this goal.

The second problem, equity, is exemplified by the Garrison diversion project. Even if the benefit-cost ratios had shown that costs exceeded benefits, residents of North Dakota were convinced that the project would compensate for losses imposed on them when the Pick-Sloan project was built. Irving Fox's criticism of benefit-cost analysis points to the difficulty of reconciling actual benefits (those that exceed costs) and perceived benefits (those that affect people's pride and well-being), because they are looked upon as just deserts. "Traditional benefit-cost analysis misses the dynamic character of the situation . . . and [thus] fails to measure the benefits, because the impact a large venture has upon the psychology of the people of the region is not susceptible to engineering-economic analysis" (Fox, 1966: 275).

In essence, efficiency and equity are often confused by government agencies and the general public, alike. The Garrison case has been particularly difficult to solve to everyone's satisfaction, because North Dakotans who advocate the project argue that equity should outweigh considerations of national economic accounts factored into benefit-cost ratios. These residents' ancestors were told that water resources developments would be forthcoming. It was perceived to be part of a deal, in which residents gave up their lands to Pick-Sloan dams in exchange for indirect benefits to their heirs.

The third criticism, project and program quality, is perhaps the easiest to grasp and, in theory, should be the easiest to rectify. Economist Paul Downing, an authority on environmental economics, defines the problem as follows:

> It is expensive to quantify all benefits and costs. . . .
> There are differences of opinion about how the value
> of certain items should be treated. We cannot expect
> benefit-cost analysis to give us a definitive answer about
> the desired level of environmental quality. What it can
> do is to eliminate policy options that are clearly outside
> the range of economic acceptability (Downing, 1984:
> 110).

In other words, if used correctly, benefit-cost analysis can compare mitigating measures for solving water problems, a sort of policy trade-off analysis, according to Downing. If agencies are compelled to weigh alternative measures of alleviating problems of flooding, agricultural irrigation, and so on, then policy makers will be presented with more than one alternative to solve a problem. While refinements in benefit-cost analysis since the early 1950s have tried to accommodate Downing's very argument, they have met with less than overwhelming success. The reason for this are political, not economic, and boil down to this very problem of comparing alternatives.

The May 1962 resolution that became Senate Document 97 constituted, until formulation of the Principles and Standards for Water and Related Land Resources by the Water Resources Council in September 1973, the bible for water planners (GAO, 1974). Senate Document 97 established criteria for computing benefits in a consistent manner across water resources agencies. It required that benefit and cost estimates be supported with field data. It also encouraged more thorough analysis and testing of economic hypotheses by water resources agencies in their evaluation of proposed water projects. Of utmost importance, by requiring comparisons of economic conditions with and without the proposed project (a novel idea, which in some respects mirrors the action–no-action mode of operation of the 1969 National Environmental Policy Act), the document attempted to establish a means of comparing the net gains likely to accrue through different strategies to mitigate the same problem.

A General Accounting Office study on the use of benefit-cost analysis in seven projects then being undertaken—three by the Corps of Engineers, two by the Bureau of Reclamation, one by the Soil Conservation Service, and one by the Tennessee Valley Authority—found that none of the requirements of Document 97 was being met (GAO, 1974). Despite the wide use of benefit-cost analysis and the slim likelihood that a project could be authorized if benefits did not exceed costs, agencies were computing benefits inconsistently, were failing to support their findings with sufficient evidence, and rarely considered project costs fully in the computation of benefit-cost ratios.

At the root of the GAO's critique was the notion that the computation of benefits and costs, at some point, requires a judgment about the effects of alternative plans. The GAO hoped that the adoption of the Water Resource Council's Principles and Standards would help alleviate this problem by establishing uniformity and consistency in the selection of measurement objectives, the definition of beneficial and adverse effects, and the comparison of alternative actions. Following the GAO report, agencies contritely developed "draft implementing procedures" to conform with the council's Principles and Standards. They conceded that changes were warranted and publicly committed themselves to doing a better job of meeting these criteria (GAO, 1974).

Despite these attempted reforms, however, there were two things that water resources agencies did not do (and perhaps could not do under prevailing political conditions). First, they did not address the issue of whether what people wanted was environmentally sound. Thus they failed to conform to intuitive concepts of justice. The agencies continued to assume that the basic goal of water policy was to generate economic benefits that would accrue to the interests of the majority of citizens. If this could be done, then they argued that directly affected local populations were being adequately served by the proposal for development. If residents of a particular water resources region were willing to fight for a benefit, then the benefit was obviously one worthy of pursuit.

Second, water resources agencies did not gauge what people wanted in any systematic manner. There was no attempt to incorporate the opinions, preferences, and criticisms of the general public. If public opinion is presumed to be a valid indicator of benefit, then the means to tap that opinion should be broadened beyond the traditional iron triangle. This is one of the goals of the National Environmental Policy Act.

Unconventional Critiques: The National Environmental Policy Act as Political Theory

The National Environmental Policy Act of 1969 requires that federal agencies prepare assessments of how their proposed developments will affect the land, water, and other resources of the United States and its territories. Since 1969, many states have adopted their own versions of this act and require similar assessments by state agencies. The federal act attempts to transcend the mere cataloging of preferences by forcing decision makers to justify their preferences by criteria other than economic efficiency. More important, it establishes a systematic process of review, deliberation, and ramifications of proposed agency actions (Caldwell, 1988). Instead of merely requiring bargaining and negotiation to resolve differences among interests, the act compels each side to a dispute to make sacrifices in their preferences for the benefit of the larger community. These benefits include environmental protection, regional equity, and other factors.

There is no accurate way to determine how many environmental impact statements and records of a decision (the latter required by the Council on Environmental Quality as a means of rendering a final decision to approve or reject such projects) have actually mitigated the adverse ecological and social impacts of water projects. Many environmental impact statements have ended up on library shelves as monuments to the good intentions of reformers and testaments to the limitlessness of bureaucratic paperwork. However, the process does serve to critique conventional decision making and to reject simple benefit-cost analysis. Most of all, it forces decision makers to offer careful and balanced project plans and designs and technical analyses of factors previously given little attention.

A growing body of literature suggests that accurate environmental impact analyses can lead to a careful consideration of environmental factors and the thoughtful weighing of alternative means for achieving planning objectives. This is especially likely if methods are developed for evaluating the impact of multiple projects upon multiple resources, and not just single projects on single resources. These methods should establish policy guidance on resource use, not absolute scientific precision about impacts (Culhane, Friesema, and Beecher, 1987).[1]

In practice, many impact statements are overlong, resistant to public scrutiny, confusing, and poorly written, detracting from their usefulness

(Culhane, Friesema, Beecher, 1987; Enk and Hart, 1977). In order to serve the purpose for which it was intended, the assessment process should be viewed as a means to an end, not as an end in itself. Its original purpose was to open the process of natural resources decision making to public scrutiny so as to hold agencies accountable, assure an assessment of noneconomic factors, and increase public trust in decision makers.

Opposition to engineering solutions to water and energy problems is partly rooted in distrust of the elite that manages the technology. The National Environmental Policy Act is designed to alleviate this distrust. First, agencies are to supply several alternatives to solve resources problems. The Council on Environmental Quality, which monitors the environmental impact assessment process, requires that agencies identify their preferred alternative. This preferred alternative must be identified in all versions of the environmental impact statement in order to "present the environmental impacts of the proposal and its alternatives in comparative form, thus sharply defining the issues and providing a clear basis for choice" (CEQ Regulations).

An environmentally preferred alternative and an agency's preferred alternative for managing a problem will often differ. Nevertheless, non-environmental factors favoring a water project, such as commitments encumbered by treaty or other international agreement, might weigh heavily in a decision to proceed with construction. An example would be the U.S. commitment to assure Mexico a sufficient supply of fresh water as promised under the Colorado River Compact of 1922. If supplying this water led to overutilization of water supplies, the basin's salt problem would be further exacerbated, and a desalination plant or more dams would have to be built (Bureau of Reclamation, 1948: 50).

In some cases, the preferred alternative and an environmentally preferred alternative could be identical, although they must be identified separately to elucidate public concerns at public hearings and to assure consideration of the least environmentally intrusive of all options—the do-nothing alternative (Manheim, 1981).

Second, the act fosters trust by providing citizens with information about a resource problem and the plans to mitigate it. In this way, thoughtful preferences about alternatives may be expressed. In order for this information to be useful, however, the objectives of policy and the motives of agencies must be scrutable. In the past, these objects and motives have rarely been available to the public, because agencies often acted on preformed decisions.

To some extent, this is the reason vigorous opposition to the Blue Ridge project was not alleviated even after environmental impacts, and the means to mitigate them, were spelled out by the Federal Power

Commission. In essence, the environmental analysis was undertaken after planning for the pump storage dams was well advanced and when many adverse impacts would have been irreversible. To compound matters, the most critical changes in the evolution of the project—its enlargement in order to provide greater water storage for the dilution of water pollution—came about through informal consultation between the FPC, the Appalachian Power Company, and the Department of the Interior, without a public hearing or even congressional committee oversight or review.

When such important decisions on controversial projects are made in apparent secrecy, citizens often feel that public debate, discussion, and deliberation are being circumvented and that policies are made under duress or coercion. The process mandated by the 1969 National Environmental Policy Act is supposed to avoid such impasses through public hearings at the inception of a project (scoping meetings) and public hearings after initial plans are formulated.

Finally, the act is designed to improve public trust by assuring that policy makers can be held accountable for decisions. Unfortunately, this is one area where public policy specialists have failed to learn from political philosophy. While the specialists tend to consider the policy-making process as a way for heighten public acceptance of government decisions, political philosophers tend to focus on the veracity of an agency's commitment.

It is one thing for agencies to alleviate public opposition to their proposals by holding public hearings. It is quite another for these agencies to do what they said they would do during these hearings. The principal limitations of such public hearings are that they polarize views and that they are a one-way flow of information—from the citizen to the government or vice versa (Kasperson, 1986). Rarely do they lead directly to a reduction of risks to the environment, to constructive dialogue about social goals and the means to achieve them, or to the alleviation of undesirable impacts.

Public trust requires a reasonable assurance that an action taken by government to mitigate a problem, such as the adverse impacts of a water project, will in fact accomplish what its proponents claim. The mere perception by the public that government agencies are competent to resolve hazards is ethically insufficient, because it provides no means for holding officials to account, establishes no rules for ascertaining whether trust reposed was trust earned, and because appearance and reality can diverge.

The 1969 Environmental Act begins from the premise that agency officials have the capacity to make decisions to which they can be bound, that they are free to order their actions in various ways, that they are cognizant of the consequences of their decisions, and that they do not make these decisions under duress or coercion. The acceptance by policy makers of liability for policy failure is implied.

According to Marvin Manheim, who has had extensive experience applying these axioms to EIS work in the field of transportation, liability for policy failure can best be assured by identifying beneficial as well as adverse impacts of a proposed project and by accommodating equity and uncertainty concerns through explicit compensation (Manheim, 1981). How do we go beyond theory to actual decision making? Two changes in the assessment process may help regional tiering of impact statements for water projects and encouragement of wide public participation through extension of the scoping process.

An environmental impact statement is not, strictly speaking, a regulatory tool. It is not even legally binding. In agency decision making, that role is reserved for the record of decision, a report issued by the natural resources agency to the Council on Environmental Quality explaining why it selected a particular alternative and how it plans to address concerns uncovered in the final environmental impact statement. The EIS is a vehicle for ascertaining the impacts of a specific activity. While not a regulatory device, it can serve as a planning instrument if modified in appropriate ways.

The issuance of an environmental policy statement by water resources agencies prior to initiation of a water development program would be a step in this direction. In turn, written assessments by individual states of their most significant ecological characteristics, including detailed atlases inventorying the water and land resources they deem most critical, could encourage accurate assessments of potential impacts. The environmental policy statement could prevent costly litigation by implementing corrective measures during early stages of planning. It would act as a gauge for assessing and anticipating impacts. This process could be assisted through a technique called tiering (Enk and Hart, 1977).

Tiering is the preparation of several EISs to accommodate different geographical levels of planning. During the heyday of the Water Resources Council, public works agencies had lengthy experience in preparation of management plans at national or so-called framework levels, as well as at river basin, subbasin, and local levels of planning. As a result, tiering would not be particularly difficult nor would it entail unprecedented operating practices. However, it might entail the revival of river basin commissions or other regional planning instruments, which currently lie dormant or, in some cases, are nonexistent.

A regional environment impact assessment would, in effect, always be in process, and reviewing agencies would need only concentrate upon the impacts of a specific location and project. Presumably, they would have reviewed the plans from which the project stemmed. By limiting the geographic range of an EIS, public participation in the review and comment phase might also be encouraged (Enk and Hart, 1977).

Another method for improving the review process, scoping, is not to be confused with the narrowing of public concerns through local hearings prior to the undertaking of an environmental impact assessment. As used in this context, it refers to bringing together those groups most likely to be affected by water resources developments at the outset of EIS preparation. The technique is widely used for risk-laden programs whose impacts extend over large areas.

The Blue Ridge dam project on the New River is an illustration: the use of scoping in this case would have meant that the Appalachian Power Company would have consulted with affected groups in the New River valley prior to the proposed enlargement of the project. Recall that opposition began only after it was announced that many more additional relocations and inundations of property would take place. In essence, the integration of affected groups in the planning process helps to focus attention upon the adverse impacts ordinarily missed by proponents of projects—in this case the complexity of the project's purposes in the eyes of the public, the destruction of a scenic wonder not accommodated by benefit-cost calculations, and of greatest consequence, the impossibility of compensating for some forms of losses.

It has even been suggested that scoping be extended to include review by other agencies (Enk and Hart, 1977). At present, affected or interested agencies assess environmental impact analyses only after plans have been formulated by lead agencies. Again, recalling the Blue Ridge case, scoping might have allowed the EPA to express its doubts about the use of pollution dilution prior to the FPC's endorsement of the technique, a technique that opponents condemned for falling short as a method of water pollution abatement.

Dam Safety: Benefit-Cost Considerations and the Imperatives of Risk, Health, and Welfare

In recent years, dam safety has become a major public concern as aging structures upstream of populated areas have begun to show signs of structural vulnerability. In a few cases, the failure of impoundments following floods or hurricanes has heightened this concern. Even though these are not new projects, benefit-cost considerations cannot be avoided.

The prevailing federal practice is to determine during inspection or repair which dams pose the greatest risk to public safety. The Corps of

Engineers is currently struggling with the question of how much to invest in emergency planning as opposed to hazard reduction (reinforcing impoundments). Both decisions are based on a risk-cost assessment (Schilling et al., 1987), a targeting of resources where need is greatest and where benefits to the greater number of citizens will accrue.

While dam failure, even on a limited scale, is improbable, its potentially catastrophic results place a considerable burden on policy makers invested with public trust. As a result, dam safety exemplifies the need for policy assessments that are unbiased and not preformed and the need for decision makers who are politically accountable, so that the public can be assured that public safety will not be compromised in either the construction or the operation of the dam.

Before 1972, a comprehensive safety inspection program existed in the United States only for federally constructed dams. The Corps of Engineers and the Bureau of Reclamation periodically inspected their own dams as well as those belonging to other federal agencies or licensed by the Federal Power Commission (now the Federal Energy Regulatory Commission). With the exception of a few states directly victimized by catastrophic dam failure (California being the most notable example), state dam inspection programs were practically nonexistent (Platt et al., 1980).

In 1972, the Dam Inspection Act authorized the secretary of the Army (through the Corps of Engineers) to undertake a national program of dam inspection. This act limited the efforts of the corps to (1) compiling an inventory of federal and nonfederal dams; there are some 90,000 dams of any consequence in the United States, of which 68,153 were considered major enough to be included in the corps's inventory by 1980 (Schilling et al., 1987: 66; Jansen, 1980: 96), (2) surveying state and federal agency capabilities, practices, and regulations pertaining to dam safety, (3) developing guidelines for inspections and evaluations of dams, and (4) formulating recommendations for a "comprehensive national dam safety program" (Jansen, 1980: 96).

In 1977, partly as a result of the previous year's Teton Dam failure in Idaho, President Jimmy Carter issued an executive order to strengthen this program. The corps was ordered to perform a visual inspection of 9,000 high-risk dams—older dams upstream of densely populated areas. Reports on safety were to be given to state governors, who would then decide on appropriate action. In addition, a "foundation integrity analysis" was performed on those dams that failed visual inspection (Platt et al., 1980).

Three major problems have emerged in this program. First, no single federal agency can adequately inspect all of the 49,000 or so major dams in the United States (dams whose crest is twenty-five feet or more above the streambed). One possible solution is to encourage states to shoulder more of the responsibility for dam inspections. Some movement in this area has taken place.

Proponents of dam safety argue that there should be periodic state inspection of existing dams as well as state regulation of the construction of new dams, especially privately owned dams not regulated by the federal government. Another option is a scoping process, which would include consultation with developers, downstream residents, environmental groups, and other relevant organizations and interests before a dam is constructed. The scoping process could also serve as emergency preparedness in the event of catastrophic failure (Platt et al., 1980).

California, which has experienced catastrophic dam failures, has undertaken a program that approximates this suggestion. The exceptional nature of this program is exemplified by the fact that California spends more on dam inspection than all other states combined (Platt et al., 1980). Under the program, California demanded additional foundation studies of the Auburn Dam, a proposed federal project, due to concern over possible seismic sensitivities in the vicinity of the dam.

This bring us to the second problem. Under the Dam Inspection Act, the Corps of Engineers determines what constitutes a high-risk dam. The corps defines risk by reference to potential loss of life and potential economic losses from dam failure. By making such an assessment up front, the corps is able to determine how much to invest in planning for dam failure, in building new dams, and in repairing old ones. It could be argued, cynically, that the less spent on dam safety, the more money there is available for new water project planning, the preferable activity of water resources agencies. In reality, however, the corps has no choice but to limit spending on dam safety. The large number of dams in the United States, their complex patterns of ownership, and the variety of rehabilitation needs—ranging from stability and seepage to inoperable components and spillway disrepair—make the task of dam safety exceedingly difficult and expensive. Table 7.1 depicts the hazard potential of nonfederal dams under criteria determined by the corps.

The purpose of this classification system is to determine how best to target limited resources. By way of contrast, the Bureau of Reclamation takes the view that, whenever a population is at risk from one of its dams, emergency planning should be emphasized. (Emergency planning includes warning of an impending flood, evacuation of the population, restricting dam building in flood zones; and improving dam inspection.) This difference in approach is probably due to the failure of the Teton Dam in 1976. Since the corps has had no comparable failure in any recently constructed dam, it has taken a more conservative approach. In short, the corps's approach to dam safety is to sample dams posing

Table 7.1 Expected Loss of Life and Economic Loss Caused by Unsafe
Dams, According to Corps of Engineers' Estimate of Hazard Potential

Hazard Potential	Expected Loss of Life	Expected Economic Loss
Low	None: no permanent structures for human habitation downstream	Minimal: Undeveloped or temporary structures or agriculture
Significant	Few: no urban development, no more than a few inhabitable structures	Appreciable: notable agriculture, industry, or structures
High	More than a few	Excessive: extensive community, industry, or agriculture

Source: Schilling et al., 1987, p. 67.

a high hazard to human life (Schilling et al., 1987: 67). Not only does
this approach fulfil legislative intent, it controls the cost of inspection.

While the corps's approach may make economic sense, it prompts
questions about policy equity, the third problem entailed in the dam
safety program. Many noninspected dams are old, in gross disrepair,
and located in places where neither state governments nor private owners are willing to invest time or effort in rehabilitation. Merely counting
the people at risk does not solve this problem, because about half of all
high-risk dams are so small that failure of any one of them would place
few people at risk; however, losses in the immediate vicinity would be
catastrophic.

By contrast, few federal dams, which do undergo a risk-cost process
of rehabilitation, are included in the high-risk category (Schilling et al.,
1987: 69). Table 7.2, which depicts ownership of unsafe dams, illustrates the dimensions of this problem. In order to adequately encompass
the concerns of people living downstream of these dams, greater attention needs to be given to determining appropriate risk. Voluntary consent to risk, sometimes used as one measure of acceptability, would be
impossible to implement, even if it could be made fair through democratic procedure, because the public is not fully knowledgeable about
the criteria that defines an unsafe dam. While virtually everyone can
agree that dam safety stands apart from philosophical considerations
about water resources development, it is not fair that the safety of a few
people living downstream of small dams be ignored because the consequences of failure are less than for a major dam burst.

Table 7.2 Ownership of Unsafe Dams According to Corps of Engineers and Federal Emergency Management Agency

Owner	Percentage of Total
Federal agency	0.4
State or local government	26.4
Water resources development district	8.4
Private camp, club, civic organization	3.5
Church, hospital, school	1.5
Water and irrigation company	6.8
Corporation	19.0
Property (owner association or individual)	33.4
Other (not identified)	0.6

Source: Schilling et al., 1987, p. 68.

This problem is compounded by the fragmentation of responsibility for dam safety, a situation that mirrors the fragmentation of other water policy responsibilities. According to a Federal Emergency Management Agency survey, several federal agencies share responsibility for about 3,000 federal and 5,000 nonfederal dams, while states regulate an additional 80,000 or so (Schilling et al., 1987: 68). A partial solution to both the fragmentation problem and the problem of determining public concern over dam safety is offered by the Water Resources Development Act of 1986 (Schilling et al., 1987: 70).

Under a survey conducted by the Interstate Conference on Water Policy, state officials who are expert on safety issues were asked for their input regarding dam safety programs. Four needs for improvements were most commonly identified: (1) federal cost sharing for the establishment of state inspection programs, (2) federal training of state inspectors, (3) federal agency consultation with states on design and safety matters prior to agency dam construction or approval of private construction, and (4) a federal research program on inspection and monitoring (Schilling et al., 1987: 70).

Title XII of the Water Resources Development Act addresses some of these concerns. Training and assistance is included in the legislation, but funding is provided only to update the nonfederal dam inventory. Because most safety problems lie in nonfederal dams, continuing investigation of acceptable levels of risk are needed. A report by the National Council on Public Works helped generate reform in dam safety beyond those outlined in the Water Resources Development Act. "The states did not view the introduction of risk-cost analysis principles as

a useful component of technical assistance, nor did they see it as a way
for evaluating the overall issue of 'how safe is safe enough'" (Schilling
et al., 1987: 70). Instead, the report suggests that continuing research
is needed to develop more cost-effective decision-making techniques
regarding repair. It would appear that states believe any risk to downstream populations should be mitigated.

In short, dam safety illustrates how efficiency can be misused. Once
it is established that dams ought to be safe and that people ought to be
protected from their collapse, then the only matter for decision is how
to provide effective safety margins economically. Efficiency cannot be
used to determine if the goal of maximum public safety is worth pursuing; that assumption is rooted in values basic to our very way of life
and our intuitive concept of justice.

Conclusions: The Difficulty in Finding Alternatives to Benefit-Cost Analysis—Values in Conflict

In 1973, the Water Resources Council's Principles and Standards for
Water and Related Land Resources supplanted Senate Document 97 as
the basis for multiobjective natural resources planning by federal public
works agencies (WRC, 1973). Prior to its demise, the council issued
what would be its final iterations on improving guidelines for computing
benefits and costs (Eisel, Seinwill, and Wheeler, 1982).

These improved principles, standards, and procedures attempted to
force agencies to pay particular attention to the obligations of water
project beneficiaries to those who fund the projects, the conditions under which water project beneficiaries should help finance improvements
to water resources, and how environmental impacts can be economically computed. The upshot of these improvements in principles and
standards, which are still used by the Office of Management and Budget
as well as by some members of Congress to assess the viability of water
projects, is careful elucidation of benefit and cost measures for recreation, hydropower, navigation, and irrigation.

The principles and standards require, among other things, measurement of the willingness of recreational users of water to pay for improvements, measurement of the costs of pollution imposed by recreation, measurement of the willingness of hydropower users to pay for
more electricity and for alternate means of generating power, and measurement of the real costs of navigational improvements relative to alternative modes of shipping goods once federal outlays for dredging and
damming of navigable streams are accounted for (Eisel, Seinwill, and
Wheeler, 1982). The problem, however, is inconsistent adherence to
these standards by water resources agencies.

A 1982 GAO report on the Corps of Engineers' Elk River project in Jackson County, Oregon, illustrates that many of the same errors of measurement in benefit-cost analysis noted in the 1974 GAO report still applied in the 1980s. Unrealistic projections of the benefits for flood control, recreation, and water supply, the employment of outdated data, and inadequate consideration of recovery of project costs through hydropower revenues were but a few of the GAO's criticisms of the corps's benefit-cost studies (U.S. House of Representatives, 1987).

Why is adherence to standards so hard to obtain? Ultimately, it is because benefit-cost analysis and other methods of assessing social gains and losses from natural resources development are not defended on ethical grounds. Instead, they are seen as political tools to make proposed projects credible. This is why merely changing emphases and priorities of a program or the definitions of costs, benefits, and risks fails to produce a policy able to address water shortages or pollution.

Principles and standards should not be used to avoid conflict—that is, to coopt the opposition by adding more and more features to appease more and more interests. The resolution of differences over the objectives of water policy requires a commitment to a combination of scientific method and ethical justification, which I term *reasonable fallibility*. In essence, reasonable fallibility predicates that all policy decisions are fallible. Science cannot tell us with absolute certainty the benefits, costs, and risks of various decisions. Likewise, few ethical positions in the political arena are totally without stakeholder bias or the perception of personal gain. Policies should strive to minimize the scope of an action, to build iteratively upon lessons learned from prior developments, and to impose the lowest impacts based upon scientific guidance, not absolute scientific certainty.

William Lord, a former staff economist in the Office of the Secretary of the Army, suggests that a principal source of inaccuracy in benefit-cost analysis is "adding more features to a project in order to include positive net benefits for a wider range of interests" (Lord, 1980: 6). While this obviously makes sense within the rules of the game of distributive politics, where agencies try to increase local support for a project in order to attain congressional approval, it erroneously presumes that there are no losers in the game of building water projects.

The real purpose of principles and standards is to insure that factual information is used as a basis for public policy. No amount of standards can assure efficient and equitable policy, however, if value conflicts over why a project should be undertaken remain unresolved. Lord himself concedes that scientific method is not very effective when proponents and opponents of a policy cannot come together over values.

Concluding that there is probably no durable solution to this problem,

Lord argues that the "objective grounds for conflict over water resources development has been increasing. This is [also] true of social goals and values" (Lord, 1980: 10). While solutions are elusive, however, it is clear that, as the objective bases for conflict increase, the need to transcend a merely preferential negotiating framework becomes more apparent. No longer will merely carving the water resources pie into more pieces act to improve policy. Organizational values must themselves be changed to conform to a broader perspective of social need and environmental impact.

What we are left with are two possible directions for reform. While most attempts at reform have so far met with resistance, many of these attempts were misplaced or misguided. They have concentrated upon agency reorganization, issuing more rules, or merely opening up the game to more participants.

An alternative to reorganization is regional contractualism, in which the decision-making framework is incrementally modified to allow establishment of decentralized, self-sufficient water resources regions, which plan and implement their own management systems through user fees imposed upon residents of each region. The biggest obstacle this type of reform will face in the short run is the resistance of established water resources agencies, which view themselves as stewards of natural resources. These agencies define regional interest and national interest according to a limited set of economic criteria.

This brings us to the second possible direction for reform, the elimination of technological elitism. The sooner it is recognized that the behavior of water resources agencies is rooted in strongly held values, the better reformers will be able to anticipate resistance to change. More important, all the parties to a water resources conflict will realize that narrow conspiracy theories do not adequately or fairly explain the failure of government to correctly use benefit-cost analysis, to follow the spirit of the National Environmental Policy Act, or to resolve value conflicts through adherence to principles and standards.

Essentially, policy failures are as much the result of rigid ideologies unsympathetic to ecological considerations as they are the result of distributive politics. While this does not make prospects for reform any easier, it should make reformers more realistic about their own goals.

8 Practitioners of Water Policy: Technological Elitism as a Policy Ethic

These guys are engineers, and all they're doing is plans. . . . When you've got guys who haven't seen a shovel of dirt in ten years, you have a morale problem.
—TOM SKIRBUNT, SENATE WATER COMMITTEE

The Corps has 45,000 civilians and 1,200 military. . . . We're not especially cheap, but you can't get ability cheaply. It's unthinkable to let that [talent] wither on the vine.
—JOSEPH A. BRATTEN, CORPS OF ENGINEERS

Water Policy as the Product of a Closed and Undemocratic Process

The ideological basis for American water policy has, for the most part, been efficiency. Moreover, what is considered to be efficient has also been assumed to be socially beneficial. This is largely because the principal agency charged with making and implementing water policy is the Corps of Engineers. The corps was originally given this authority because the need to engage in internal improvements was considered a matter of national security, for which a military organization was best equipped. The corps retained this authority because, over time, the task of managing water resources was seen as sufficiently complex to require supervision by military engineers rather than civilians. Because the profession of civil engineering in the United States was to a great extent nurtured by the military, this enhanced the authority of the corps to manage water resources. In short, while early frontier experiences gave the corps expertise in water resources management, later national needs for a skilled organization able to manage natural resources helped it gain independence from the army as a whole and political influence with Congress.

The training, socialization, and history of the corps has shaped a conservative and, at the same time, dynamic organization, resistant to change yet eager to solve problems in ways that conform to its own peculiar sense of the national interest. While the Bureau of Reclamation, the Corps of Engineers' chief rival in water policy, is a civilian agency, it favors economic modernization through water resources development. The Corps of Engineers set the values in natural resources policy, and other agencies emulate its example. This emulation is understandable given the corps's success in building a network of political influence, in setting water policy, and in constructing water projects.

None of these agencies want to destroy natural resources or to exclude interest groups from participation. Were this the case, it would be easy to challenge current policy. Instead, these agencies are guided by an ideology that is simply too narrow to accommodate the entire range of social concerns about natural resources. The reasons this ideology is resistant to change is the focus of this chapter.

Engineering, Political Development, and the Army Corps of Engineers: National Security and Natural Resources

Since 1824, the Army Corps of Engineers has been the principal steward of the water resources of the United States. Even when it has shared this responsibility with other agencies, it has been difficult to talk about major water policy problems without somehow accounting for either how the corps will be involved in their resolution or why they choose not to be. The Pick-Sloan plan, for example, was really a compromise plan between the Bureau of Reclamation and the corps, which had competing interests in the Missouri valley. The key components of that plan, including the controversial Garrison diversion project, shared characteristics favored by both agencies. The components of Pick-Sloan most often criticized by environmentalists were the unfinished Bureau of Reclamation irrigation plans, not the completed flood control and power components built by the corps.

For better than a generation, political scientists who have studied U.S. water policy have attributed the power of the corps to structural factors unique to the U.S. government. These factors include the fragmented, decentralized representation in Congress (the branch of government closest to the corps through the actions of public works committees, which traditionally encourage river and harbor improvements); the idiosyncrasies of subsystem politics, or iron triangles; the absence of rule-making institutions with adequate authority in polities where interest groups are both specialized and numerous; and the corps's organizational unity derived from its long experience in water resources management (Ferejohn, 1974; Truman, 1971; Marshall, 1966; Drew, 1970).

Each of these explanations offers important insights into water policy but does not pay sufficient attention to the origins of the corps's authority. This authority arose from an inadequate administrative capacity in American natural resources policy, which led to a role expansion of the military into politics. This role expansion, unthreatening to other civilian political institutions or to civil political authority, originated at a time when the national concerns were internal improvements and the governing of natural resources.

The corps remained paramount in this area because, in the absence of widely held and commonly understood values over natural resources use, water policy remained sufficiently complex to require the expertise of skilled extragovernmental specialists (Rourke, 1984). This was especially true during the greater part of American history when the national government remained severely limited in its power to promote a centralized economy (Skocpol and Finegold, 1982).

During the New Deal, dam building and comprehensive river basin planning proceeded on an unprecedented scale. The planning capacity of the national government thus grew, as did the possibility of inclusion into policy making of elements formerly excluded. These elements would eventually challenge the corps on various projects and policy goals. Unfortunately, these changes in society at large did not necessarily induce changes in the corps (or the Bureau of Reclamation, which often adhered to the corps's goals).

This role expansion of the military constitutes an American variant of a pattern known to comparativists as civic action. Civic actions are activities not germane to the normal activities of the armed forces that promote economic development (Perlmutter and Leo Grande, 1982; Glick, 1967). The civic action framework illuminates the development of the corps's activities, the unique way it has lent its expertise to policies without challenging overall civilian authority, and the types of policies it has pursued.

The Corps's Entry into Water Policy: National Security in Another Light

The principal responsibility for the exploration and surveying of this nation's interior fell to the neutral and competent military scouts and topographical engineers trained at West Point. Among the better known of these expeditions were those of Lewis and Clark in the Missouri River valley in 1804–5, Zebulon Pike's Arkansas headwaters expedition of 1806–7, Stephen H. Long's central Rocky Mountain–Yellowstone scientific survey in 1819–20, and John Wesley Powell's post–Civil War

Colorado River hydrographic survey (Goetzmann, 1959; Clarke and McCool, 1985). The distinguished efforts of a small but vital military topographical engineering unit during the War of 1812 prompted Congress to establish the Board of Engineers for Internal Improvements in 1824 and to allocate funds for widening the channel of the Ohio River. President James Monroe appointed two army engineers to this three-man body, because the corps was the only agency with the necessary technical expertise (Clarke and McCool, 1985).

Anticipated dangers from hostile Indians, unfamiliar terrain, and uncertain international boundaries compelled these missions to rely upon military officers, rather than civilian explorers. In an important historiography of these expeditions, William Goetzmann contends that, in a nation with few trained engineers or surveyors and even fewer resources to devote to internal improvements, the Corps of Topographical Engineers (COTE, a branch of the Army Corps of Engineers formed in 1838) played a vital role in advancing western settlement.

In addition to mapping the interior, COTE constructed roads, improved navigation, staffed West Point and shaped its curriculum, and dealt with conflicts between local and national factions, who saw the corps, variously, as a public works agency responsible to settlers or as a military unit accountable to Congress (which, in actuality, it was). Because the interests in frontier development of members of Congress and their constituents tended to be the same, Congress overlooked budget constraints and encouraged public works.

By the early twentieth century, responsibility for most river and harbor improvements fell to the corps's Civil Works Directorate (successor to the Board of Internal Improvements) because the regional prosperity, integration, and political unity that would ensue were viewed as components of national security. As Francis Rourke notes, the corps produced tangible achievements easily recognized and appreciated by laypersons through methods difficult for nonspecialists to comprehend (Rourke, 1984: 94).

Evidence for the linking of development and national security is offered by official corps chronicles. In 1903 and again in 1916, the corps strongly endorsed the efforts of private consortia to develop a hydropower project on the Tennessee River at Muscle Shoals, Alabama. A license for this project was vetoed by President Theodore Roosevelt on grounds that it constituted an "exclusive franchise" (*Congressional Record*, 1903). During World War I, the corps successfully argued that a hydropower project at Muscle Shoals would provide electricity for a nitrates plant to produce high explosives for munitions, explosives otherwise obtainable only by importation (Hobday, 1969: 67).

One former chief of engineers notes that the corps's projects, in historical perspective, resemble the civic action efforts of the armed forces in developing nations because of their concern for regional development. The corps's civil works accomplishments have been substantial:

> Deep-draft harbors have opened the cities of our sea-coasts and Great Lakes to the flow of international commerce, and inland waterways have linked vast internal regions together through a low-cost transportation system. . . . Beneficial effects of these investments have played an important role in development of major regions of the nation. (Gribble, 1974)

Another, more subtle, concern may underlie the nation's use of the military for civil works, and that is the avoidance of an elite, aloof armed forces. West Point as a civil engineering training center allayed fears that a suppressive, segregated caste, a sort of American praetorian guard, would develop (Weigley, 1973).

Civil-Military Conflict and the Corps of Engineers:
The Special Case of Hydropower

In addition to its traditional expertise in civil engineering, the Corps of Engineers has developed political skills. Such "bureaucratic superstars" (Clarke and McCool, 1985) are often asked to lend their political skills to various political objectives. When national development objectives change, an agency like the corps "rarely turns down an opportunity to expand its horizons," even if that opportunity is unexpected (Clarke and McCool, 1985). The corps's efforts in the field of hydropower exemplify this fact.

Hydropower represents the first large-scale effort in the United States to develop a national energy policy. While several agencies with varying mandates participated in this initiative, the participation of the corps was, to a large degree, unintended. This participation was initiated in the early 1900s by Major Francis R. Shunk, who was affiliated with the Mississippi River division of the corps, and the cities of Minneapolis and St. Paul, Minnesota.

In 1899, interests in and around the Twin Cities urged Congress to appropriate funds to modify a navigation dam on the Mississippi River for the purpose of generating electricity. Influenced by the Progressive Movement and its emphasis on public stewardship of resources, Congress appointed a study commission to look into the engineering feasibility of the request. As a result of this investigation, the Corps of Engineers recommended the construction of a higher impoundment at lock and dam number one on the Mississippi River (Merritt, 1979: 142).

Despite the engineering feasibility of the proposal, however, Congress was reluctant to appropriate funds, since many believed that such a project should be built privately and that the federal government should not be in the business of producing electricity. However, the Twin Cities refused to relinquish land to private developers for construction of power dams. When at the same time Major Shunk asked the corps for funds to appraise the power potential of the Mississippi River main stem, Congress succumbed. Shunk became the first Corps of Engineers' officer to design and build a hydroelectric dam (Merritt, 1979: 143).

Shunk, who envisioned a national-local partnership on behalf of a broader public interest in water resources development, recommended that the federal government build power facilities and then lease them to private utilities. Shunk was sensitive to the fact that investor-owned utilities were being formed and that the private sector distrusted federal intervention in this area (Merritt, 1979: 142–45). Shunk was also aware that Congress would not deny approval of a water project that had local support, a phenomenon the corps has exploited ever since.

Although Congress authorized the corps to consider the inclusion of hydroelectric facilities in project studies as early as 1909, there was considerable debate within and without the corps over how this objective should be pursued, as evidenced by conflicts over the efficacy of combining irrigation, flood control, and power in single projects (Clarke and McCool, 1985). Many engineers believed that dams designed explicitly for storing water to generate power were inconsistent with the alleviation of floods. Others believed these goals could be reconciled.

According to Arthur E. Morgan, an original board member of the Tennessee Valley Authority and a long-time critic of the corps, this conflict was precipitated by the corps's lack of an "inclusive engineering outlook," a holistic approach to solving water resources problems. He attributes this lack of a broad outlook to the corps's narrow West Point training. "All of the characteristics of West Point: the sheltered and isolated atmosphere, the rigid repression, the antiquated curriculum, the rote method of learning, [and] compulsory obedience [produce] graduates who are not independent or creative thinkers" (Morgan, 1971: 17). However, many civilian engineers also opposed combining several water resources management objectives in a single storage project (L. Johnson, 1974: 193).

The underlying cause of this problem of combining objectives was the failure of Congress to establish an unambiguous policy for water resources development. A 1909 congressional act required the corps to "consider the potential for [hydroelectric] power in all preliminary surveys for navigation projects," thus placing navigation ahead of power. Not until a 1912 report by the National Waterways Commission was this conflict resolved. Once Congress made its will known, the corps "quickly moved to capture the program" (Clarke and McCool, 1985: 16).

Thus was established the corps's congressional link and its freedom from cabinet scrutiny. Later efforts to expand the corps's role by granting it the authority to act in areas of national concern increased the corps's ability to defy executive branch control of its activities and enabled it to exercise considerable discretion in regional development. Both of these freedoms exacerbated conflicts with other agencies (Brown, 1980: 27).

The civil works function of the corps also avoided cabinet-level scrutiny by first garnering influential local support for its projects. Major Shunk had set the precedent, by mobilizing local support in Minneapolis and St. Paul for hydroelectric power. Congressional support followed, and the cabinet was bypassed. Subsequently, the grassroots efforts of the corps itself were aided by a powerful, locally organized group supportive of corps policies, the National Rivers and Harbors Congress. This group comprised former corps officers, members of Congress, contractors, state and local officials, and water user groups. The group also works at the congressional level to gain support for project funding and against spending cuts and attempts to combine the corps with the Bureau of Reclamation or to turn it into a civilian agency.

In essence, the feasibility of hydropower projects with strong local backing were tested at the district level, then at the division level. Positive reactions at these levels would prompt a request to the secretary of the Army for construction funds. In many instances, positive local reaction engendered virtually automatic approval at the departmental level (Mazmanian and Nienaber, 1979: 17–18; Brown, 1980: 27). The power of the corps and its local and congressional allies is exemplified by the fact that, in 1949, Defense Secretary James Forrestal did not participate in the recommendation to transfer the water resource functions of the corps to the Department of the Interior (Truman, 1971: 337, 410).

Understandably, the fact that such reorganization never took place led to conflicts between the corps and the rival Bureau of Reclamation— and further underscores the short shrift paid to comprehensive regional planning, apart from the economic feasibility of particular water projects.

Insights into the Corps of Engineers' Values from Comparative Politics

Specialists in American politics are reluctant to draw comparisons between the Corps of Engineers and military institutions involved in natural resources politics in other nations. First, the exercise of military authority in American domestic politics takes place without violent coups d'état or interference in legitimate constitutional processes. Second, although the corps is formally a military organization, it is heavily staffed with civilians, is uninvolved in traditional national security matters, and competes lawfully for budget authorizations with civilian agencies. Its values and sources of authority are thus thought to be explainable by public administration models of interagency conflicts and political fragmentation characteristic of American pluralism (Mazmanian and Nienaber, 1979: 9; Seidman, 1970: 44–49).

Crossnational comparisons are, however, useful. They show that sources of expertise for addressing natural resources problems are partially dependent upon a polity's level of political development and, furthermore, that a government's capacity to initiate natural resources policies without fear that the policies will be overturned by other interests also depends on the level of political development.

Henry Bienen's model of civil-military relations predicated upon interest group relations may be relevant for the United States (although this model may be irrelevant to lesser developed societies). Where institutions have well-developed boundaries, distinct patterns of socialization and recruitment, and specialized, independent vehicles for training, "personal, ideological, and policy networks may exist across . . . boundaries" (Bienen, 1983: 8). In all cases, the level of a polity's development, determined by the complexity of its institutions and the perceived legitimacy of their boundaries, establishes the parameters for civilian control and stability.

Francis Rourke focuses on the manner in which expertise constitutes a means for bureaucratic advancement. He asserts that, while in all polities "scientists and military officers are in a highly advantageous position . . . to command respect for their talents," the ascendancy of the military profession tends to be more characteristic of lesser developed societies, since the military's influence is not offset by other groups (Rourke, 1984: 93). In short, one result of political development is the proliferation of expertise, which then challenges the monopoly on expertise possessed by the armed services.

How do these comparisons relate to U.S. natural resources policy? In societies undergoing modernization, economic development is a principal imperative of government. The armed forces often play a pivotal role in meeting the challenge of economic development precisely because they are disciplined, hierarchical organizations, have finely honed skills and a sense of esprit de corps, and are relatively isolated from other bureaucracies (Peters, 1978: 118).

If political modernization is rapid, the military's acceptance of state intervention, coupled with its puritanical outlook, may make it a more "supple instrument of political modernization than the civil service, embodying to a greater degree the qualities of dynamism, empiricism, and know-how." In the early nineteenth century, the corps clearly embodied these traits, partly as a result of the army's role as protector of white settlers and peacekeeper along the frontier, a role that rubbed off on all components of the military, to some degree (Heady, 1979: 260; Unruh, 1982).

In sum, in the early stages of political development, the military begins as an organization concerned largely with matters of life and death and the protection of the nation-state from attack or invasion. Later, it may evolve into an organization concerned with internal matters only indirectly related to national security. It was in this way that the army Corps of Engineers, in a fashion that parallels the behavior of the armed forces in developing countries today, became concerned with natural resources policy.

The Capacity of State Regulation and the Preeminent Role of Natural Resources in Political Development

Modernization is a principal goal of developing nations. The preeminent tasks in modernization include the exploitation of natural resources, the development and settlement of the nation's interior, and the harnessing of energy. R. L. Siegel and L. B. Weinberg have identified several stages of natural resources development common to industrialized societies.

In the incipient stage, the goals are conservation and public health. Strategies are pursued that conserve renewable resources and promote their systematic exploitation. Other strategies aim at destroying disease-carrying insects or rodents or clearing out their natural breeding areas (Siegel and Weinberg, 1977). The incipient stage represents the first attempt by centralized, national political authority to allocate money, time, and personnel to problems of territorial scope. Such state intervention is usually prompted by the inadequacy and haphazardness of subnational policies. In short, this stage corresponds to conditions in the United States in about the 1820s, with its territorial expansion and improvements in inland navigation and transport.

The lack of a coherent national development strategy in the United States in its incipient stage encouraged the granting of authority to an agency already in place—the Army Corps of Engineers.

But why the corps? Why not a civilian agency? One explanation is that internal improvements to rivers and harbors and, later, the development of hydropower and other water resources needs were identified with national security. They were viewed as a means of strengthening the military, gaining national economic independence, and securing borders. This would be consistent with Siegel and Weinberg's analysis of the formation of public policy.

An additional explanation of the use of the military in resources development is to be found in the political character of the United States in this early stage of development. The national government was unable to mobilize the administrative authority to address problems of internal development. The ability to mobilize such resources is termed *state capacity*, and it refers to a government's authority to regulate without fear of opposition by powerful, organized interests. For much of the nineteenth century and well into the twentieth, state capacity for natural resources management was weak in the United States. Policies designed to control water resources and, particularly, to develop inland waterways had to rely upon "extragovernmental specialists and organizations," such as the Corps of Engineers, for their implementation (Skocpol and Finegold, 1982: 261).

According to Theda Skocpol and Kenneth Finegold, with whom the term *state capacity* originates, the United States was essentially a stateless polity for much of its history. In other words, before the 1930s, it was virtually unable to initiate strong administrative imperatives in areas such as the management of natural resources. The advent of strong business regulation and natural resources planning (such as river basin commissions) during the New Deal changed this condition.

Civilian agencies were formed to manage these activities, in a deliberate attempt to increase the size, authority, and fiscal resources of government (Skocpol and Finegold, 1982). This attempt to overcome a stateless condition has parallels among present-day developing countries, especially in Latin America.

The advent of powerful agricultural interest groups, land grant colleges, and a handful of statistical experts in the federal government laid the groundwork for a climate favorable to government intervention in the American economy (and created a precedent for the growth of rival agencies to the Corps of Engineers, such as the Bureau of Reclamation and the Soil Conservation Service). A parallel process appears to be occurring in some Latin American states today. "The broadening of military education [in Latin America] to include studies of society and the economy as a whole as well as techniques of economic planning [has created a class of] new military professionals" (Skocpol and Finegold, 1982: 276). A sort of corporate identity with the goal of national economic and political development has led to vigorous pursuit of civic actions by the armed forces. Such activity is very common in an administratively weak polity.

Skocpol and Finegold do not draw parallels between the armed forces in Latin America and the Corps of Engineers. Nevertheless, it is clear from their analysis that the weakness of state capacity in the United States during the early nineteenth century warrants an interpretation of the corps's activity in water resources as a form of civic action. The geographical, technical, political, and administrative obstacles to interior development in the United States in the nineteenth century parallel the dilemma facing many developing countries grappling with the need to exploit natural resources, tame their interiors, control and regulate settlement and industrialization, and establish effective systems of transportation (Glick, 1967). Until 1824, it was not even clear if the U.S. federal government had the constitutional authority to undertake navigable improvements on rivers (Clarke and McCool, 1985). Moreover, the minuscule size of the national government, elite resistance to internal improvements (or in some cases, internal settlement), restrictive credit policies, and the vastness of the frontier were all deterrents to civic improvements and the exploitation of natural resources.

Further evidence for this interpretation is the contrast between the weak national government and strong, local, property-rights-based institutions, which opposed national political control of resources. Weak state capacity is attributable to the absence of knowledgeable administrative groups able to impose their will upon regulated groups (Skocpol and Finegold, 1982: 260–61). The paucity of such expertise in the United States was one source of reliance upon the Corps of Engineers for internal improvements. It also led to the corps becoming embroiled in the conflicts between the demands of settlers and Congress's desire to shape the pattern of development.

Corps activities in natural resources contrast with the experience of western European societies during this same formative period. European states had formed powerful central governments before the notion of a weak state characterized by checks and balances and strong individual rights had taken hold. They managed to form strong governments partly because they were territorially smaller, had fewer obstacles to internal communication, did not have to contend with expansion across hostile territories, and were much older than the United States.

For example, in Great Britain, the monarchy, with the acquiescence of parliament, developed significant powers to regulate the use and exploitation of forests as early as the sixteenth century. Restrictions on timber harvesting were enforceable due to the size and strength of the government and the common, widespread belief that resources were held under the stewardship of the Crown. Moreover, restrictions on use of resources were prompted by an appreciation of the value of wood to national security—for example, for shipbuilding (Cronon, 1983: 20–21).

In France, similar efforts at integrated resource policies were made possible due to the assumption that national preemptory rights over private property were both necessary and proper. The establishment of grist mills on streams supervised by agents of the Crown in the late Middle Ages, the imposition of decrees governing the disposal of human wastes upon the soil during the Renaissance, and actions to prevent depletion of forests in the mid-nineteenth century exemplify the French state's capacity for administrative intervention in natural resources matters. Of particular significance is the fact that these regulations granted considerable discretion to civil servants in enforcement, a continuing feature of French environmental policy.[1]

In the United States, by contrast, an appreciation of the value of natural resources to national security took longer to develop, because an "administrative will to intervene," resulting from competence in natural resources policy, was lacking. Usually, this competence is developed, according to Skocpol and Finegold, by the forging of a "unified administrative leadership" committed to intervention (Skocpol and Finegold, 1982: 275–76). In water and energy policy, development of this competence awaited such policy entrepreneurs as Major Francis Shunk, who urged an expanded federal role in hydroelectric power development in the Twin Cities of Minneapolis and St. Paul.

A final observation on the parallel between the activities of the Corps of Engineers in water resources development and the civic action efforts of military establishments in developing nations is worthy of note, mostly because of what it says about the causes and consequences of this activity upon the overall health of a polity. In developing nations, civic actions are often defended as a necessary response to the fragmentation of civil government, the inadequacy of civilian expertise in practical aspects of development, and the ineffectiveness of policy implementation due to political factionalism (Glick, 1967).

In countries such as Argentina and Chile, the armed forces have long been engaged in civil works programs (Milenky, 1980). Forest clearing, forest management, farm machinery operation and training, supervision of technology intensive industries, and railroad and aircraft fabrication, for example, have been pursued by the armed forces of these countries since the early nineteenth century. These activities predate the direct intervention of the armed forces in governing, underscoring the fact that, as in the United States, they were initially seen as compatible with civilian control of the armed forces and even appropriate for the furtherance of a democratic commitment among the officer corps.

In the United States, of course, unlike many developing nations, the civilian government remained supreme. The military was called upon to assist the government in the management of natural resources because the government lacked the ability to implement their development, not the right to do so (at least after 1824). The Corps of Engineers never questioned civilian control of its budget, personnel allotments, or policy authorizations. Instead, true to its mission in this area, it has only challenged the means for implementing these goals.

What all of this illustrates is that, in nations with institutionalized, stable, political authority provided by strong political parties, cohesive civilian leadership, and legitimate organizations for the peaceful settlement of conflict, intervention by a faction of the military in politics may be limited to policy areas where its expertise is appropriate. For American natural resources policy, Corps of Engineers' policies in water resources development are distinctly military, characterized by a resistance to public scrutiny, a dogged adherence to a narrow set of criteria for policy evaluation, and a resistance to change.

Conclusions: Technological Elitism, Efficiency, and the Corps of Engineers

In the implementation of water policy, the Corps of Engineers' efforts are virtually indistinguishable from those of civilian natural resources agencies. Its program authorizations and budget allotments are taken up separately from those of defense-related programs and are usually dealt with by congressional committees that oversee civilian resources agencies. Moreover, most employees in the corps's Civil Works Directorate are civilians.

However, the civil works program of the corps is directed by some 300 officers chosen from the top 8 percent of the graduates of West Point. In addition, major policy decisions are still formulated by this military elite, who represent the corps before Congress. The corps remains under the nominal supervision of the Department of the Army (Mazmanian and Nienaber, 1979: 9), and "the military aura lent to [the corps's] functions significantly add to the agency's prestige" (Clarke and McCool, 1985: 15). The corps's demeanor toward economic development, its use of benefit-cost analysis as a tool to achieve that purpose, and its vigorous resistance to policy change are all related to the problem of organizational ideology.

It is, perhaps, a bit too easy to attack the corps's use (or misuse) of benefit-cost analysis. Judging by the number of criticisms, it is clear that the corps has been an easy target for project foes who consider the corps's emphasis on cost efficiency narrow, shortsighted, and contemptuous of environmental impacts. Benefit-cost analysis presumably exemplifies the traits the corps aspires to: independence, lack of political partisanship, and engineering rationality. In other words, the very characteristics of benefit-cost analysis that invite attack by critics—its imperialism, mathematical rigidity, and attempts at precision in computation of gains and losses—are what the Corps finds attractive.

Ironically, this dogged attitude exemplifies the corps's desire to rise above a simple response to majoritarian preferences or pluralism in the articulation of policy, in order to be methodical, deliberative, and intellectually disciplined. However, while apolitical in these respects, the corps offers no alternative Madisonian vision of decision making, important to a democratic theory of environmental decision making in the American context. Its perspective is decidedly elitist and remains wedded to an econometric, market-based, traditional benefit-cost approach.

Not unlike the military in developing countries when engaged in civic action, the corps prides itself on filling economic voids by apolitical means. In other words, it achieves its goals in water resources development without reliance upon outside capital, through creating an infrastructure that will inspire private investment, and by submitting itself to a rigorous process that accounts for national needs separate from the wishes of a single group (Linville, 1981). If this attitude seems naive and even insensitive to conditions of change or of intangible benefits and costs, it simply may be the case that the corps cannot conceive of an alternative methodology.

This doggedness is characteristic of military-run organizations, which are likely to see themselves as impartial arbiters of national good able to equitably accommodate diverse interests. Say what one will about the truth of this claim of impartiality, civilian bureaucracies have a harder time justifying such a claim. Moreover, impartiality is closely identified in U.S. culture with economic efficiency. In fairness to the corps, their claim to impartiality is also bolstered by the fact that, during a period of national development, when civilian institutions were insufficiently prepared to meet the challenges of natural resources development, the corps likely was "the only well-trained elite and efficiently organized institution" to be found (Rourke, 1984: 93). A large component of the corps's elite training and organizational structure was geared to insuring technical objectivity and an adamant refusal to take sides on partisan issues.

Along these same lines, the corps's insistence on speaking for such national needs has invested it with a high public visibility, which has augmented its ability to charge critics with representing the goals of narrow factions. In regions where its own plans overlap with those of other water resources agencies, it has been especially adept at justifying its proposals by the need to serve large and diverse constituencies and to promote national economic growth.

The corps has resisted changes that would void its historical mandates to improve navigation or provide flood control. The assumption of the corps has been that, if a function served the nation well in the past, only compelling reasons could detract from the need to pursue it now. This is exemplified by the corps's resistance to reorganizations of water resources agencies, which would force a merger of the corps with civilian agencies like the Bureau of Reclamation.

Finally, organizational ideology, important to all bureaucracies, is particularly critical in explaining the corps's organizational conservatism. Military organizations are characteristically resistant to innovation and only gradually accept structural reform of the rules they are accustomed to working under (Mazmanian and Nienaber, 1979; Jackman, 1976).

In the early twentieth century, while organizational coherence in the corps was high, there was a great deal of commitment to water resources development but only slow response to environmental changes. Thus, when it came to hydropower development and the use of impoundments to control flooding, the corps tended to be a policy follower rather than a policy innovator. Thus the corps remains slow to adopt preservationist, nonstructural solutions to water resources problems today, despite the National Environmental Policy Act and other reforms.

Perhaps no example of water policy exemplifies this resistance to change better than the corps's policy toward wetlands. Technically, the corps shares authority for the protection and management of wetlands with the Environmental Protection Agency. In Mississippi, the corps is embroiled in a fight with environmental groups over a $2 billion effort to drain half of the state's remaining four million acres of delta hardwood bottoms located in an area north of Vicksburg and close to the Mississippi River—the Yazoo River basin project (Husar, 1988).

Opposition revolves around the impact of this project upon migratory waterfowl throughout the Mississippi flyway. The corps is determined not to alter its plans unless compelled to do so by Congress, even though the state already has a surplus of marginally productive farmland and even though the wetlands provide a natural flood reservoir. The plans for this drainage project were laid by the Flood Control Act of 1936. The corps has cited this fact as reason not to apply recent conservation legislation to the project's evaluation.

The U.S. Fish and Wildlife Service has expressed reservations about the project, because of the possible effects of siltation and pesticide runoff upon nearby Yazoo National Wildlife Refuge if the land is farmed. A coalition of environmentalists, hunters, farmers, and landowners, similar to that formed in response to the New River project, has also lobbied hard against the project. Nevertheless, the corps continues to defend the project on traditional economic development grounds. In fairness to the corps, many of these economic values are supported by the state's congressional delegation, which is ambivalent toward the project (Husar, 1988).

It is too early to forecast the outcome of this battle. But in the past when the corps has shifted ground on such controversies, it has done so in order to enhance, or at a minimum preserve, its power as an autonomous military organization, which makes it unique among U.S. natural resources agencies. The corps's insistence upon a differentiation from civilian society is predicated upon preserving a distinct ideology, inculcated through specialized training and expertise. This all serves to remind us that, while present-day corps activities in water resources management are identical to those performed by civilian agencies, its military ideology makes its style of water resources management distinctive.

In the final chapter, it is suggested that changes in the corps's ideology will not come about easily and that the only assured means of changing the direction of water policy is through changing the dominant social values justifying decisions. This will lead to changes in the organizational processes through which decisions are made. Among other things, this means the rejection of mere engineering solutions to water problems; the tempering of hierarchical command over resources with decentralized, coordinated planning; and an emphasis upon policies that do not entail environmental disruptions or structural solutions.

Such policies may also prove to be economically efficient, insofar as they will save water and use it more wisely. However, they will not necessarily lead to new supplies of water, the dominant strategy of water resources agencies. These new policies include conservation and reuse of water, a balance among in-stream uses, and an increase in state and local influence in policy making. These policies would not necessarily challenge the ideology of agencies like the corps, but they would challenge the authority such agencies have had in formulating and implementing water policy.

9   Ideals and Realities in Establishing an Environmental Ethic

All ethics . . . rest upon a single premise: that the individual is a member of a community of interdependent parts. . . . The land ethic . . . enlarges the boundaries of the community to include soils, waters, plants, and animals or, collectively, the land.
—ALDO LEOPOLD

Regional Contract: The Basis for a New Ethic in Water Policy

There will always be a tension between ideals and political realities in natural resources policy. The narrow perspectives of many participants in the policy process, coupled with faulty measures of benefits and costs and uncertainty over environmental risks and impacts, make adherence to any set of ideals difficult. While this might seem an obstacle to reform, it should be borne in mind that policy change, although difficult to achieve, is not impossible. Water policy has never been immutable. Awareness of problems not well perceived at earlier stages of our national history has already led to reforms in benefit-cost analysis, environmental impact analysis, social preference assessment, and administrative reorganization.

Following the framework for reform outlined in chapter 3, I propose that a realistic point of departure for more ambitious change would be a nationwide system of regional, self-sustaining, water management authorities. These authorities would systematically address the needs of water consumers. Water use would be based upon a social contract consented to by users. Furthermore, each water management authority would seek conformity between political institutions and the disposition and character of natural resources in its region. This could be done by establishing these authorities in a combined political-hydrological framework.

Three principles would guide these authorities: (1) the rights of users to fair and equal use of the water, (2) the interdependency of natural resources, based upon the character and disposition of these resources in a region as well as historical patterns of development, and (3) the obligations of users to abide by the rules for allocation of water and of the costs of locating, supplying, cleaning and transporting water. Following John Rawls (1971), decision-making rules for the use and allocation of water would be guided by the premise that water is an essential good. While water resources can be divided or allocated among several people, each person's use has some impact upon the quality and quantity available to the next user. Thus, one individual use or abuse of water affects the opportunities of others to take care of their needs.

Pareto optimality would guide the selection of policies for the use and development of water resources. No change in use, allocation, or development would be permitted unless it could be demonstrated that the change that makes some members of society better off would not make others, whether in the same or another water resources region, worse off. Inequalities of supply could, however, be justified if it could be shown that, ultimately, such inequalities would result in an increase in structural efficiency, which would make everyone in society better off. For example, a new irrigation project could be justified, even if the burden of cost would be borne by everyone (not just the direct users of the project's water), if its aim was to produce more food and no alternative way of producing this food were available.

These rules for allocating and distributing water and related land resources should take precedence over the practical means for achieving them. Furthermore, these rules should be based upon a veil of ignorance (Rawls, 1971), behind which our ethical responsibilities would be the same no matter what our station in life. The social contract embodying these rules would aspire to cost effectiveness and an acceptance of ambiguity and uncertainty.

Each user system should strive for the most social benefit at the least environmental damage and economic expense, especially to the poor. In practice, all of these goals should be achieved simultaneously, since policies most intrusive environmentally usually adversely affect the poor disproportionately. Those who lose their land and homes to dams and reservoirs and who suffer most from the impacts of increased salinity or pollution tend to have less direct influence upon the policy-making process. Moreover, many of these people are poor, which is precisely why they are the least powerful members of society.

We further suggest that each stakeholder within the regional authority should consider what policies would benefit the poorest members of society. These policies would allocate water resources on a principle of universal equity rather than on principles of first discovery or first use (prior appropriation doctrine) or land adjacency (riparian doctrine). Without such an agreement, the eventual disposition and distribution of resources could lead to intolerable disadvantages for some of us. Moreover, the achievement of the goals composing our individual ways of life is dependent upon an equitable allocation and distribution of resources. Thus, rights to the resource should be based upon demonstrable need or, in other words, the degree to which the resource constitutes a social primary good—a good required regardless of one's concept of his or her own good.

This Rawlsian position is consistent with a Madisonian democratic perspective, which obligates participants to reject narrow self-interest and to articulate preferences, not on the basis of passion or material gain, but on the basis of what would make them better citizens. The perspective concedes that we are finite, fallible creatures with only a limited understanding of nature, as well as of ourselves. It is based upon a preemptory criterion, which says that before we can make decisions designed to promote the good, we must first choose a procedure for defining the right (i.e., for deciding what kind of allocation would be fair to everyone).

An additional feature of the social contract I am advocating for water use departs from the Rawlsian framework, however—the rights of other living creatures. I contend that every living creature, not just people, has a right to clean, abundant water in order to survive and develop in the manner optimal for its species. Otherwise, we jeopardize the natural balance and risk the consequences of species extinction. Unfortunately, these stakeholders are unable to participate in the social contract.

The acceptance of ambiguity and uncertainty in water policy will require self-restraint and an abandonment of self-interest, to which natural resources agencies and the American public are unaccustomed. The need for this self-restraint is dictated by the weight of experience, as shown by the case studies. Wise use of resources hinges upon our understanding of nature and of the long-term impacts of human activity upon the environment. These case studies indicate that we should opt for modest confidence in our ability to manage nature. We simply cannot continue to overdevelop and overutilize water resources with impunity. Over the long term (beyond fifty years), we may begin to see effects upon regional water resources from global warming, which is caused in part by a doubling of the carbon dioxide in the atmosphere. The impacts of global warming upon rainfall, cloud patterns, sea level, and estuaries could profoundly affect water for agriculture, industry, the generation of electricity, and other uses (Bach, 1984; Shepard, 1986; Jager, 1986; Report of the International Conference, 1986).

Studies of the dust bowl in the Great Plains during the 1930s, for example, suggest that no amount of tinkering with irrigation or methods of cultivation can prevent or alleviate the effects of regional drought, which comes and goes in unpredictable patterns every few decades (Worster, 1979). What is worse, however, is that our attempts to forestall these impacts may only worsen the effects. The implications of this fact for an environmental ethic shall be discussed later; for now it is important to remember that many civilizations with as much, if not more, confidence in their ability to manage nature as we have either learned these lessons the hard way or never learned them at all. They depleted their water supplies and no longer exist.

We cannot modify nature without irreparable harm. If each water user recognizes the limits of human reason and of our understanding of the character of natural processes, we will attain what I term a doctrine of reasonable fallibility. This doctrine, exemplified by a number of pioneering environmental philosophies discussed in this chapter, encourages the incorporation of ecological considerations in policy. It does this by encouraging smaller, less intrusive impacts. Generally, the smaller a water project, the more likely that its negative impacts can be averted or even reversed at some future time.

But even small-scale projects, such as those proposed under recent hydropower schemes, can produce significant, irreversible impacts upon both society and nature. Sudden increases in cheap hydropower, especially in developing areas, can lead to a desperate search for energy intensive industries, dramatically upsetting their politics and culture (Abrahamson, 1975; Deudney, 1981; Hayes, 1977). This does not take into account the numerous environmental impacts, mentioned throughout this volume, that these projects also impose. In many developing countries, for example, deforestation has caused soil erosion and, thus, the sedimentation of reservoirs, which have lost their storage capacity as a result. Compounding this problem, failure to manage the watersheds leading into the reservoirs has also affected their usefulness, reducing their ability to generate electricity and to sustain fish and wildlife (L. Brown, 1981: 38; Eckholm, 1982: 173).

Before proceeding with a discussion of the regional authority framework, a caveat is in order. Even if the goals of equity, Pareto optimality, and protection of sensitive and unique features of the natural environment prove politically unattainable in the short term, as long-term premises of policy (over a course of time consistent with the anticipated impacts of, for example, global warming on water resources—fifty years and beyond), there are many reasons to endorse them, including the fact that other democratic polities have shown them to be workable. The centerpiece of this approach could be revival of the now dormant river basin commission concept. An example of a promising form of river basin organization is that of France.

Reviving the River Basin Commission:
A Comparative Perspective

France's river basin organizations were established in 1964. While by no means devoid of problems, they can be instructive as to how to organize the U.S. regional management of water. Six river basin agencies, based upon France's major drainage basins, are empowered to assist municipalities and industrial enterprises in meeting national water quality standards. These agencies use a variety of methods, including such economic incentives as loans, grants, and fines. The process for establishing, enforcing, and implementing these incentives is complex and includes several political and administrative actors in addition to river basin organizations.

Because of France's long experience in managing pollution, coupled with the mixed success of previous efforts, the French have tended to be receptive to innovative management schemes. Unlike former U.S. river basin commissions, French river basin agencies are primarily concerned with control of water pollution rather than the development of water resources. While these agencies possess no authority to enact pollution standards—which are formulated by the *Ministère de l'Environnement* (Environment Ministry) headquartered in Paris—they do possess considerable discretion in the way they implement such standards, unlike their U.S. counterparts.

Water resources regulation and development begins with the Environment Ministry. The ministry issues pollution and waste withdrawal standards applicable to all regions and departments (roughly equivalent to American counties) throughout France. Implementation of these standards are monitored by a series of inspectorates appointed by and accountable to the ministry. There are inspectorates for the various industries, for the agricultural sectors, and for the so-called classified establishments.

Below the ministry and its inspectorates are local commissars, referred to as *prefets* prior to the advent of the Mitterrand government in 1981. Commissars, who are elected by local residents, are accountable to bureaucrats in Paris. They work with national inspectorates in discovering breaches of law and in levying fines and other penalties established by the ministry (Chambolle, 1981: 36).

The role of the basin agencies is to establish a system of charges for consumers and polluters of water in proportion to the amount of water drawn or degraded, in order to reduce the ultimate costs of pollution control to society and, thus, to make the task of the ministry easier. These charges, which function as a form of economic inducement, are intended to alleviate the need for the ministry to have to resort to more formal penalties.

Charges are paid by all water users in a basin and are levied by a complex formula based upon weight (not volume) of pollution and estimates of cost for decomposition. They average out to about two dollars (U.S.) per person, per year. Currently, these charges are levied upon farms, municipalities, and industries after a formal process of consultation between the ministry and interest groups representing each of these sectors (Chambolle, 1981: 34; Saglio, 1980: 76; Barde, 1975: 101).

Each basin, as noted previously, conforms to a distinct hydrographic region not merely based upon the disposition of water resources but also "suited to the economic requirements of the area" (Barde, 1975: 99). Revenues collected by basin agencies are placed into an account managed by the multimember *Agence financière de bassin* (Basin Financial Agency). This agency determines how best to spend these revenues to improve water quality and quantity problems in that region (Barde, 1975: 100).

In essence, the money raised by each *Agence financières de bassin* belongs to that basin to spend for projects as necessary. The function of the agency is to authorize expenditures for pollution abatement and water supply projects in conformance with prearranged, multiyear plans for meeting water resources objectives. The interesting part of this process is the manner in which these objectives are established. First, the *Agence financière de bassin* draws up its multiyear plan for pollution control and the construction of water projects with the assistance of *comités de bassin* (basin committees) (Chambolle, 1981: 34).

The *comités de bassin* are advisory boards made up of equal numbers of water users and representatives of departments and local governments in a given watershed (Barde, 1975: 100). They offer input on the calculation of polluter charges, negotiate how pollution standards shall be met within a basin agency's own timetable, and allow direct citizen input on major issues. Although their opinions are nonbinding, their role has proven to be invaluable in legitimizing the decisions of basin authorities. Central ministry authority in France has long depended upon prior consultation with affected groups (F. Wilson, 1983).

Under the government's current decentralization reforms undertaken by the Socialists beginning in 1981, this process of direct consultation has been extended further. Members of nature protection societies, environmental interest groups, and local and regional councils who have been appointed to these committees have occasionally functioned as investigative arms of Environment Ministry inspectorates, reporting violations of the national water pollution code to the government (Chambolle, 1981).

Such activity could be viewed as a form of administrative cooptation: a way of disarming opposition to government policy by organized interest groups by making them feel they are part of the decision-making process. It is clear, however, that the authority possessed by basin agencies is quite real. For example, although local commissars must formally consent to expenditures of funds by the basin agencies, let bids for water projects, and approve water quality standards even if these decisions were already recommended by advisory committees, the commissars rarely veto these decisions. They recognize that the consensus was often arrived at painstakingly. Moreover, basin agencies have become self-managing authorities able to utilize such economic incentives as pollution "taxes" upon industry, industrial grants, and even ten-year loans for establishing pretreatment waste-handling facilities (Chambolle, 1981: 35).

How effective have these authorities been? And could they work as effectively in the American context? To answer the first question, since 1980, organic waste discharges in France have declined an average of 4.4 percent a year, and 50 percent of toxic waste discharges have been eliminated through an aggressive pretreatment program (Chambolle, 1981: 37). Moreover, regional diversity in the management of water resources is accommodated, since economic incentives are determined by regional authorities (F. Anderson et al., 1977: 62).

If such a scheme were implemented in the United States, several institutional changes would have to be introduced. First, the federal government's role would be largely limited to mitigating conflicts between regions, to establishing minimal standards for water quantity (largely in the realm of in-stream flow maintenance and groundwater supply), and to exercising preemptory rights to halt practices by states, localities, individuals, or industries that are detrimental to national needs. National needs preempt regional needs in so far as the former include ensuring Pareto optimality and equity among regions. Given the fact that the American political system is federal, as opposed to the unitary structure of France, a number of constitutional issues that might arise would be difficult to surmount. Nevertheless, the federal government does have significant legal powers over navigable streams, which could be used to overcome such resistance.

Water laws governing surface water rights and groundwater are largely state based. Even with recent groundwater policy reform, implementation guidelines still focus on state initiatives. Thus, one implication for water law is that federal powers to control navigable streams would now have to be more aggressively extended to water conservation and pollution control. While this is precisely the direction federal water law has begun to take, resistance has been strong and will likely continue without an overall change in public attitudes toward land use policy.

The second implication is that the role of the construction agencies (Corps of Engineers, Bureau of Reclamation) would need to be significantly curtailed. They would construct projects initiated by regional authorities; they would not formulate policy alternatives. The third implication, and probably the most important, is that states and water resources regions would have to begin conceiving of themselves as coherent decision-making entities. There would appear to be so little precedent for such a concept that, on the surface at least, little hope might be invested in achieving this goal.

In reality, however, regionalization of water policy through shifting policy innovation to states and regions is not radical. Aside from declines in federal government willingness to continue funding massive water projects and a recent preference for imposing cost sharing upon states, recent studies suggest that placing additional responsibility upon regions to seek common, comprehensive solutions might produce better policy. The river basin commission boundaries used by the Water Resources Council in the 1960s and 1970s could be a starting point for such a policy innovation. These commissions successfully encompassed the overlap of states and river basins by allowing states to be included in more than one region.

According to Helen Ingram and others who have focused upon the water policy problems of the Four Corners states of the Southwest, innovation and regional initiative for water resources management are beginning to occur. Traditionally, residents of the Southwest have looked to federal agencies like the Bureau of Reclamation to solve water resources problems through the building of massive dams. In recent years, however, the lack of good dam sites, the depletion of groundwater, and environmentalist opposition to further destruction of scenic rivers and the natural habitat of rare and endangered species have prompted a search for new water policies.

Despite growing urbanization in that part of the United States, agriculture continues to use large amounts of water. As a result, state legislators and voters are faced with increasingly difficult choices— either forcing all users to conserve water or transferring water from lower value uses to higher value uses (Ingram, Laney, McCain, 1979,

1980). Ingram and her colleagues are clear about the reluctance of voters and their elected representatives to force any water user to cut back on water use. The dominant pattern of thinking in the Far West toward water remains acquisitive: how to find more of it and how to use it for economic expansion. There is a resistance to perceiving the relatedness of land and water resources and an insistence on maintaining fragmented administrative and legal control of water (Richard, 1978).

Ingram also concludes that state legislatures will probably forgo any active role in formulating a solution to regional problems. Why then, the optimism about the possibility of regional innovation? First, all relevant policy actors agree that water scarcity is a serious problem. They also view the prospects for outside assistance to resolve it as very dim. This is slowly leading residents and legislators throughout the region into a common perception of the need to do something about balancing water supply for energy, agriculture, and urban use within their own legal and political frameworks. This has been noted by other scholars as well (Richard, 1978).

Second, while there is also no immediate prospect for the erosion of the traditional distributive politics model of policy formulation in this or any other region, Ingram and her associates find hope in one trend. The same fragmented policy structure that inhibits comprehensive management by allowing administrative capture by concerted, vocal interests also provides openings for "end runs" around established patterns (Ingram and Ullery, 1980). While this is a far cry from a massive shift of power to a regional authority, it suggests that changes are possible. The very existence of French river basin agencies suggests that alternatives to water management in developed polities are available. These alternatives can prompt us to move away from mere polemic and begin addressing instruments likely to generate real change. Furthermore, such alternatives are rooted in democratic perspectives, which view policy makers not as delegates responding to amorphous, inarticulate preferences but as representatives charged with making difficult choices based on a demonstration of national needs, which requires prioritizing policy values.

Equitably Dividing Benefits and Costs

Water is not free. Using water imposes costs on oneself as well as others. Groundwater must be mined and transported great distances. Surface water, once used, becomes polluted and must be cleaned to be useful to others and to not harm the environment. The public choice approach shows the need to treat the character and cost of a resource as a function of not merely technology but of resource disposition, availability, and demand. To optimize public preferences in the allocation and use of water, the joint-user system should be viewed as a group of consumers who pool their resources for mutual benefit. Somewhat analogous to a publicly owned utility, the delivery system for water thus becomes self-sustaining.

Because the criteria for justifiable policy—efficiency, equity, feasibility, minimal transaction costs, and noneconomic values—may be unique in different regions, they would be subject to different emphases, depending upon their setting. Ideally, the interdependency of resources would shape the types of technology to be applied to their development. In the absence of cost controls, users might opt for the most expensive projects with little regard for their long-term impacts. The Colorado River salinity problem, for example, could have been avoided under a regionally based system, since one responsibility of water management authorities would be to facilitate input by a broad array of interests, including environmental professionals likely to anticipate geological impacts.

In addition, the fees supporting water projects would come from the users themselves, encouraging conservation of water and use of appropriate technology. Penalties might be imposed to assure compliance with national policy objectives for water quality and in-stream flow. However, regionally based water utilities would ensure that these penalties are imposed with regard to regional capabilities of implementation as well as regional, institutional, and individual capacity to pay. In some regions, such incentives might work better than in others.

Benefits and costs would be linked to fiduciary responsibility. A purely technocratic outlook toward water resources development could be avoided, and noneconomic issues would be more effectively incorporated into decision making. This framework would be incorporated into the regional-hydrological framework previously discussed.

Reasonable Fallibility as an Environmental Ethic

One of the greatest ironies of environmental policy is that, despite the staggering increase in our knowledge about the hydrology, geology, biology, and economics of water, we still know very little about the long-term social and environmental impacts of our development and exploitation of it. This gap in knowledge sometimes produces extraordinary, almost desperate, attempts to resolve water problems. Many environmentalists, viewing our uncertainty as a stark warning about our inherent inadequacy as a species, suggest that the best way of addressing this problem is to combine preservationist and conservationist approaches into a single policy. This would entail using what we have already developed more efficiently and leaving as much of the remaining natural environment in as pristine a condition as possible.

But we cannot solve water problems fairly and equitably by merely conserving what we already have and locking away undeveloped resources. While this alternative might be acceptable to those living in abundance, it would only heighten the inequities suffered by those whose reasonable rights to water have not been fulfilled—the native American tribes adjacent to the Garrison diversion project, for example, or the Appalachian dirt farmers whose water use is restricted by scenic river designation. Thus, from one vantage point, Garrison might seem like merely another pork barrel project designed to placate powerful, well-organized interests. From another vantage point, however, the project might be viewed as an entitlement to native American tribes and white farmers formerly excluded from the benefits of western water resources. Thus, the undesirable environmental impacts of this type of project have to be weighed against the rights of certain groups.

Likewise, both the defunct Blue Ridge project and the New River scenic river proposal need to be viewed not as choices to either exploit a river's resources or preserve them but as differing attempts to balance economic and noneconomic values against the rights of those in direct proximity to the river to choose how they want to use it. Oftentimes, the issues in these controversies are more complex than the choice between development and nondevelopment. The real questions are, How much should we develop? and To what degree are impacts tolerable and beneficial and still in accordance with certain criteria?

One way to get beyond a narrow juggling of conservationist and preservationist approaches is to better understand how our present environmental crisis and our environmental values are a function of the way we live. Part of the reason it is so difficult to establish a genuine environmental ethic is that it would have to compete with a far more popular ethic toward the use of natural resources and whose core values are antithetical to conservation and preservation. This ethic, capitalism, often encourages profligate consumption, as Donald Worster (1979) has shown. Its core values toward nature are (1) *nature is capital*; a set of economic commodities to be developed and exploited and that have no mystical, spiritual, or intrinsic value of their own, (2) *people have a right and even an obligation to use nature for self-aggrandizement* in order to fulfill their right to conquer and subjugate the Earth (the highest economic rewards in a capitalist society go to those who have reaped the bounty of nature most fruitfully), and (3) *society should allow individuals unlimited freedom in exploiting nature*. Not only will the community absorb the environmental costs of this activity, but society will benefit from this economic exploitation in the long run through more and better goods.

Even if one were to quibble with Worster's singling out of capitalism for these faults (it is clear, for example, that similar views toward exploitation characterize many Marxist-Leninist societies, a point Worster concedes), the singling out of capitalism is still justified. Capitalist societies were the first, and remain among the most efficient, societies to promote an acquisitive ethic toward nature. They have also produced injurious environmental impacts throughout the world—in developed countries, in present and former colonies of developed countries, and in other nonindustrialized countries. Moreover, the disconformity of capitalism's dominant outlook toward nature has partly contributed, in conjunction with our Enlightenment concepts of science (Bennett, 1987), to such environmental disasters as the dust bowl on the Great Plains during the 1930s through encouraging cash crop, bonanza farming.

Where the capitalist order can be faulted is in its naive confidence in its ability to bend the natural order to human design. It is this overconfidence, and not mere greed, that poses an obstacle to the establishment of a different environmental ethic. Ironically, this overconfidence also makes the task of developing a different ethic just a bit easier. Worster offers one point of departure for replacing overconfidence with reasonable fallibility, a view that is increasingly being termed deep ecology. I will discuss this view and two others as well—the extended anthropogenic rights approach and ecofeminism.

Deep Ecology and the Rejection of Gratuitous Policy

Most environmental critiques of water policy and other natural resources policies start from a human-centered premise, a premise in some respects identical to that held by those who are being criticized. The purpose of preserving the environment, these critiques argue, is to promote human welfare. This can be done more effectively by preserving nature rather than exploiting it. One shortcoming of this view is its ethical narrowness; it ascribes only extrinsic or utilitarian value to the environment. It assumes, in other words, that water and other land resources exist largely for our benefit and that human beings are lords and masters of the earth. This shallow ecology view shares with the narrow, majoritarian view of democracy a preference for justifying environmental protection from the standpoint of economic self-interest, instead of from the standpoint of how our interactions with nature enlighten and ennoble our very being, or by conceding that nature, too, has rights.

The deep ecologist urges adoption of a broader life-centered view of ecology, which begins not from a spaceship earth premise about the need to protect resources for the benefit of human civilization but from the need to protect, preserve, and develop the biological rights of every organism. To understand the premises of the deep ecologist, exemplified by Worster's view of water and land resources, it is best to begin with its philosophical roots. These are outlined succinctly by Paul Taylor (1981).

To Taylor, the foundations of a life-centered view of environmental ethics begin with a respect for nature on nature's own terms, as objects and beings with intrinsic as opposed to extrinsic value. This view has three components: (1) every living thing is deserving of consideration simply by virtue of being part of Earth's community of life, (2) every living thing has intrinsic good, and (3) every living thing has a right to fulfill its life purpose, whatever that purpose may be (Taylor, 1981). This life-centered view is part preemptory, part meliorative, and thus represents a major departure from the social contract view. This view contends that nature has a telos, as do human beings.

Why should we adopt these views? According to Taylor, there is no socially beneficial reason why we should do so. In the short term, it might be prudent to protect wildlife, avoid the clear-cutting of trees, and resist polluting rivers. This would all be beneficial to the economic well-being of certain segments of society. In the long run, however, we could easily advance our goals as acquisitive individuals by simply exploiting nature in a calculating manner without regard for these consequences. We could, if we were motivated solely by meliorative ends, allow someone else to worry about these externalities of our behavior. Or, we could find a way to include them in the utilitarian calculation beyond the present generation.

The reason we should follow these rules, insists Taylor, is for preemptory reasons—because each and every creature has inherent worth and dignity quite apart from considerations of benefit and cost. In short, Taylor's view is a sort of Kantian categorical imperative toward nature. Further than Kant, however, who extended this imperative to creatures who can demonstrably think and reason, Taylor presumes that animals should be encompassed by this same imperative, even if their ability to think or reason is open to contention. We should treat each and every creature as we would wish to be treated, as ends in themselves and not as a means to fulfill the ends of others. We should accept such premises as a necessary corollary of being human and because others also accept them. We should consciously accept certain obligations because we are not solely meliorative creatures.

What follows from this view, according to Taylor, is that human and nonhuman elements of Earth's community hold equal claims to existence (though not necessarily equal ability to participate within the framework of policy); that each and every one of us is part of a complex, interdependent web; and that each and every one of us has a telos to fulfill (Taylor, 1981).

How can this theory be tied to a regional contractarian approach to natural resources? The possibility of a connection is afforded by Worster's view of the dust bowl. The dust bowl was directly attributable to capitalism's human-centered ethos and its naive overconfidence toward human ability to subdue nature with impunity. Great Plains farmers rarely perceived nature as having any needs of its own. It was assumed that nature's development could be shaped to society's needs. Even a more prudent approach to that region's development might not have prevented the dust bowl—it might only have delayed it or, perhaps, lessened its severity. But a deep ecology approach could well have averted the impacts of the dust bowl on human populations by avoiding land use patterns and economic intrusions that made communities vulnerable to the impacts of wind and drought. It would have respected the character of the land and its seeming refusal to be subjugated to human will. On the other hand, such an approach would also have discouraged settlement of the Great Plains, giving a far different flavor to the economic development of this nation's interior.

In the nineteenth and early twentieth centuries, farmers on the southern Great Plains assumed that they—in their personal struggle to advance their stations in life by taming the wild frontier and forcing it to yield its bounty—could literally compel the land into submission. If the rains refused to come, it was said, cultivate the land more intensively. If other obstacles arose, then hold to your belief in rugged individualism and persist in the face of adversity. This persistence was viewed as a moral virtue under capitalism and the Judeo-Christian tradition, alike (Taylor, 1981).

This rigid, naive optimism was not attributable merely to social Darwinist greed, a belief that unlimited riches would be granted to those earnest enough to prevail. After all, most Great Plains farmers were satisfied simply scratching out a modest living. Instead, it was animated by a religious fervor that was itself a part of capitalism, a belief that the world is preordained to promote the welfare of civilization.

The disaster of the dust bowl was less that it revealed the folly in believing that nature could be subjugated than that few recognized the folly. As Worster concludes, most farmers living on the Great Plains today have yet to learn to accept these basic facts about nature. Capitalism's human-centered outlook toward the environment has kept farmers from viewing drought as anything but a temporary aberration, which can be overcome with continued hard work, better government support, more irrigation projects, and more efficient attempts to tame the land. This point of view does not accommodate the fact that the region has incessant winds, low humidity, loose soil, flat land, no trees, and little rainfall. These characteristics are not curses to be condemned or scourges to be tamed. They need to be accepted on their own terms and to be adjusted to. One need not like this region, but one must respect it.

How can this deep-ecology ethic help build an environmental ethic? What can it teach us about water policy? The Garrison diversion case is relevant to this debate. The so-called free market cannot possibly encompass the management of so complex a set of resources. Nature does not respond as a commodity. For comprehensive management of water and land resources, deep ecology posits that political institutions should conform to the character of the natural resources of a region. Like it or not, these characteristics may be fundamentally unalterable.

In the Garrison diversion case, for example, while no deep ecology ethic was openly espoused by any side to the conflict, it was at least acknowledged early on that the water resources of the upper Great Plains should be managed as an integrated, coherent unit in which each party respects the water rights of the other. Indirectly, nature was acknowledged to have an inherent dignity, insofar as both the United States and Canada agreed to leave water resources in the same usable state they were found in before human intervention. The overconfidence of the Bureau of Reclamation's proposal conflicted with this principle.

The bureau displayed unjustifiable optimism in its ability to control Missouri River biota intrusions into the Hudson Bay drainage. Canadians could not share this confidence, because from their vantage point it appeared that the United States was violating, for their own meliorative gain, preemptory rules designed to protect both drainage basins. To this day, no one can say for certain which party's view of Garrison's impacts is correct. The point of that case study, however, is to show that differing degrees of confidence in the ability to prevent these intrusions of biota through human-made devices lay at the core of the debate. The question was not merely how safe was safe enough but, given the disproportionate cost upon Canadians (so they argued), how fair was safe enough?

The centralization of water resources administration in a remote, national government agency places authority too far out of the relevant region and too far out of touch with that resource's problems. Residents of a natural resources region need to be given the responsibility to manage the resources upon which their livelihood depend. Forcing them to absorb a bigger share of the costs and risks of exploitation might

infuse such responsibility. North Dakotans could ignore the sustainability of the water resources of the upper Great Plains because, by and
large, they were not paying for the Garrison project. Its costs were diffused throughout society. Moreover, there was an already pervasive belief, especially on the U.S. side, that anything that tamed the Great
Plains and lessened the impact of periodic drought was good, especially
if such actions would compensate for lands already taken by the state.

Society, like nature, exhibits a penchant for fragmentation and diversity. Pluralism, diversity, and conflicting uses should be welcomed, not
abhorred. A wise environmental ethic does not require uniformity. Policy centralization and a unified approach to natural resources management place extraordinary confidence in our ability to understand
complex natural processes. An ethics of respect for nature requires a
respect for diversity, an acceptance of uncertainty, and a willingness to
accept doubt.

A principle of American democratic theory, rooted in the Madisonian
tradition, is that we are all a part of a coherent, interlocking community.
While we are distinct individuals, our individual ways of life are tied
to each through our actions toward ourselves and nature. This is exemplified by culture, language, and the dynamics of social learning. A
rational, reflective individual in such a context should behave toward
the environment as he or she would expect others to act. This individual
would reject both a purely managerial perspective on natural resources,
which sees nature as nemesis, as plastic, or as benign (Bennett, 1987)
and a view of nature as idyllic, harmonious, and ordered. I opt for a
view between these two positions: while nature is amenable to some
human control, it resists total control. This is one reason why we are
fallible.

In addition to the fact that we never know where or when we shall be
born, and thus have no way of knowing what would be in our self-
interest and good for the environment, we also inhabit a cultural and
linguistic milieu that inhibits us from ascertaining absolute justice.
Concepts of justice rooted purely in a culturally neutral rationalism,
devoid of historical context, attribute to rationalism a greater power to
resolve ethical ambiguity than it can bear (MacIntyre, 1988).

I contend that our reasonable fallibility is attributable to two related
sources with relevance for environmental policy. First, we inhabit a
culture where practical rationality, socialization, and history filter our
perception of what is reasonable. Second, we fail to factor the role of
nature into our decisions. Just as culture filters our perceptions of what
is just, so should natural abundance or scarcity.

The environmental ethics cited in this book, such as deep ecology,
animal rights, and ecofeminist views, prescribe specific criteria for ac-

commodating reasonable fallibility in the implementation of policy. They suggest that our behavior be based upon guarantees that we not treat nature and our fellow humans as capital for our own personal self-aggrandizement. I suggest, therefore, that these diverse environmental approaches be viewed as a means of maximizing the range of policy alternatives about natural resources, to facilitate accountability in policy, and to provide optimal information about impacts.

In essence, none of these views offers a complete, absolutely valid explanation for how nature and society interact. However, taken together, these approaches may collectively suggest something about the fallibility of the predominant attitudes toward nature held by water policy agencies. Divergent environmental ethics, like divergent political philosophies, help clarify and challenge the established epistemologies of contemporary political practices, pointing to shortcomings not ascertainable within the framework of those individual philosophies (MacIntyre, 1988; Parekh, 1968).

Animal Rights and Animal Wrongs: Extended Anthropogenic Rights and Water Policy

Most environmental debates are struggles between technocrats and preservationists. Technocrats argue for a human-centered approach to ecology and ask the utilitarian question, Within what policy alternatives do the greatest benefits and the least costs lie? Even some preservationist approaches place human-centered goals, such as aesthetics and recreation, high on the list of reasons to preserve and protect the environment. One of the more provocative approaches to an environmental ethic, and an approach derivative from deep ecology, is the animal rights approach, which may also be termed an extended anthropogenic rights view.

The view is most succinctly argued by Tom Regan. Regan rejects the utilitarian approach to ecology partly for the same reasons Taylor does, because it fails to encompass the inherent dignity of all beings. However, Regan believes that most alternatives to utilitarianism, while having merit in a human-centered ethical system, are inadequate as guides to ecology. For example, a social contract view, such as that of Rawls, is not easily applicable to nature or to animals. Animals do not appear to understand explicit or tacit agreements to do or not to do certain things. It is difficult to invest them with rights when it is clear that they cannot function as stakeholders in the political arena (Ackerman, 1980). It is also unlikely that inanimate objects are capable of understanding our claims. As a result, it is not possible to compel nature to agree with arrangements that humans establish to manage the land and water resources upon which nature as well as we depend (Regan, 1983).

Regan, using a rights-centered view, predicates that, despite the vast apparent differences between humans and animals, both of us share one characteristic in common, which gives to us moral standing: we experience our individual lives, possess consciousness of them, and appear to place an importance upon our individual welfare. While we do not know if this is true of all animals, we do not need to know it to be true to apply this rule. All we need to know is that it is virtually impossible to deny that all animals may share this impulse. Again, this is a reflection of our reasonable fallibility.

This sense of importance is displayed by our ability to feel, to recall, and to expect things from our environment (Regan, 1983). Like Taylor's ethics of respect for nature, Regan claims that animals have intrinsic value apart from human calculations. Unlike Taylor, however, Regan also appears to be suggesting that animals, as experiencing subjects of their existence, are in possession of certain anthropogenic characteristics that make them more humanlike than is usually acknowledged.

For environmental policy, one implication of this view is that a radical restructuring of our attitudes toward nature are called for. Because animals are sentient creatures, they have certain inalienable rights, even if they are unable to demand those rights in a political arena. A true animal rights advocate would not think in terms of merely giving farm animals more space, or laboratory animals bigger and cleaner cages, but of completely abolishing sport hunting and fishing, commercial livestock agriculture, and animal experiments.

For water and land resources, Regan is less clear about what kinds of policies his animal rights position would require. It seems certain, however, that any water resources development that would lead to the possible extinction of a species or to the killing of fish through spillway structures or penstocks represents nothing less than murder. All human activities likely to produce such impacts are patently immoral. We are able to survive without killing members of other animal species. Animals, on the other hand, probably cannot survive without doing so. They have a mitigating excuse for killing. We do not.

Ignoring for the moment the practicality of Regan's view for present-day public policy, it would appear that he has introduced an important issue into this debate, which cannot be ignored. If we refuse to extend to other sentient beings the rights we claim for ourselves simply because it is economically inconvenient to do so or because it violates tradition, then how do we apply these principles to ourselves? Among the problems presented by this approach are (1) the limited utility of traditional rights-based theories to help us articulate appropriate behavior toward nature, (2) the practical as well as conceptual limitations in making distinctions among living creatures in terms of social welfare, and (3) our lack of confidence in the principle itself.

The real value of Regan's analysis is that it points out the need to think very carefully about the symbiotic relationship between rights and obligations in an environmental ethic and the limitations of a purely rights-based concept of justice for an environmental ethic. Conceived in this way, many of Regan's claims have practical value for water policy. The Blue Ridge controversy exemplifies this practicality. Proponents of a scenic river were in a sense suggesting that all rivers, although inanimate, manifest their essence in wild, untamed states. Rivers are, metaphorically speaking, sentient. To dam a scenic river is to irreversibly destroy it. To do so for short-term material gain to some segment of society, moreover, is always wrong, because once the usefulness of that short-term purpose is exhausted, the denial of the river's existence remains. Our rights to that river's water, in other words, impose obligations upon us to protect its character.

A possible objection to this view is that rivers, unlike animals, are not aware or conscious of their existence. However, as Paul Taylor would remind us, that it hardly the point. If the realization of the good of a river lies in coursing through rapids, then who are we to deny that good? If we were to argue that the river would constitute a better resource if it were tamed and harnessed (as the Federal Power Commission and Appalachian Power Company argued during the licensing proceedings for Blue Ridge), one question that could be reasonably posed is, What places us in the position to know the good of a river?

This is not the place to argue for the complete applicability of rights-based theories of ethics to nonhuman entities. Suffice it to say that any process of decision making that encourages these questions will likely encourage a broader view of nature than the view derived from benefit-cost calculations alone.

Ecofeminism: Mother Nature Is Not Enough

Although humans may be generically similar, culturally imposed distinctions among us have taken on ethical trappings. Gender has long been an accepted and acceptable basis for distinguishing rights and duties toward the use of the environment. Moreover, attitudes toward the environment have often been shaped by gender. In Western culture, men are taught to use and exploit nature, while women are taught to nurture and sustain Mother Earth. An approach that challenges the legitimacy of these prevailing socialization patterns, and that has possible implications for water resources policy, is ecofeminism.

Ecofeminism links the exploitation of the earth with the subordination of women by contending that the attitudes guiding both sets of behavior are determined by political instruments of domination controlled by men. Ecofeminists further contend that the connections between ecology movements and feminist movements (their common emphases upon liberation from oppression and their search for a democratic-participatory ethos) pose an extraordinary challenge to ethics. In essence, a male-dominated political and economic world is also an inherently exploitive one, which regards both the feminine gender and the Earth as mere devices for reproduction and sustenance. Patriarchal sources of power produce a radical disassociation of mankind from nature. This disassociation is rooted in a quest for dominance and superiority, a quest to control aspects of the world seen as mentally, emotionally, and physically inferior (Merchant, 1981; Hendrix, 1987).

The ecofeminist points to three parallels between feminism and ecology. First, some of the leading ecological figures in the late nineteenth and twentieth centuries have been women. Ellen Swallow-Richards, the founder of the science of ecology, built much of her career upon the development of a science of industrial health and hygiene. This science was based upon experimental research and focused upon improving air and water quality in the home and workplace. Known for a time as home ecology (Merchant, 1981), it provided one of the earliest means for women to enter the field of science.

The work of Rachel Carson on the dangers to the food chain from pesticides and other by-products of a grossly wasteful consumer society parallels the work of Betty Friedan, the noted feminist author. Friedan pioneered recognition of the connections between inner growth and development, self-assertiveness, and liberation from the stifling social controls of that same consumer society. In Carson's case, the argument was made that dangers from pesticides and other chemical substances not only were dangerous to health and welfare but were violations of basic rights and the integrity of our bodies.

In addition, women researchers have often taken the lead in studies of chemical wastes, have been some of the most noted activists in organizing political opposition to the siting of chemical hazards, and have often led the so-called appropriate technology movement, a refutation of large-scale, environmentally degrading, technologies in favor of personal skills able to provide people with direct control over their economic destiny.

A second connection, more problematic, is the identification of traditionally feminine characteristics with ecological symbols—as in virgin lands and Mother Nature. While an acknowledgment of this connection could lead to greater appreciation for the way in which women have traditionally sustained nurturing values toward the environment in Western society, they may also reinforce negative stereotypes. These same feminine attributes, when applied to nature, "are suggestive of sexual assaults that render both women and nature passive and submissive" (Merchant, 1981: 8).

A final connection is philosophical. Just as ecology assigns equal importance to all components of the ecosystem, so does feminism assign equality to men and women. Thus, Earth is a home, which should be cherished and valued equally by members of both sexes. And it should be viewed as engaged in a steady-state process of growth, death, decay, and in some respects, rebirth.

How might ecofeminism help us to develop an environmental ethic? First of all, the political process that produced natural resources policies has been overwhelmingly controlled by men. Ecofeminists can help us to understand how the approaches of male-dominated professions, like engineering, and of male-dominated agencies, like the Corps of Engineers, tend to reinforce values that are authoritarian and patriarchal. Those thinkers might also prompt us to consider if policies would be better if there were more women engineers implementing them. Likewise, they might enhance our understanding of the political dynamics of the iron triangle of policy making, comprising congressional committees, water agencies, and interest groups, which tends not only to be male dominated but characterized by distinctly masculine traits of clubbishness and closed informality.

Their perspective can also help to focus attention upon the sources of distrust toward public agencies charged with stewardship over natural resources. American water policy has often been biased toward masculine activities, such as sport fishing, hunting, and power boating. Large-scale hydropower generation through giant dams has come to symbolize the achievements of generally male-dominated labor activities.

More important than these symbolic critiques, however, is the need for a reemphasis upon process in natural resources policy. Because the perspective of ecofeminists is rights oriented, as are those of animal rights advocates and deep ecologists, the ends they promote are similar: respect for all living things, restoration of the environment, and minimal intrusions upon nature. Ecofeminists differ, however, due to their human-centered value system.

Ecofeminists place a heavy reliance upon (1) examining the long-term consequences of environmental impacts, stemming from their concern with the interconnectedness of nature, human equality, and the dignity of both genders, (2) self-management and direct democracy, stemming from the home-centered foci of their early concerns, and (3) open decision making, with full and free discussion of all available alternatives,

from their belief that the dynamic processes of change and
cessitate a free flow of information (Merchant, 1981). This
phasis is, I believe, the one universalizing factor of the eco-
erspective directly relevant to water policy.

The process of analyzing environmental impacts before the undertaking of water projects exemplifies the open-ended process of decision
making urged by ecofeminists. Any effort that broadens participation
in decision making enhances the representation of minorities and the
disenfranchised; experts and nonexperts alike would play a part in making decisions. Ecofeminism might offer a prescription for expansion of
the scoping and tiering process for gauging impacts. It could also illuminate the need for an emphasis upon consent to risks, like those addressed by the federal dam safety program. While ecofeminism would
not guarantee better policy, it might ensure the consideration of a
greater number of alternatives and a greater diversity of perspectives,
each of which has some claim to legitimacy.

Finally, ecofeminism illuminates the culturally based, gender-biased
character of benefit-cost and other microeconomic approaches to policy
analysis. An approach to nature animated by impulses to dominate and
subjugate cannot accept a notion of reasonable fallibility. As has been
seen, benefit-cost analyses often assume an infallibility of method
that does not exist. This assumption of infallibility may very well have
a nonrational basis rooted in socialization patterns and culturally
shaped perspectives toward animals, inanimate objects, minorities, and
women.

Directions for the Future: Toward
an Environmental Ethic

To achieve good public policy, participants in the policy-making process
must want good policy. As one recent book on the policy-making process phrases it, "The behavior of public-spirited individuals is motivated
by an honest effort to achieve good public policy" (Kelman, 1987: 208).
At the same time, of course, a democratic policy process must be prepared to accommodate differing and sometimes contradictory opinions
on what constitutes good policy. Wanting is not the same as having,
however. The policy-making process must incorporate conditions that
facilitate public spiritedness. These conditions must invest the policy-
making process with a perspective that compels participants to think
about the impacts of policy on ourselves in other than a purely material
sense. Good public policy makes us better persons through making
possible dignified, orderly survival on this planet with all other living
creatures. It cautions us to be aware of our limitations and our moral

obligation to leave this planet as we found it. Moreover, it educates us to want to leave a better legacy for our children by reasoning beyond our immediate wants.

A principle theme of this book is that U.S. natural resources policy, while partly animated by public spiritedness, has also been animated by a sometimes conscious, at other times subconscious, gratuitousness. Because the process of policy making has not served to school individuals to behave as deliberative, contemplative citizens of a polity and has instead encouraged the solving of problems on an ad hoc, disjointed, fragmented basis designed to serve the material needs of the greatest number of citizens, it has failed the test of public spiritedness.

To restore such public spiritedness requires that we begin with clear needs, based upon the conditions that make us capable of becoming fully human, of fulfilling our capacities for justice to the fullest. We should use those needs as a basis for formulating policies comprehensively, coherently, fairly, and with due regard for the very environment that nurtures and sustains us. Specific recommendations have been made throughout this book for the reform of water law, the practice of engineering, the application of benefit-cost analysis, and the use of environmental impact assessment. Moreover, case studies from a variety of settings have been drawn upon to illuminate environmental, economic, and other problems that stem from the failure to consider all relevant factors in the formulation of public policy.

What is also needed, however, is a commitment to a structurally efficient framework for public policy. Comprehensive planning, through centralized rules to protect the environment and regionally based instruments for the implementation of such rules, will not solve all water problems. There are additional criteria that must be utilized; I call these criteria *reasonable fallibility rules for decision making.*

The first of these rules is recognition of the fact that intangible cultural and historical factors, over and above the character of a natural resource, establish important parameters for a policy's success or failure. As was seen in the Blue Ridge case, the arguments offered on behalf of a hydropower project on the New River might have been perceived as reasonable elsewhere but, for a variety of reasons indigenous to the valley, doomed the project from the start. Policy makers must be sensitive to the traditions, expectations, and most important, established patterns of land and water use characteristic of a region before embarking on either water resources development or preservation. Neither goal can be democratic if it does not take into account the opinions of those directly affected as well as the welfare of society as a whole. As Alasdair MacIntyre notes, it will never be easy to decide on a given-case basis which of these goals—sensitivity to historic conditions or the need for economic development and growth—should take precedence. No moral standard articulated for either position will be absolute or infallible. The position opposite to our own allows us to see the fallibility of our own point of view and to broaden it. We may then be more willing to compromise (MacIntyre, 1988).

The second rule of reasonable fallibility is that, contrary to the assumptions of many policy approaches—including the public choice approach, which has proven useful as a point of departure for many of the arguments in this book—historic patterns of resource use are an important determinant of public acceptance of a particular system for natural resources management. The perception that contamination of transboundary waters affects the welfare of Canadians and Americans equally, coupled with the long-standing amity between these two nations, encouraged the formation of the International Joint Commission for management of these resources.

On the other hand, the same traditions militated against Canadian acceptance of any plan imposing risks upon the environment of Manitoba that did not include their prior consent. This was Canada's major objection to Garrison. In essence, when conditions that encourage public trust are established, unilateral decisions designed to benefit one side or the other are destined to be seen as unjust. This should not have been surprising. Moreover, to expect that the preemptory concerns of one side—North Dakota farmers—should overrule all other considerations outside the Missouri River valley, was shortsighted. A lesson in this policy-making process is that, by reasoning together in a tentative, cautious manner, we can change the struggle for power from a contest in which each side is threatened by the position of the other to a process by which we confront the scarcity and fragileness of resources as vulnerable entities we hold in common (Ackerman, 1980). Thus, no single meliorative or preemptory principle can resolve natural resources problems justly.

Likewise, while the salinity of the Colorado River could have been anticipated through careful study of the region's geology and geography, the patterns of exploitation established under the Colorado River Compact inhibited the accommodation of such impacts by means other than more dam building.

A final rule: while the risks to health, welfare, and the environment of natural resources development are measurable and often immutable, a public's perceptions of these risks are not. For example, although French citizens allow nuclear power to be developed by an elite of scientists, bureaucrats, and elected officials, they prefer that water resources management be shared with local and regional officials. A people's attitudes toward some environmental policies are shaped by imperfect knowledge of their consequences; as knowledge of their impacts becomes clearer, opposition to some policies and acquiescence toward others may develop. When this occurs, the allocative efficiency of a policy may be hindered, its transaction costs may grow, its equity may be challenged, and its overall feasibility may be called into question. This is one reason policies are never fixed.

The lesson in all of this is that reasonable fallibility depends upon accepting the limitations of information about known impacts ahead of meliorative considerations of economic benefit. Not only is this lesson applicable to water policy, but it appears to be relevant for nuclear power, hazardous and toxic wastes, and problems such as global atmospheric warming. Clearly, we need an environmental ethic for all of these policies. Perhaps water policy can provide a starting point.

Notes

1 Values, Political Theory, and Environmental Policies

1. For an original analysis of the establishment of an American frontier culture, see Jordan and Kaups, 1989.

2 Ethics and U.S. Water Policy

1. The following discussion on scenic resources is based on a personal communication with Dr. Richard E. Chenoweth, Department of Landscape Architecture, University of Wisconsin, Madison, 6 November 1989.
2. This connection has been recognized in many quarters and is becoming a source of opposition to subsidy politics (Schmidt, 1982, 1983). The origins of this transferability principle are traceable to Kendrick Dam, a 1930s reclamation project (Hart, 1957, p. 116).
3. A good example of this issue is offered by recent accounts of semiserious proposals to restore the Tuolumne River in California by the destruction of John Muir's hated Hetch-Hetchy Dam and draining its reservoir (Pope, 1987).

3 Law, Engineering, and the Absence of Environmental Principles in Water Policy

1. This distinction comes from an interview with George Gould, a professor of water law at the McGeorge School of Law in Stockton, California, as quoted in Neumann, 1985.
2. For a general history of American engineering that emphasizes professionalism, social responsibility, and ethics, see Layton, 1986.

4 The Great Plains Garrison Diversion Project and the Search for an Environmental Ethic

1. By comparison, the Colorado River–Big Thompson Project, completed in 1947, which transfers water through the Continental Divide, irrigates approximately 630,000 acres and has storage reservoirs whose capacity exceeds 710,000 acre-feet. The Grand Coulee–Columbia basin project, completed in 1940, irrigates over 1 million acres and has a water storage capacity that exceeds 5 million acre-feet. Comparable figures for the Garrison diversion project are 250,000 acres of irrigated land and 340,000 acre-feet of storage (Houck, 1954: 23; Bureau of Reclamation, 1957: iv).
2. Sixty-two percent of North Dakota farmers depend upon groundwater for domestic uses, while 87 percent of Manitobans depend upon this resource (Freshwater Foundation, 1985: 6).
3. For example, estimates indicate that a fish screen for the McClusky Canal that would prevent biota transfer could cost upwards of $2 million, while a closed-loop system could add another $22 million (Oettig, 1977: 44).

5 The Pathology of Structural Reform in Water Policy: Ethics and Bureaucracies

1. For a discussion of these agencies and their authority, see the Power Planning and Conservation Act of 1980.

6 The Blue Ridge Pump Storage Project: Conservation, Preservation, and the Search for an Environmental Ethic

1. Since 1977 the Federal Power Commission has been called the Federal Energy Regulatory Commission and has been part of the U.S. Department of Energy.
2. For a discussion of this cooptation problem, see Bernstein, 1965. A good discussion of the Federal Power Commission and its relation to investor-owned utilities is contained in Beil, 1973.
3. Schoenbaum, 1979, p. 50. Grayson County, Virginia, stood to lose $3 million a year in agricultural production alone, while APCO's estimate for total recreational benefits for the project in the three counties where land would be inundated was $3.4 million a year (Kenworthy, 1974e).
4. The Blue Ridge project may have been the first challenge to the low-flow

augmentation (pollution dilution) principle in a nongovernment water project (Kenworthy, 1971). Since the mid-1970s, the Army Corps of Engineers has moved away from endorsing the practice (*National Parks and Conservation*, 1977; Kenworthy, 1973d; Schoenbaum, 1979, pp. 65ff.; Federal Water Pollution Control Act Amendments of 1972).

5. Specifically, the Federal Power Commission was criticized for accepting APCO's environmental impact statement without suggesting modifications. Meanwhile, APCO was cited for not only failing to find housing for more than 10 percent of the families who required relocation but also for offering to pay only half the actual cost that each family incurred in finding suitable housing (Kenworthy, 1973a).

7 Benefit-cost Analysis as an Inadequate Substitute for an Environmental Ethic

1. While the body of literature on impacts is large, a good summary is found in Bain et al., 1986; and Culhane, Friesema, and Beecher, 1987.

8 Practitioners of Water Policy: Technological Elitism as a Policy Ethic

1. For an overview of French policies in this area, see Deudney, 1981, pp. 6–7; Feldman, 1989; Siegel and Weinberg, 1977; and Whitehead, 1985.

References

Abrahamson, Dean E. 1975. *Environmental Cost of Electric Power.* Washington, D.C.: Scientists Institute for Public Information.

Abramavitz, Alan I. 1980. "The United States: Political Culture Under Stress." In Gabriel Almond and Sidney Verba, eds., *The Civic Culture Revisited.* Boston: Little, Brown, pp. 177–211.

Ackerman, Bruce. 1980. *Social Justice and the Liberal State.* New Haven: Yale University Press.

Anderson, Charles W. 1979. "The Place of Principles in Policy Analysis." *American Political Science Review* 73 (September): 711–23.

Anderson, F. R. et al. 1977. *Environmental Improvements through Economic Incentives.* Baltimore: Johns Hopkins University Press for Resources for the Future.

Bach, W. 1984. *Our Threatened Climate: Ways of Averting the CO_2 Problem through Rational Energy Use,* trans. Jill Jager. Dordrecht, FRG: D. Reidel.

Baines, M. B. et al. 1986. *Cumulative Impact Assessment: Evaluating the Environmental Effects of Multiple Human Developments.* ANL/EES-TM-309. Argonne, Ill.: Argonne National Laboratory, July.

Barber, Benjamin R. 1984. *Strong Democracy: Participatory Politics for a New Age.* Berkeley and Los Angeles: University of California Press.

Barde, J. 1975. "An Examination of the Polluter Pays Principle." In *The Polluter*

Pays Principle: Definition, Analysis, Implementation. Paris: Organization for Economic Cooperation and Development, pp. 93–117.

Bay, Christian. 1978. "From Contract to Community: Thoughts on Liberalism and Post-Industrial Society." In Fred Dallmayer, ed., *From Contract to Community: Political Theory at the Crossroads.* New York: Marcel Dekker, pp. 29–46.

Beatley, Timothy. 1989. "The Role of Expectations and Promises in Land Use Decisionmaking," *Policy Sciences* 22 (March): 27–50.

Beil, Marshall. 1973. "Power for the People: Electricity and the Regulatory Agencies." In Mark J. Green, ed., *The Monopoly Makers: Ralph Nader's Study Group Report on Regulation and Competition.* New York: Grossman, pp. 193–226.

Bennett, Jane. 1987. *Unthinking Faith and Enlightenment: Nature and State in a Post-Hegelian Era.* New York: New York University Press.

Bennis, Warren. 1966. *Beyond Bureaucracy.* New York: McGraw-Hill.

Bergsrud, F. G. 1978. "Better On-Farm Water Management." In *The Water Conservation Challenge.* St. Paul: Upper Mississippi River Basin Commission, pp. 60–61.

Bernstein, Marver H. 1965. *Regulating Business by Independent Commission.* Princeton: Princeton University Press, 1965.

Berry, D., C. Cox, and P. Wolff. 1983. "Managing Rafting Rivers," *Water Spectrum* 15 (Spring): 10–17.

Bienen, Henry. 1983. "Armed Forces and National Modernization: Continuing the Debate," *Comparative Politics* 16 (October): 1–16.

Biniek, Joseph P. 1985. "Benefit-Cost Analysis: An Evaluation." In Sheldon Kaminiecki et al., eds., *Controversies in Environmental Policy.* Albany: State University of New York Press, pp. 136–52.

Brasher, P. 1988. "Lost Heritage: Tribes Seek Millions for Flooded Homeland," *Fargo Forum,* 6 March.

Braybrooke, David, and Charles Lindblom. 1963. *A Strategy of Decision: Policy Analysis as a Social Process.* New York: Free Press.

Brown, D. Clayton, 1980. *Rivers, Rockets, and Readiness—Army Engineers in the Sunbelt: A History of the Ft. Worth District, Corps of Engineers, 1950–1979.* Washington, D.C.: Government Printing Office.

Brown, Lester R. 1981. *Building a Sustainable Society.* New York: Norton.

Brown, R. Steven. 1986. "Environmental and Natural Resource Problems: The Role of the States." In *The Book of the States, 1986–1987.* Lexington, Ky.: Council of State Governments, pp. 401–05.

Brunner, R. D. 1980. "Decentralized Energy Policies," *Public Policy* 28 (Winter): 71–90.

Bureau of Reclamation. 1948. *Boulder Canyon Project Final Reports.* Part 1. *Introductory, General History and Description of Project.* Boulder City, Nev.: U.S. Dept. of Interior.

———. 1957. *Colorado–Big Thompson Project.* Vol. 1. *Planning, Legislation, and General Description.* Denver: U.S. Dept. of Interior.

———. 1983. *Draft Supplemental Environmental Impact Statement, Garrison Diversion Unit.* Billings: U.S. Dept. of Interior.

Burke, Major Robert L. 1964. "Military Civic Action," *Military Review* 44 (October): 62–72.

Burke, R., and J. B. Heaney. 1975. *Collective Decision-Making in Water Resource Planning.* Lexington, Mass.: D. C. Health.

Bushy, C. E. 1955. "Regulation and Economic Expansion." In *Water: The Yearbook of Agriculture, 1955.* Washington, D.C.: Government Printing Office, pp. 666–76.

Cahn, Robert. 1978. *Footprints on the Planet: A Search for an Environmental Ethic.* New York: Universe Books.

Caldwell, Lynton K. 1975. *Man and His Environment: Policy and Administration.* New York: Harper and Row.

———. 1981. "Survivalist Policies: Ecological-Environmental Factors." Unpublished paper. American Political Science Association meeting. New York City, September.

———. 1988. "Environmental Impact Analysis (EIA): Origins, Evolution, and Future Directions," *Policy Studies Review* 8 (Autumn): 75–83.

Cass, Ed. 1981. "How Long Can You Tread Water?" *Water Spectrum* 13 (Fall): 8–16.

Caulfield, Henry P., Jr. 1978. "Policy Goals and Values in Historical Perspective." In D. F. Peterson and A. B. Crawford, eds. *Values and Choices in the Development of the Colorado River.* Tucson: University of Arizona Press, pp. 113–20.

———. 1984. "U.S. Water Resources Development Policy and Intergovernmental Relations." In J. G. Francis and R. Ganzel, eds., *Western Public Lands.* New York: Rowman and Allanheld, pp. 215–31.

CEQ Regulations. 40 C.F.R. chap. 5, sec. 1502.14.

Ceriacy-Wantrup, S. V. 1964. "Benefit-Cost Analysis and Public Resource Development." In *S. C. Smith and E. N. Castle, eds., Economics and Public Policy in Water Resources Development.* Ames: Iowa State University Press, pp. 9–24.

Chambolle, Thiery. 1981. "Controlling Industrial Water Pollution in France, and the Role of the River Basin Authorities," *Industry and Environment, United Nations Environment Program* 7 (July/August/September): 34–37.

Chenoweth, Richard E. 1989a. "Image-Capture Computer Technology and Aesthetic Regulation in Rural Riverway Planning and Management." Unpublished paper. Department of Landscape Architecture, University of Wisconsin, Madison.

———. 1989b. Personal communication with author, 6 November.

Chenoweth, Richard E., and Bernard Niemann. 1988. "Human Values of Landscape Corridors: Law, Policy, Economics, and Aesthetics." Abstract of unpublished paper presented before the annual meeting of the American Association for the Advancement of Science, Boston.

Chenoweth, Richard E., and James Pardee. 1988. "Visual Simulations of Alternative Futures for the Proposed Lower Wisconsin State Riverway." Proposal to the Wisconsin Department of Natural Resources, Madison.

Chenoweth, Richard E., Wayne G. Tlusty, and Bernard J. Niemann. 1982. *Public*

Rights to Scenic Resources: Infringement Is Sufficient Cause for Denial of Lowland Sand and Gravel Operations in Wisconsin. Miscellaneous Publication 17, Agricultural Experiment Station. St. Paul: University of Minnesota.

Chisholm, R. *Theory of Knowledge.* 1966. Englewood Cliffs, N.J.: Prentice-Hall.

Clarke, Jeanne N., and Daniel McCool. 1985. *Staking Out the Terrain: Power Differentials among Natural Resources Management Agencies.* Albany: State University of New York Press.

Clarkson, R. N. 1983. Garrison Focus Office, Winnipeg, Manitoba. Personal correspondence with author, 14 April.

Cochran, Clarke E. 1977. "Authority and Community: The Contributions of Carl Friedrich, Yves Simon, and Michael Polanyi," *American Political Science Review* 71 (June): 546–58.

Conservation Foundation. 1984. *State of the Environment: An Assessment at Mid-Decade.* Washington, D.C.: Conservation Foundation.

Corps of Engineers. 1972. Souris-Red-Rainy River Basin Commission. *Souris-Red-Rainy River Basin Comprehensive Study.* Moorhead, Minn.: U.S. Army Corps of Engineers.

———. 1973. *Missouri River Division Reservoir Control Center.* Omaha: U.S. Army Corps of Engineers.

———. 1978. *The Role of Conservation in Water Supply Planning.* Fort Belvoir, Va.: U.S. Army Corps of Engineers.

———. 1979. Board of Engineers for Rivers and Harbors. *Manual for Water Resource Planners.* Washington, D.C.: Government Printing Office.

———. 1981. Huntington District. *Feasibility Report, Draft Main Report and Environmental Impact Statement.* Vol. 1. *Summersville Lake Modification Study.* Huntington, W.V.: U.S. Army Corps of Engineers.

Cotgrove, S. 1982. *Catastrophe or Cornucopia.* Chichester, U.K.: John Wiley and Sons.

Cronon, William. 1983. *Changes in the Land: Colonists and the Ecology of Colonial New England.* New York: Hill and Wang.

Cropsey, Joseph. 1977. *Political Philosophy and the Issues of Politics.* Chicago: University of Chicago Press.

Crosson, Pierre, 1982. *The Cropland Crisis: Myth or Reality?* Baltimore: Johns Hopkins University Press for Resources for the Future.

Culhane, P. J., H. P. Friesema, and J. A. Beecher. 1987. *Forecasts and Environmental Decisionmaking: The Content and Predictive Accuracy of Environmental Impact Statements.* Social Impact Assessment Series 14. Boulder: Westview.

Davis, David Howard. 1982. *Energy Politics.* 3d ed. New York: St. Martin's.

Davis Peter V. 1983. "Selling Saved Energy: A New Role for the Utilities." In Dorothy S. Zinberg, ed., *Uncertain Power: The Struggle for a National Energy Policy.* New York: Pergamon, pp. 182–98.

Davis, P., and J. Cunningham. 1977. *State Laws Pertaining to Water and Related Land Resources.* Jefferson City: Missouri Department of Natural Resources, Clean Water Commission.

Derthick, Martha. 1970. *Between State and Nation.* Washington, D.C.: Brookings.

Deudney, Daniel. 1981. *Rivers of Energy: The Hydropower Potential.* Worldwatch Paper 44. Washington, D.C.: Worldwatch Institute.

Dewey, John. 1954. *The Public and Its Problems.* Chicago: Swallow.

———. 1963. *Liberalism and Social Action.* New York: Capricorn Books.

Dickson, David. 1981. "Limiting Democracy: Technocrats and the Liberal State," *Democracy* 1 (January): 61–79.

Downing, Paul B. 1984. *Environmental Economics and Policy.* Boston: Little, Brown.

DRBC (Delaware River Basin Commission). 1961. *DRBC Compact.* Trenton, N.J.: DRBC.

———. 1978a. *Water Code for the DRBC.* Trenton, N.J.: DRBC.

———. 1978b. *Annual Report of the DRBC.* Trenton, N.J.: DRBC.

Drew, Elizabeth. 1970. "Dam Outrage: The Story of the Army Engineers," *Atlantic Monthly* (April): 51–62.

Dror, Yehezkel. 1968. *Public Policy Making Re-Examined.* Scranton, Penna.: Chandler.

DRP (President's Departmental Reorganization Program). 1971. *The Proposed Department of Natural Resources: A Review and Report.* Washington, D.C.: Government Printing Office, March.

Dubos, Rene. 1980. *The Wooing of Earth.* New York: Scribners'.

Dworkin, Ronald. 1977. *Taking Rights Seriously.* Cambridge: Harvard University Press.

Eckholm, Erik P. 1982. *Down to Earth: Environment and Human Needs.* New York: Norton.

Eckstein, Otto. 1958. *Water Resource Development: The Economics of Project Evaluation.* Cambridge: Harvard University Press.

Eisel, Leo M., Gerald D. Seinwill, and Richard M. Wheeler, Jr. 1982. "Improved Principles, Standards, and Procedures for Evaluating Federal Water Projects," *Water Resources Research* 18 (April): 203–10.

Energy and the Environment: Unfinished Business. 1985. Washington, D.C.: Congressional Quarterly Press.

Enk, Gordon, and Stuart Hart. 1977. *Beyond NEPA Revisited: A Re-examination of the Responses of Federal Agencies to NEPA.* Washington, D.C.: Institute of Man and Science.

Environment Reporter—Current Developments. 1981. 28 August.

Fargo Forum. 1982a. "Federal Judge Removes Major Garrison Hurdle." 16 October, sec. A.

———. 1982b. "Cooperative North Dakota–Saskatchewan Dam on Souris River Proposed." 8 December, sec. B.

———. 1983a. "Guy Says North Dakota Owed Water Development." 13 February, sec. D.

———. 1983b. "Report Says Canada's Fears of Garrison Largely Unfounded." 4 May, sec. A.

———. 1983c. "Column Reports Agency Ignores Anti-Garrison Data." 4 October, sec. A.

———. 1987. "End of Big Dam Era Seen." 24 January.

Feldman, David L. 1987a. "Comparative Models of Civil-Military Relations and the U.S. Army Corps of Engineers," *Journal of Political and Military Sociology* 15 (Fall): 43–53.

———. 1987b. "The Defeat of the Blue Ridge Pump-Storage Project as Microcosm of Environmental Policy Change," *Policy Sciences* 20 (Fall): 235–58.

———. 1989. "France's Environmental Policy." In Fredric Bolotin, ed., *International Public Policy Sourcebook*. Vol. 2, *Education and Environment*. Westport, Conn.: Greenwood, pp. 235–55.

Ferejohn, John A. 1974. *Pork-Barrel Politics: Rivers and Harbors Legislation, 1947–1968*. Stanford: Stanford University Press.

Florman, Samuel C. 1976. *The Existential Pleasures of Engineering*. New York: St. Martin's.

Ford, Daniel F. 1984. *The Cult of the Atom: The Secret Papers of the Atomic Energy Commission*. New York: Simon and Schuster.

Fox, Irving K. 1966. "Policy Problems in the Field of Water Resources." In A. V. Kneese and S. C. Smith, eds., *Water Research*. Baltimore: Johns Hopkins University Press, pp. 271–89.

Frankena, William K. 1963. *Ethics*. Englewood Cliffs, N.J.: Prentice-Hall.

Frasure, C. W., and L. M. Davis, eds. 1977. *Eight Years, Official Statements and Papers, the Honorable Arch A. Moore, Governor of West Virginia*. Vol. 3. Charleston: State of West Virginia.

Freedman, Warren. 1987. *Federal Statutes on Environmental Protection*. Westport, Conn.: Greenwood.

Freeman, J. Lieper. 1965. *The Political Process: Executive Bureau–Legislative Committee Relations*. New York: Random House.

Freshwater Foundation. 1985. *Watershed Stewardship in the Red River Basin*. Moorhead, Minn.: International Coalition for Land/Water Stewardship in the Red River Basin—Freshwater Foundation.

Freudenburg, W. R., and R. K. Baxter. 1985. "Nuclear Reactions: Public Attitudes and Policies toward Nuclear Power," *Policy Studies Review* 5 (August): 96–110.

GAO (General Accounting Office). 1974. *Report to the Congress: Improvements Needed in Making Benefit-Cost Analyses for Federal Water Projects, B-167941*. Washington, D.C.: General Accounting Office.

GDCD. 1986. *The United States, Canada, and Garrison Diversion*. Carrington, N.D.: GDCD.

Gianessi, L. P. et al., 1986. "Non-point Source Pollution: Are Cropland Controls the Answer?" *Journal of Soil and Water Conservation* (July/August): 215–18.

Glick, Edward B. 1967. *Peaceful Conflict: The Non-Military Uses of the Military*. Harrisburg, Penna.: Stackpole Books.

Goetzmann, William. 1959. *Army Exploration in the American West: 1803–1863*. New Haven: Yale University Press.

Goslin, Ival V. 1978. "Colorado River Development." In D. F. Peterson and A. B. Crawford, eds., *Values and Choices in the Development of the Colorado River Basin*. Tucson: University of Arizona Press, pp. 18–60.

Gramlich, Edward M. 1981. *Benefit-Cost Analysis of Government Programs*. Englewood Cliffs, N.J.: Prentice-Hall.

Gribble, Lt. General William C., Jr. 1974. "Perspectives on the Army Engineers Water Management Mission," *Water Spectrum* 6:1–9.

Griffiths, A. Phillip. 1958. "Justifying Moral Principles," *Proceedings of the Aristotelian Society* 58:103–24.

Hart, Henry C. 1957. *The Dark Missouri.* Madison: University of Wisconsin Press.

Hayes, Dennis. 1977. *Rays of Hope: The Transition to a Post-Petroleum World.* New York: Norton.

Hays, Samuel P. 1958. "The Mythology of Conservation." In H. Jarrett, ed., *Perspectives on Conservation.* Baltimore: Johns Hopkins University Press, pp. 40–45. Revised edition, 1961, pp. 171–80.

Heady, Ferrel. 1979. *Public Administration: A Comparative Perspective.* 2d ed., revised and expanded. New York: Marcel Dekker.

Hendrix, Kathleen. 1987. "A New Global Vision Called Ecofeminism," *Los Angeles Times,* 2 April.

Hobbes, Thomas. 1957. *Leviathan,* pts. 1 and 2. Ed. Herbert W. Schneider. Indianapolis: Bobbs-Merrill.

Hobday, Victor C. 1969. *Sparks at the Grassroots: Municipal Distribution of TVA Electricity in Tennessee.* Knoxville: University of Tennessee Press.

Holmes, Beatrice H. 1979. *A History of Federal Water Resources Programs and Policies, 1961–1970.* Washington, D.C.: Economics, Statistics, and Cooperatives Service, U.S. Department of Agriculture.

Houck, Fred A. 1954. "Grand Coulee Dam–Columbia Basin Project." In *Dams and Control Works,* 3d ed. Washington, D.C.: Government Printing Office, pp. 21–32.

Howe, Charles W. 1979. "The Coming Conflicts over Water." In *Western Water Resources: Coming Problems and the Policy Alternatives.* Boulder: Westview, pp. 15–38.

Husar, J. 1988. "Battle in Mississippi Still Raging over U.S. Draining of Wetlands," *Chicago Tribune,* 3 March.

IGDSB (International Garrison Diversion Study Board). 1976. *Report to the International Joint Commission.* Washington, D.C.: IJC–Garrison Diversion Study Board.

IJC (International Joint Commission). 1977. *Transboundary Implications of the Garrison Diversion Unit.* Washington, D.C.: IJC.

Ingram, Helen. 1978. "The Politics of Water Allocation." In D. F. Peterson and A. B. Crawford, eds., *Values and Choices in the Development of the Colorado River.* Tucson: University of Arizona Press, pp. 61–75.

Ingram, Helen, Nancy Laney, and John R. McCain. 1979. "Water Scarcity and the Politics of Plenty in the Four Corner States," *Western Political Quarterly* 32 (September): 298–306.

———. 1980. *A Policy Approach to Political Representation: Lessons from the Four Corners States.* Baltimore: Johns Hopkins University Press for Resources for the Future.

Ingram, Helen, and Scott J. Ullery. 1980. "Policy Innovation and Institutional Fragmentation." *Policy Studies Journal* 8 (Spring): 664–82.

Jackman, R. W. 1976. "Politicians in Uniform: Military Governments and Social Change in the Third World," *American Political Science Review* 70 (December): 1078–97.

Jager, Jill. 1986. "Climatic Change: Floating New Evidence in the CO_2 Debate," *Environment* 28 (September): 38–41.

Jansen, Robert B. 1980. *Dams and Public Safety.* Washington, D.C.: U.S. Department of the Interior.

Johnson, J. E. et al., 1962. *Negative Impacts of Garrison and Oahe Reservoirs on the North Dakota Economy.* Fargo: North Dakota State University Extension Service.

Johnson, L. R. 1974. *The Falls City Engineers: A History of the Louisville District Corps of Engineers.* Washington, D.C.: Government Printing Office.

Johnson, Ralph W. 1968. "The Changing Role of the Courts in Water Quality Management." In T. H. Campbell and R. O. Sylvester, eds., *Water Resources Management and Public Policy.* Seattle: University of Washington Press, pp. 196–203.

Jordan, Terry G., and M. Kaups. 1989. *The American Backwoods Frontier: An Ethnic and Ecological Interpretation.* Baltimore: Johns Hopkins University Press.

Kalleberg, Arthur, and Larry Preston. 1975. "Normative Political Analysis and the Problem of Justification: The Cognitive Status of Basic Political Norms," *Journal of Politics* 73 (August): 650–84.

Kasperson, Roger. 1986. "Six Propositions on Public Participation and Their Relevance for Risk Communication," *Risk Analysis* 6:275–81.

Kelman, Stephen. 1987. *Making Public Policy: A Hopeful View of American Government.* New York: Basic Books.

Kenworthy, E. W. 1971. "Pollution-Dilution Issue in Blue Ridge Power Plan," *New York Times*, 11 November.

———. 1972. "FPC Curb Asked in Waste Control," *New York Times*, 6 February.

———. 1973a. "FPC Criticized over Blue Ridge," *New York Times*, 16 April.

———. 1973b. "Mizell, N.C. Representative, Acts to Block Huge Power Project," *New York Times*, 22 October.

———. 1973c. "Project to Dam Carolina River to Flush Out Pollution Is Fading," *New York Times*, 22 October.

———. 1973d. "EPA Staff Is Critical of Blue Ridge Power Project," *New York Times*, 5 November.

———. 1974a. "Project to Build Two Dams on Carolina River Protested," *New York Times*, 10 February.

———. 1974b. "Morton in Shift on Power Plant," *New York Times*, 6 April.

———. 1974c. "FPC Approves Power Project: Opponents in Congress Angered," *New York Times*, 15 June.

———. 1974d. "Labor Federation Joins Utility in Lobbying for Dam on New River," *New York Times*, 21 August.

———. 1974e. "Battle for Future of a River," *New York Times*, 8 December.

———. 1976a. "Reagan Wants Carolina Dam Included in U.S. Scenic River System," *New York Times*, 15 February.

————. 1976b. "Ford Expected to Back Scenic River Plan on North Carolina Trip," *New York Times*, 8 March.

Keys, David L. 1984. "National Environmental Policy, Foreign Policy, and the GDU," *Environmental Professional* 6:223–34.

Kleinman, A. P., and F. B. Brown. 1980. *Colorado River Salinity: Economic Impacts on Agricultural, Municipal, and Industrial Users*. Denver: U.S. Department of the Interior.

Knudsen, T. J. 1987. "Bureau of Reclamation Forsakes Construction for Conservation: With Giant Dams All Built, Agency Seeks New Work," *New York Times*, 8 November, sec. E.

Kohlberg, Lawrence. 1970. "Education for Justice: A Modern Statement of the Platonic View." In N. F. Sizer and T. R. Sizer, eds., *Moral Education*. Cambridge: Harvard University Press, pp. 57–83.

————. 1971. "From Is to Ought: How to Commit the Naturalistic Fallacy and Get Away with It." In T. Mischel, ed., *Cognitive Development and Epistemology*. New York: Academic Press, pp. 183–84.

————. 1981. *Essays in Moral Development*. Vol. 1. *The Philosophy of Moral Development*. New York: Harper and Row.

Laycock, George. 1975. "New River, Old Problems," *Audubon* 77 (November): 62.

Layton, Edwin T., Jr. 1986. *The Revolt of the Engineers: Social Responsibility and the American Engineering Profession*. Baltimore: Johns Hopkins University Press.

Leopold, Aldo. 1966. *A Sand County Almanac*. New York: Oxford University Press.

Lepawsky, A. 1950. "Water Resources and American Federalism," *American Political Science Review* 44 (September): 631–49.

Linville, Major R. P. 1981. "Assisting the Third World in the 1980's," *Military Review* 61 (December): 8–20.

Lloyd, T. 1969. "A Water Resource Policy for Canada." In J. G. Nelson et al., eds., *Water: Selected Readings on the Process and Method in Canadian Geography*. Toronto: Methuen, pp. 277–93.

Loch, J. S. et al. 1979. *Potential Effects of Exotic Fishes on Manitoba: An Impact Assessment of the GDU*. Fisheries and Marine Service Technical Report 838. Winnipeg: Manitoba Department of Fisheries and the Environment.

Locke, John. 1963. *Two Treatises of Government*. Ed. Peter Laslett. New York: New American Library.

Lord, William B. 1980. "Water Resources Planning: Conflict Management," *Water Spectrum* (July): 2–11.

Lowi, Theodore J. 1979. *The End of Liberalism: The Second Republic of the United States*. 2d ed. New York: Norton.

Luten, Daniel B. 1980. "Ecological Optimism in the Social Sciences," *American Behavioral Scientist* 24 (September/October): 125–51.

McConnell, Grant. 1966. *Private Power and American Democracy*. New York: Vintage.

MacIntyre, Alasdair. 1988. *Whose Justice? Which Rationality?* London: Duckworth.

MacNeil, N., and H. W. Metz. 1956. *The Hoover Report, 1953–1955.* New York: Macmillan.

Macpherson, C. B. 1978. "The False Roots of Western Democracy." In F. Dallmayr, ed., *From Contract to Community: Political Theory at the Crossroads.* New York: Marcel Dekker, pp. 17–28.

MacRae, Duncan, Jr. 1971. "Scientific Communication, Ethical Argument, and Public Policy," *American Political Science Review* 65 (March): 343.

Madison, James. 1961. "Federalist no. 10." In *The Federalist Papers.* Ed. Clinton Rossiter. New York: New American Library.

Manheim, Marvin L. 1981. "Ethical Issues in Environmental Impact Assessment," *Environmental Impact Assessment Review* 2 (December): 315–34.

Mann, Dean. 1985. "Democratic Politics and Environmental Policy." In S. Kaminiecki et al., eds., *Controversies in Environmental Policy.* Albany: SUNY Press, pp. 3–36.

Mansbridge, J. J. 1983. *Beyond Adversary Democracy.* Chicago: University of Chicago Press.

March, J. G., and J. P. Olson. 1983. "Organizing Political Life: What Administrative Reorganization Tells Us about Government," *American Political Science Review* 77:281–96.

Maritain, Jacques. 1951. *Man and the State.* Chicago: University of Chicago Press.

Marshall, Hubert. 1966. "Politics and Efficiency in Water Resources Planning." In A. V. Kneese and E. C. Smith, eds., *Water Research.* Baltimore: Johns Hopkins University Press, pp. 291–310.

———. 1978. "Rational Choice in Water Resources Planning." In D. F. Peterson and A. B. Crawford, eds., *Values and Choices in the Development of the Colorado River Basin.* Tucson: University of Arizona Press, pp. 403–23.

Maslow, Abraham F. 1954. *Motivation and Personality.* New York: Harper and Brothers.

———. 1968. *Towards a Psychology of Being.* 2d ed. New York: Van Nostrand.

Mather, J. R. 1984. *Water Resources: Distribution, Use, and Management.* New York: John Wiley and Sons.

Mazmanian, Daniel A., and Jeanne Nienaber. 1979. *Can Organizations Change? Environmental Protection, Citizen Participation, and the Corps of Engineers.* Washington, D.C.: Brookings.

MDNR (Manitoba Department of Natural Resources). 1982. *Garrison: An Environmental Threat to Manitoba.* Winnipeg: MDNR.

Menzies, J. R. 1969. "Water Polution in Canada by Drainage Basins." In J. G. Nelson et al., eds., *Water: Selected Readings on the Process and Method in Canadian Geography.* Toronto: Methuen, pp. 213–33.

Merchant, Carolyn. 1981. "Earthcare: Women and the Environmental Movement," *Environment* 23 (June).

Merritt, Raymond H. 1979. *Creativity, Conflict, and Controversy: A History of the St. Paul District, U.S. Army Corps of Engineers.* Washington, D.C.: Government Printing Office.

Milenky, E. S. 1980. "Arms Production and National Security in Argentina," *Journal of Inter-American Studies and World Affairs* 22 (August): 267–88.

Mill, John Stuart. 1962. *On Utilitarianism and Other Writings.* Ed. Mary War-
nock. New York: New American Library.

Miller, T. R. 1985. "Recent Trends in Federal Water Resource Management: Are
the 'Iron Triangles' in Retreat?" *Policy Studies Review* 5 (November): 395–
412.

Missouri Law Review. 1954. 19:138–46.

Mizell, Wilmer. 1972. "The Blue Ridge Power Project," *Congressional Record*
118 (12 September): 30393–94.

Moody, Sid. 1983. "U.S. Corps of Engineers May Have Reached Bend in River,"
Fargo Forum, 30 October, sec. A.

Morgan, Arthur E. 1971. *Dams and Other Disasters: A Century of the Army
Corps of Engineers in Civil Works.* Boston: Porter Sargent.

Mosher, Lawrence. 1984a. "Localities Begin to Challenge Government's Water
Policy Vacuum," *National Journal,* 28 January: 164–68.

———. 1984b. "Polluted Groundwater Clearly a Problem, but Few Agree on
Extent or Solution," *National Journal,* 2 February: 223–25.

Muir, John. 1970. *Our National Parks.* New York: AMS Press.

Munton, D. 1982. "Water—A Canadian View." In *The Interbasin Transfer of
Water . . . The Great Lakes Connection.* Milwaukee: Wisconsin Coastal Management Council, pp. 169–74.

Murphy, J. T. 1974. "Political Parties and the Porkbarrel: Party Conflict and
Cooperation in House Public Works Committee Decisionmaking," *American
Political Science Review* 68 (March): 169–85.

Nation. 1976. "Power to Ruin," 14–21 August, pp. 100–101.

Neumann, Jim. 1985. "Conflicts over Water Rights Increase as Demand Increases. *Fargo Forum,* 15 December, sec. D.

New York Times. 1965. "Appalachian Power Files Plans for Two Plants."
2 March.

———. 1971a. "Pollution Curb Stirs a Dispute." 8 August.

———. 1971b. "FPC Hears Foes of Power Plant." 12 November.

———. 1976a. Full-page ad by APCO defending Blue Ridge project. 9 January.

———. 1976b. "Ervin Says AFL-CIO Acted to Block Vote on Scenic River."
22 June.

Nisbet, Robert. 1962. *Community and Power.* New York: Oxford University
Press.

Nozick, Robert. 1974. *Anarchy, State, and Utopia.* New York: Basic Books.

NWC (National Water Commission). 1968. *Compendium of State Water Laws.*
Washington, D.C.: Government Printing Office.

———. 1973. *Final Report, Water Policies for the Future.* Port Washington, N.Y.:
Water Resource Information Center.

Oettig, R. B. 1977. "How the Garrison Dam Project Affects Canada," *Canadian
Geographic Journal* 95 (October/November): 38–45.

Office of Groundwater Protection. 1985. *Overview of State Groundwater Program Summaries.* Washington, D.C.: Environmental Protection Agency.

———. 1986. *Fact Sheet: Groundwater Provisions of the SDWA Amendments of
1986.* Washington, D.C.: Government Printing Office.

Olson, Mancur, Jr. 1965. *The Logic of Collective Action: Public Goods and the Theory of Groups.* Cambridge: Harvard University Press.

Ostrom, Elinor, and Vincent Ostrom. 1971. "Public Choice: A Different Approach to the Study of Public Administration," *Public Administration Review* 31:203–16.

Ostrom, Vincent. 1971. "Institutional Arrangements for Water Resources Development." Washington, D.C.: National Technical Information Service.

Palmer, Tim. 1982. *Stanislaus: The Struggle for a River.* Berkeley and Los Angeles: University of California Press.

Parekh, Bhikhu C. 1968. "The Nature of Political Philosophy." In P. King and B. C. Parekh, eds., *Politics and Experience: Essays Presented to Professor Michael Oakeshott on the Occasion of His Retirement.* Cambridge: Cambridge University Press, pp. 153–207.

Perlmutter, A., and W. Leo Grande. 1982. "The Party in Uniform: Toward a Theory of Civil-Military Relations in Communist Systems," *American Political Science Review* 76 (December): 778–89.

Perrow, Charles. 1984. *Normal Accidents.* New York: Basic Books.

Peters, B. Guy. 1978. *The Politics of Bureaucracy: A Comparative Perspective.* New York: Longman.

Peterson, Iver. 1984. "Dakota Water Project Is Cut by Reagan Panel," *New York Times,* 16 December.

Pinkett, Harold. 1978. *Gifford Pinchot: Public and Private Forester.* Urbana: University of Illinois Press.

Platt, Rutherford et al. 1980. *Intergovernmental Management of Floodplains.* Boulder: Institute of Behaviorial Science.

Pope, C. 1987. "Undamming Hetch Hetchy," *Sierra* 72 (November/December): 34–38.

Powledge, Fred. 1982. *Water: The Nature, Uses, and Future of Our Most Precious Resource.* New York: Farrar, Straus, Giroux.

President's Advisory Commission on Water Resource Policy. 1955. *Water Resources Policy.* Washington, D.C.: Government Printing Office.

Priscoli, Jerry D. 1981. "People and Water: Social Impact Assessment Research," *Water Spectrum* 13 (Summer): 8–17.

Rawls, John. 1971. *A Theory of Justice.* Cambridge: Harvard University Press.

Red River Valley Historical Society. 1981. *Garrison Diversion: Opposing Views.* Fargo: Heritage Press.

Regan, Tom. 1983. *The Case for Animal Rights.* Berkeley and Los Angeles: University of California Press.

Region 7. 1980. U.S. Environmental Protection Agency, "Water Resources Development Issues and Options Papers." Preliminary draft. Washington, D.C.: Government Printing Office.

Reisner, Mark. 1981. "Are We Headed for Another Dustbowl?" *Readers' Digest* (May): 87–92.

———. 1986. *Cadillac Desert: The American West and Its Disappearing Water.* New York: Viking.

Report of the International Conference on the Role of Carbon Dioxide and of

Other Greenhouse Gases in Climate Variations and Associated Impacts. 1986. Report 661. Geneva: World Meteorological Organization.

Richard, John B. 1978. "The Scramble for Water: Agriculture vs. Other Interests in Wyoming," *Policy Studies Journal* 6 (Summer): 519–23.

Rieve, S. 1981. "Garrison History: A Manitoba View." In *Garrison Diversion: Opposing Viewpoints.* Fargo: Heritage Press, p. 13.

Robie, Ronald B. 1980. "The Impact of Federal Water Policy on State Planning: A Cautionary Example," *American Water Works Association Journal* 72 (Feb.), pp. 70–73.

Rothblatt, D. N. 1971. *Regional Planning: The Appalachian Experience.* Lexington: Heath.

Rourke, Francis E. 1984. *Bureaucracy, Politics, and Public Policy.* 3d ed. Boston: Little, Brown.

Rousseau, Jean Jacques. 1967. *The Social Contract,* ed. Lester B. Crocker. New York: Washington Square.

Rowen, Herbert. 1977. "The Role of Cost-Benefit Analysis in Policymaking." In R. H. Haveman and J. H. Margolis, eds., *Public Expenditure and Policy Analysis.* Chicago: Rand McNally, pp. 552–59.

Royce, Josiah. 1936. *The Philosophy of Loyalty.* New York: Macmillan.

Saglio, J. F. 1980. "How to Include Environmental Concerns in the Decision Making Process." In *Environmental Policies for the 1980's.* Paris: Organization for Economic Cooperation and Development, pp. 63–80.

Schilling, Kyle et al. 1987. *The Nation's Public Works: Report on Water Resources.* Washington, D.C.: National Council on Public Works.

Schmidt, William E. 1982. "Groups United against Reagan Policy on Hydroelectric Rates," *Fargo Forum,* 24 October, sec. A.

———. 1983. "More Snow Is Sought to Feed Colorado River," *New York Times,* 6 March.

Schoenbaum, Thomas J. 1979. *The New River Controversy.* Winston-Salem: John F. Blair.

Seidman, Harold. 1970. *Politics, Position, and Power: The Dynamics of Federal Organization.* New York: Oxford University Press.

Selznick, Phillip. 1966. *TVA and the Grassroots.* New York: Harper and Row.

Sheinbaum, Ervin. 1983. "Storm King: Bureaucratic Pluralism in Regulatory Administration," *Southeastern Political Review* 11:111–26.

Shepard, M. 1986. "Earth's Climate in Transition," *EPRI Journal* (June): 18–60.

Siegel, R. L., and L. B. Weinberg. 1977. *Comparing Public Policies: The United States, the Soviet Union, and Europe.* Homewood, Ill.: Dorsey.

Simison, R. L. 1984. "Debate Is Growing Over a Proposal to Sell Water from Colorado River," *Wall Street Journal,* 19 November.

Simon, Yves. 1960. "Common Good and Common Action," *Review of Politics* 22 (April): 202–44.

Skocpol, Theda, and Kenneth Finegold. 1982. "State Capacity and Economic Intervention in the Early New Deal," *Political Science Quarterly* 97 (Summer): 255–78.

Smith, R. A., R. B. Alexander, and M. G. Wolman. 1987. "Water Quality Trends in the Nation's Rivers," *Science* 27 March: 1607–15.

Sproule-Jones, Mark. 1982. "Public Choice Theory and Natural Resources: Methodological Explication and Critique," *American Political Science Review* 76:790–804.

Stanfield, R. L. 1985. "Enough and Clean Enough?" *National Journal*, 17 August: 1876–87.

Stokes, Samuel N. et al. 1989. *Saving America's Countryside: A Guide to Rural Conservation.* Baltimore: Johns Hopkins University Press.

Talbot, Alan. 1972. *Power along the Hudson: The Storm King Case and the Birth of Environmentalism.* New York: Dutton.

Taylor, Paul. 1961. *Normative Discourse.* Westport, Conn.: Greenwood.

———. 1981. "The Ethics of Respect for Nature," *Environmental Ethics* 3 (Fall): 197–218.

Time. 1976. "Saving the New." 27 September, pp. 68–71.

Toulmin, Stephen. 1950. *An Examination of the Place of Reason in Ethics.* New York: Oxford University Press.

Truman, David B. 1971. *The Governmental Process.* New York: Knopf.

Unruh, John D., Jr. 1982. *The Plains Across: The Overland Emigrants and the Trans-Mississippi West, 1840–1860.* Urbana: University of Illinois Press.

U.S. House of Representatives. 1983. Testimony of Dr. Raymond C. Loehr. Subcommittee on Natural Resources, Agricultural Research, and Environment, of the Committee on Science and Technology, 97 Cong. 2d sess. *The Research Needs of the Clean Water Act.* Washington, D.C.: Government Printing Office.

———. 1987. Subcommittee on General Oversight, Northwest Power, and Forest Management, of the Committee on Interior and Insular Affairs. 99 Cong. 1 sess. *Oversight Hearing: New Federal Hydroelectric Projects in the Pacific Northwest, October 5, 1985.* Washington, D.C.: Government Printing Office.

Uslaner, Eric M. 1989. *Shale Barrel Politics: Energy and Legislative Leadership.* Stanford: Stanford University Press.

U.S. Senate. 1912. *Final Report of the National Waterways Commission.* S. Doc. 469. 62 Cong. 2d sess.

———. 1962. *Policies, Standards, and Procedures in the Formulation, Evaluation, and Review of Plans for Use in Development of Water and Related Land Resources.* S. doc. 97. 87 Cong. 2d sess. Washington, D.C.: Government Printing Office.

———. 1976. Subcommittee on Environment and Land Resources, of the Committee on Interior and Insular Affairs. *Hearings on S. 158. Designation of New as Segment of National Wild and Scenic Rivers System, May 20–21.* Washington, D.C.: Government Printing Office.

———. 1978a. Committee on Energy and Natural Resources. *An Analysis of the President's Water Policy Initiatives.* Washington, D.C.: Congressional Research Service.

———. 1978b. Committee on Public Works. 96 Cong. 1 Sess. *The Water Resources Development Act of 1979*, pt. 5. Washington, D.C.: Government Printing Office.

———. 1985. *What is the Most Effective Water Policy for the United States?*

Sdoc. 99-2. 99 Cong. 1 sess. Washington, D.C.: Congressional Research Service.

————. 1987. Select Committee on Indian Affairs; and U.S. House of Representatives, Committee on Interior and Insular Affairs. 100 Cong. 1 sess. *Final Report and Recommendations of the Garrison Unit Joint Tribal Advisory Committee.* Washington, D.C.: Government Printing Office.

Viessman, Warren. 1978. *The Water Resources Policy Study: An Assessment.* Washington, D.C.: Congressional Research Service.

Walzer, Michael. 1983. *Spheres of Justice: A Defense of Pluralism and Equality.* New York: Basic Books.

Warne, William B. 1973. *The Bureau of Reclamation.* New York: Praeger.

Waterbury, John. 1979. *Hydropolitics of the Nile Valley.* Syracuse: Syracuse University Press.

Webster, Bayard. 1969. "Two Dams Planned to Ease Pollution," *New York Times,* 26 October.

Weigley, Russell F. 1973. "Commentary." In M. D. Wright and L. J. Paszek, eds., *Soldiers and Statesmen: Proceedings of the Fourth Military History Symposium, USAF Academy.* Washington, D.C.: Office of Air Force History, 1973, pp. 48–49.

Wheeler, William B. 1986. *TVA and the Tellico Dam, 1936–1979: A Bureaucratic Crisis in Post-Industrial America.* Knoxville: University of Tennessee Press.

White, Gilbert. 1969. *Strategies of American Water Management.* Ann Arbor: University of Michigan Press.

Whitehead, C. 1985. "European Community Environmental Policy Is Model for Other Nations." *Europe* 250 (September/October): 31.

Wildavsky, Aaron. 1979. *Speaking Truth to Power: The Art and Craft of Policy Analysis.* Boston: Little, Brown.

Wilson, Frank L. 1983. "French Interest Group Politics: Pluralist or Neo-Corporatist?" *American Political Science Review* 77:895–910.

Wilson, L. V. 1978. *State Water Policy Issues.* Lexington, Ky.: Council of State Governments.

Wilson, R. H. 1973. "Towards a Philosophy of Planning: Attitudes of Federal Water Planners." Socioeconomic Studies Series. Washington, D.C.: Office of Research and Monitoring, Environmental Protection Agency, March.

WMO. 1986. *Report of the International Conference on the Assessment of the Role of Carbon Dioxide and Other Greenhouse Gases in Climate Variations and Associated Impacts.* 1986. Report 661. Geneva: World Meteorological Organization.

Worster, Donald. 1979. *Dust Bowl: The Southern Plains in the 1930s.* New York: Oxford University Press.

————. 1985. *Rivers of Empire: Water, Aridity, and the Growth of the American West.* New York: Pantheon.

WRC (U.S. Water Resources Council). 1968. *First National Assessment: The Nation's Water Resources.* Washington, D.C.: Government Printing Office.

———. 1973. *Principles and Standards for Water and Related Land Resources.* Washington, D.C.: Water Resources Council.

———. 1978. *Second National Assessment: The Nation's Water Resources.* Washington, D.C.: Government Printing Office.

Young, Oran. 1982. *Resource Regimes: Natural Resources and Social Institutions.* Berkeley and Los Angeles: University of California Press.

Index

Designed by Martha Farlow

Composed by Brevis Press in Trump Medieval with Futura Bold display

Printed by Thomson-Shore, Inc., on 50-lb. Glatfelter Eggshell and bound in
Holliston Roxite A